The Anarchy of Bl

BLACK OUTDOORS
Innovations in the Poetics of Study

A series edited by J. Kameron Carter and Sarah Jane Cervenak

The Anarchy of Black Religion

A Mystic Song

J. Kameron Carter

Duke University Press
Durham and London   2023

© 2023 DUKE UNIVERSITY PRESS. *All rights reserved*
Printed in the United States of America on acid-free paper ∞
Project editor: Lisa Lawley
Designed by Courtney Leigh Richardson and
Typeset in Portait and Canela by Westchester Publishing Services

Library of Congress Cataloging-in-Publication Data
Names: Carter, J. Kameron, [date] author.
Title: The anarchy of Black religion : a mystic song / J. Kameron Carter.
Other titles: Black outdoors.
Description: Durham : Duke University Press, 2023. | Series: Black
outdoors | Includes bibliographical references and index.
Identifiers: LCCN 2022048865 (print)
LCCN 2022048866 (ebook)
ISBN 9781478025030 (paperback)
ISBN 9781478020042 (hardcover)
ISBN 9781478027027 (ebook)
Subjects: LCSH: Race—Religious aspects—Christianity. | Racism
against Black people—United States. | Racism—Religious aspects—
Christianity. | Evangelicalism—Political aspects—United States. |
White supremacy movements—Religious aspects—Christianity. |
Religion and politics—United States—History—21st century. | Political
culture—United States—History—21st century. | BISAC: SOCIAL
SCIENCE / Black Studies (Global) | RELIGION / General
Classification: LCC BL65.R3 C36 2023 (print) | LCC BL.R3 (ebook) |
DDC 230.089—dc23/eng20230407
LC record available at https://lccn.loc.gov/2022048865
LC ebook record available at https://lccn.loc.gov/2022048866

Cover art credit: Renee Gladman, *Untitled (brown, blue)*, 2020. From the
series *Suddenly We Have the Feeling: Scores, 2019-2022.* 8½ × 11 in. © Renee
Gladman. Courtesy of the artist.

For Charles H. Long,
belated teacher and friend (in memoriam)

and for Kennedi, Madison, and now Atlas

"Anarchism" is an open and incomplete word, and in this resides its potential.

—Saidiya Hartman

Contents

Acknowledgments

It is a joy and gift, an honor and privilege, to do what I do. I mean learning, teaching, pondering, imagining, dreaming, and writing. This book, which is about the spiritual vocation of black radicalism and which unfolds between the notions of anarchy (as spiritual craft) and mysticism (as political activity), offers a perfumed trace of that imagining and dreaming. But in no way do I do what I do alone. Here's a nowhere-near-exhaustive list of folks who've helped me—some up close, others more from afar—in one way or another to imagine, dream, and write this book. They are colleagues, friends, and loved ones in the tender relation of anarchy.

The seeds that would germinate into this book surely go back to my time on the faculty of Duke University and the many fruitful conversations, sometimes on walks through Duke Forest or at coffee shops or the Mad Hatter, with colleagues and friends, some of whom are yet at Duke and others of whom, like me, have moved on. They are Esther Acolatse, Rey Chow, Valerie Cooper, Michaeline Crichlow, Joseph Donahue, Tom Ferraro, Amy Laura Hall, Michael Hardt, Sharon Holland, Tsitsi Jaji, Willie James Jennings, Kimberly Lamm, Nathaniel Mackey, Jarvis McInnis, Ebrahim Moosa, Fred Moten, Anthea Poitier-Young, Luke Powery, Ebony Marshall Turman, William C. Turner Jr., Priscilla Wald, Lauren Winner, and Joseph Winters.

I wrote this book while at Indiana University (IU) Bloomington, my current academic home, and have no doubt that the welcome, embrace, and encouragement I have received from colleagues and friends there have aided me in writing this book. I must mention, specifically, colleagues in religious studies and in my affiliate departments of English and African American and African diaspora studies: Maria Hamilton Abegunde, Heather Blair, Candy Gunther Brown, Carolyn Calloway-Thomas, Constance Furey, David Haberman, M. Cooper Harriss, Laura Carlson Hasler, Nur Amali Ibrahim, Sarah Imhoff, Michael Ing, Kevin Jacques, Meredith Lee, Rebecca Manring, Patrick Lally Michelson, Richard Nance,

Judith Rodriguez, Jeremy Schott, Stephen Selka, Rebecca Sheldon, Aaron Stalnaker, Winnifred Fallers Sullivan, and Sonia Velázquez. I must also make special mention of poet Ross Gay, who's not just a colleague at IU but has become a dear friend. I've learned from him that gratitude, delight, and basketball on the asphalt streets of North and West Philly are all of the spirituality of anarchy that I am trying to think about in this book.

Thank you to colleagues and friends beyond IU: Gil Anidjar, Jeremy Biles, Karen Bray, Mikael Broadway, Amy Carr, Raymond Carr, Eleanor Craig, Clayton Crockett, Spencer Dew, Seth Gaithers, Amy Hollywood, Brooke Holmes, R. A. Judy, Catherine Keller, Tiffany Lethabo King, Carlos Manrique, Nadia Marzouki, Leonard McKinnis, M. NourbeSe Philip, Mercy Romero, Noah Salomon, Devin Singh, Corey B. D. Walker, Dorothy Wang, Calvin Warren, Andrea White, Reggie Williams, and An Yountae.

I am grateful to those who came and listened to presentations I gave in connection with the book. Parts of chapter 2 were presented in October 2021 at the University of Chicago Divinity School to Professor Sarah Hammerschlag's graduate class on The Fetish, while parts of chapter 4 were presented in November 2021 as a talk, also at the University of Chicago Divinity School. In both settings, the comments, questions, and engagements were incredible and helped enhance aspects of the argument. I am grateful particularly for Professor Hammerschlag's and Professor Alireza Doostdar's Q&A engagements with me on poetics in relationship to my reading of Charles Long on the mathematics of the ellipse and the circle and on the grammatology of ellipsis. I'm also grateful for the vibrant exchange with Professor Mark Payne (University of Chicago, classics) on the etymological and other connections between ellipse, ellipsis, and the astrological phenomenon of eclipse among certain Greek classical writers in the context of the argument I make in chapter 4. Interlocutions with Professor Kris Trujillo (University of Chicago, comparative literature) on how mysticism functions as a literary device and reading strategy in this book and what it could mean for critical theory have also helped me strengthen the argument. I must also mention Dr. David Niremberg. Before he left as dean of the University of Chicago Divinity School to become the current director of the Institute for Advanced Study in Princeton, New Jersey, vibrant conversations with him on mathematics, religion, and the humanities, on "race" in antiquity and the Middle Ages, and finally on Charles Long and his beautiful complication of, and in many respects yet to be reckoned with, Afro-diasporic extension of the Chicago School of the study of religion have left their traces on this book as well.

I mention two final contexts in which I was privileged to present some of the material of this book. I am grateful to the current president of the American

Society for the Study of Religion, Barbara Holdrege, for inviting me to offer a talk on the imagination of matter in Charles Long's thought. Drawing on parts of chapter 2 of this book, the talk positioned Long's notion of the "imagination of matter" as bridging questions of race, settler colonial violence, and ecological catastrophe. The conversation crackled with energy and has left its traces on this book.

On the invitation of Will Storrar, director of the Center for Theological Inquiry, I was honored in March 2022 to offer the William H. Scheide Lecture on Global Concerns, where the general theme for the year was "Religion and the Natural Environment." For the lecture, I drew again on material from chapter 2. The conversation was wonderful in so many ways, but I am particularly grateful for the comments and questions offered by Dr. Peter Paris, himself a former student of Charles Long.

I am grateful to the Anticolonial Machine—Colin Dayan, Denise Ferreira da Silva, Sora Han, Lenora Hanson, Laura Harris, David Lloyd, Fred Moten, Dylan Rodriguez, and Atef Said—for reading parts of this book in manuscript form and offering truly invaluable conversation and suggestions. When I was finding my way into a different approach to the study of religion, one that did not simply "apply" ideas from black studies and poetics but one that itself is a practice of black study, this group received and intellectually held me. With them, I relearned the study of religion as a function of black study—full stop. This book bears the traces of conversations with this group of friends on topics far beyond the immediate topic of the book itself. My gratitude to you all for friendship and intellectual comradery in the beauty of incompletion is itself incomplete and always will be—completely beyond words.

Kevin Quashie and Sarah Jane Cervenak have been immense supporters of me and this project. From the time I first read Kevin's *The Sovereignty of Quiet*, which is one of the few works of scholarship that's actually moved me to tears, and reached out to him to express my gratitude and admiration of his work, he's been a friend and encourager as I worked to make this book a reality. Thank you.

And to Sarah. What can I say, except that since Fred connected us and our collaboration started in 2014, it's been about the practice and poetics of study filled with cake and laughter, as you rightly say, to facilitate imagining something else, being somewhere else, even somewhen else (if I might put it this way). With Candice Benbow and Matt Elia (the other two who fill out the crew), we have been a band of mu-wanderers in black gathering, in the anarchy of black religion.

There is also a community of friends who provided me with profound intellectual and spiritual care throughout the process of writing this book and beyond. They are Ashley Gilmore, Jeremy Gilmore, Mario Holmes, Rev. Clarence

Laney, Lisa Laney, Donyelle McCray, Mark Ramsey, Jemonde Taylor, and Denise Thorpe. I must make special mention of Genna Rae McNeil. Uncannily, God (and I have no other way of accounting for it) seems to have you check in on me always when it's most needed. My gratitude to you runs deep. Your wisdom and encouragement and love helped me get this book to the finish line and yet help me keep on keeping on.

Thank you to the two anonymous reviewers of this book. The care, attention, and suggestions you offered me have, without a doubt, made this a better book. They were a gift.

Thanks to Ryan Kendall, Lisa Lawley, James Moore, and all of the people at Duke University Press for helping to make this book a reality. I especially want to express my gratitude to Ken Wissoker, my editor at Duke. You've been superb in handling the book. I am grateful to the Editorial Advisory Board of Duke University Press for its suggestions and comments.

Finally, and most important, I want to thank my family. In everything I do, it's always with my mom (Rose) and grandmom (Hattie) still in mind. Though gone many years now, they both remain the fire in my bones. Their lives of joy—my momma's dancing and my grandmomma's organ playing and preaching—inspired me to imagine something else. I'm grateful to my dad and stepmom, who wrap me in their prayers as I do what I do. I'm grateful to my daughters, Kennedi (your art, photography, and intellectual seriousness move me; and by the way, when you gonna gimme my Christina Sharpe book back? LOL.) and Madison (us nerding out on your engineering and physics schoolwork, and on cosmology stuff, actually, helped me quite a bit on parts of this book; your genius and tenderness awe me; you're the bomb). And I can't forget my goddaughters, Jocelyn and Jaelle. During breaks from writing or while chillin' on weekends, Jaelle brought me bouquets of happiness by insisting that I play UNO with her. She's a straight-up boss who takes no prisoners and takes me down every time. But that's cool 'cuz the point is the playing. That she insisted that I play, that we dared to play—that was its own kind of anarchy; UNO and so much more sustained me through the writing.

Near the end of the writing of this book, my grandson, Atlas, to whom (with my daughters) I've dedicated this book, was born. It was bumpy getting him here, but he's here. He arrives already having to carry too much, this world demanding too much. But his name reminds me, yet again, to dream otherwise, to imagine beyond what is, to envision and enact more than this narrow now. Other worlds beyond the very notion of *world*. Kennedi and Richie, you're already amazing parents.

Finally, to my wife, friend, and partner, Felicia Cheryl. Your love and energy and tenderness and care sustained me through writing this book—and through so much more. You keep me present, reminding me of a love broad and wide, without restriction or exclusion, another name for which is God's love. You have all my heart. And yes, we takin' the train.

An Anarchic Introduction
(Antiblackness as Religion)

The sea of people [storming the US Capitol on January 6] was punctuated throughout by flags. Mostly variations of American flags and Trump flags. There were Gadsden flags. It was clear that the terrorists perceived themselves to be Christians. I saw the Christian flag directly to my front, and another had "Jesus is my savior, Trump is my president." Another, "Jesus is king."—DC POLICE OFFICER DANIEL HODGES, congressional testimony (2021)

Religion and January 6

This is a book I had not planned to write. When I was only a chapter or so away from the finish line on a different one, this one insisted on being written. Behind it lay nothing less than the harrowing events that gripped the United States and indeed the world in 2020 and 2021 and that persist into 2023, the year of this book's publication.

Regarding those harrowing events, I mean many things. We can start with the coronavirus or COVID-19 pandemic, which besides grinding the world economy to a halt on its inception has taken millions of lives planetwide and hundreds of thousands in the United States, the country from which I write. As I write this introduction, we've just brought in the 2022 New Year, and the omicron variant of the coronavirus is causing spikes in hospital admissions and a spike in deaths, principally among the unvaccinated. There are debates as to whether schools should open back up and with what requirements. In such cities as Chicago and

New York City, students themselves are criticizing the health conditions of their schools. Walking out of classrooms, they are protesting.

I also have in mind the police killings of George Floyd in Minneapolis, Minnesota; Breonna Taylor in Louisville, Kentucky; and others, as well as the killing of Ahmaud Arbery in Brunswick, Georgia, and others like him, killed by white citizens of the state who in effect deputized themselves to be police. But I also have in mind the response of activists, many operating under the banner of the movement for black lives, or the Black Lives Matter movement, to these killings with immense protests in the midst of the COVID-19 pandemic. The protests were not just US based. They were also international, with protests in the United States and abroad, larger in many instances than those of the 1960s. And, finally, I mean the fascism of then president Donald J. Trump. I have in mind here both Trump's and his administration's absolute incompetence in responding to the pandemic, leading to the loss of more lives than had to be lost, as well as his clampdown in response to the protests against police violence.

That clampdown is perhaps best symbolized by what I see as the bookend events in Washington, DC, outside of the White House, in the summer of 2020 and then on a winter day in January 2021. On June 1, 2020, amid protests in Washington, DC, against the police killing of George Floyd, law enforcement with Trump's backing used tear gas and other riot-control tactics to clear out Lafayette Park, which is across from the White House, as well as streets surrounding the park. Flanked by government officials including General Mark A. Milley, chairman of the Joint Chiefs of Staff, dressed in military fatigues, Trump then walked from the White House through the violently cleared park to St. John's Episcopal Church, where he posed for a photo op, holding a Bible (upside down no less), thus claiming a kind of religious or sacred sanction for what he'd done in reasserting police as political authority over the protesters and indeed in clearing the ground(s), or, as we also might think of it, in reclaiming, reenclosing, or resettling it.

Bookending this June 1 event is the white nationalist assault on the US Capitol building, again in Washington, DC, roughly six months later, on January 6, 2021. This was the day that the US Congress was to certify the electoral college vote following the November 2020 US national election, thus affirming Joseph R. Biden to be the forty-sixth president of the United States and making official Trump's defeat at the polls and his loss of the presidency. But as we know, a white nationalist mob, egged on by Trump and his political cronies, some of them current members of the US Congress, assaulted the Capitol building. Scaling its walls like insects to find an entry point into the building, the mob attacked the Capitol with a view to stopping the certification of the electoral college votes in favor of Biden and even "hang[ing] Mike Pence," vice president of the United States, for fulfilling his constitutional duty as vice president to oversee the certification process.

Among the many things that seized my attention as I watched it all go down—on one level shocked but on another not in the least—were the many religious symbols and signs throughout the white nationalist mob that was attacking the Capitol. Indeed, in a hearing on the January 6 Capitol assault, DC police officer Daniel Hodges testified before the US Congress about the immense presence of religious imagery throughout the "terrorist" mob during the attack. In his testimony he observed that "the sea of people [storming the Capitol] was punctuated throughout by flags. Mostly variations of American flags and Trump flags. There were Gadsden flags." He continued, "It was clear that the terrorists perceived themselves to be Christians. I saw the Christian flag directly to my front, and another had 'Jesus is my savior, Trump is my president.' Another, 'Jesus is king.'"[1]

There is much more that needs to be said about this event as a moment within the long history of the "religion of whiteness," but what I limit myself to saying now is simply that the January 6 "insurrection," as it has been miscalled (it was really a reassertion of the logic of whiteness and the fascism that since this nation's settler colonial birth has been internal to its democratic project), bookends or works hand in glove with Trump's political pastoralism, his act of political theology, through the reenclosure or the seizure of Lafayette Park back on June 1, 2020, roughly six months earlier.[2] The bookend incidents of June 1, 2020, and January 6, 2021, together form one of the most high-profile expressions of the settler colonial antiblackness of the religion of whiteness.

The Problem of Religion

I mention all of this because it is the backdrop against which this book, *The Anarchy of Black Religion*, demanded that I write it. This is a book about the religiosity of the moment, unpacked along two central lines of argumentation. In the first, I offer the beginnings of a statement about the logic of religion that is the underbelly of statecraft, indeed, the underbelly of what we have lived through and remain yet caught within as some postpandemic new normal sets in. Concisely put, I consider antiblackness as itself a mode of religion, the religion of antiblackness. That is, I explain antiblackness by thinking it in relationship to the modern invention of religion. But as I show, the modern invention of religion works in close connection with the emergence of capitalist commerce and exchange and the idea of the state as grounding "the political," on the one hand, and, on the other hand, as undergirding a racialized conception of "the human" that itself is bound up with enclosing the earth and with an imagination of matter or a way of conceiving matter through an individuating or dividing and separating logic and practice of (anti)blackening. The present struggle is over matter, over matter-ing otherwise, over rematerialization, and in this way over the social. All of this is what is at stake in the modern invention of religion. That is, at stake is the question of the human, the imagination of matter, and a violent eviscera- tion of sociality; indeed, at stake is the question of the earth itself, which entails both the loss of the ability to dwell therewith and thereon and with each other owing to a white science or political mythology of individuation or a mine-not- thine imagination of the world. Such an imagination, which is an imagination of matter, fuels practices of separation for the "ownership of the earth forever and ever, Amen," as W. E. B. Du Bois once put it.[3] But in order to understand the specific religiosity of the crises confronting us—from those just described to other, related crises, including the pressing crisis of gun violence (I write this very sentence under the shadow of the gun massacres in Buffalo, New York, and Uvalde, Texas) and the crisis of global climate change—we must release the study of what is called *religion* (including the study of what is called *black reli- gion*) from being locked up inside of the study of church history or the study of religion at the level of recognizably religious institutions and cultic orders and their attendant theological architectures.[4] To release the study of religion from such frameworks creates room for an understanding of religion as a structuring imagination of matter and culture.

This book takes on the challenge of reframing our understanding of religion. But before getting directly into the weeds of this task, I want to note at the outset that several fine works have emerged that address religion as it relates to white supremacy and thus as it relates to our present political travails. In differing ways, these works put pressure on commonsense understandings—on both sides of the political and cultural divide—of what religion is or means, on where religion is happening and where it supposedly is not happening, and on who is within religion's sphere and who, atheistically or agnostically perhaps, is not within its sphere. They implicitly call attention to the religious work that the religion-secular or the sacred-secular divide does in structuring and keeping alive racial capitalist culture.

For instance, in a provocative new book, historian of American religion Anthea Butler historicizes the Trumpism of American evangelicalism by situat- ing its emergence within the backlash to the South's defeat in the US Civil War.[5] Butler, in effect, invites a consideration of white evangelical American religion as part of what Saidiya Hartman has helped us understand as the general "after- life of slavery." More precisely, one might say that Butler reads white evangelical religion as part of the general "afterlife of the master," as part of the master(ing) or ruling class. Butler's provocative historical investigation advances an understanding of white evangelical religion and, more broadly, white nationalism as an expression of the afterlife of mastery and slavery.[6]

Biblical studies scholar Obery Hendricks also in an important new book similarly takes on white evangelicalism, though in his case from the angle of white supremacy as based in a certain weaponizing of the Bible. In so doing, white evangelicals are, as Hendricks puts it, "destroying our nation and our faith."[7] Hendricks's book, which I read alongside the much-too-underread work of towering scholar of the black culture and the Bible Vincent Wimbush on "scripturalization" as a general protocol of racial capitalism and as central to "white men's magic," is helpful in analyzing Trump's photo op in which he strikes a pose with an upside-down Bible.[8] Read with Wimbush, Hendricks helps us understand that we are not just inside of the tyranny of a certain way of approaching the Bible; rather, we are caught within a regime of scripturalization or rhetorical authority that underwrites the religion of antiblackness and thus that underwrites whiteness both in its right-wing, Christian nationalist, and white evangelical instantiations and in its more progressivist modes of liberal governance.

As a last, brief example, I mention the cultural critic, MSNBC news commentator, and African American studies scholar Eddie Glaude Jr.'s newest work, which engages writer James Baldwin. While the argument regarding religion is a bit oblique, in *Begin Again: James Baldwin's America and Its Urgent Lessons for Our Own*, Glaude demonstrates how in his own way Baldwin worked artistically to intercept American religion with a view to releasing a new kind of religiosity, a new imagination of love. Across his novels, plays, essays, and journalism, Baldwin proposed a vision of love that was nonexclusionary and in this way was revolutionarily improper. As such, it fostered an alternate religiosity, one might say, one that both broke with and yet radically extended the religiosity of his Pentecostal upbringing. Following Baldwin, Glaude makes a moving case for such "love-improper," indeed, for how such improper love—where *improper* means flight from what's politically (and otherwise) proper regarding who stands within and who outside of our circles of kith, kin, intimacy, and belonging— might allow America to "begin again" and thus renew the American democratic experiment.[9]

Again, what these books all have in common is that in their own ways they are contending with the terms of religion. That is, they are contending with the terms that inform whom one considers themselves bound or not bound to (one meaning of *religion*, or *religio*, is what binds together; *religion*, then, is a sociopolitical term) and how the question of connectedness and even kinship informs the present crises of the buckling of democratic institutions. This book joins these and similar works, though the tack I take—the approach to frying this fish, as the saying goes—is a bit different.

The Anarchy of Black Religion

The Anarchy of Black Religion surfaces that deeper philosophical, theological, and religious history that is not past but lives within and animates the present. When I say *the present*, I do indeed include in it the Trump era of entangled pandemics and what's emerging in its wake. But I also mean something more, for in truth Trump, and the Trump aftermath, which for understandable reasons has seized our cultural and political attention, is but the latest in a long train of after-effects of a longer-standing catastrophe. That catastrophe I've named *the settler colonial religion of antiblackness*. The terms in this formulation—*settler*, *colonial*, *religion*, and *antiblackness*—are vital and inseparable. In unpacking how, my goal is to take us to the foundations of this problem as bound up with the foundations of (Western) modernity. That is, I take us in this book to the foundations of modernity as a racially gendered arrangement of religion and the secular, of religion and culture. A keyword I'll be engaging to unpack this is the highly flexible Greek word *archē* (ἀρχή). More specifically, I think with and extend the already expansive work of the late scholar of religion, culture, and black life Charles Long (1926–2020) to advance an understanding of colonial and capitalist modernity as premised on an *archē*, or specific foundation and principle of sovereignty or rule (these terms being within the semantic range of the Greek word *archē*) connected with the modern invention of religion.

Far too unknown in black studies, ethnic studies, and critical theory and continental philosophy, Long rigorously argued that a "new *archē*" of being and knowing, of ontology and epistemology—indeed, a unique mythos and cosmology—had come to structure or organize the present.[10] This new *archē* emerged with and through the contacts, commerce, and exchanges that took place in the Atlantic World from the mid-fifteenth century forward in what is often called the Age of Discovery and Conquest. Differently put, a new *archē* of (human) being and knowing emerged with and through the simultaneous appearance of a people who would be called *black* and something that would be called *black religion* in the Atlantic World. Modernity is of this natal occasion. It was the occasion of the imposition of a racial capitalist cosmology upon the earth. Long contended that animating that natal occasion is a colonial *archē* that, through the emergence in the eighteenth and nineteenth centuries of a series of "sciences" intent on understanding Man, or "the human," extended or mutated into a system of knowledge about what counts as real, about "the world *as such*."[11] We've been subjected to the colonial idea(l) of "the world," made its conscripts, its uncomfortable denizens, undergone its process of "genesis." Sylvia Wynter names what I am talking about "the coloniality of being and knowing."[12] Founded in a colonial *archē*, or a principle of being, to use the language afforded us by Long, who is of Wynter's generation, modernity would in due course come to articulate a philosophical or "Enlightenment *archē*," a knowledge of the human being as a certain kind of Subject in a certain kind of world. What I am trying to communicate here is that these terms—*the human*, *the Subject*, and *world* (or as we often so easily and casually say, *the world*)—and the practices that carry them are neither self-evidently given nor innocent.

This invites a question: What manner of Subject, what manner of Man, or rather human, or rather hu/Man, is this? This is a Subject who in being, supposedly, self-determined, self-possessed, and of autonomous mind claims rationality for itself. As such, this Subject (rendered with a capital S to signal its imagined, which is also a brutal, magnanimity), can subject other things to itself. It can rule. It can own things, beginning with itself, though this properly self-possessed and self-determining Subject cannot be subjected to another. In rationally owning itself as the basis of owning things, including the capacity to lay claim to the earth itself, it declares itself to be the veritable embodiment of "freedom." And yet, it is also the case that within this cosmology, within this imagination of "the world," Man's freedom expresses a capacity of self-rule for the sake of ruling over other things. Within the world, or more precisely within such a cosmology, this is what freedom means. Freedom is a function of sovereignty and sovereignty is a function, an expression, of freedom. This is, to introduce another term, *sovereignty*.

This account of the Subject, of freedom, and of ownership is a fused adumbration of both Saidiya Hartman's and Denise Ferreira da Silva's accounts of the racial dialectic that constitutes modernity as a "scene of subjection" and a "scene of obliteration."[13] Such a dialectic, premised on settler logics of property, propriety, and properness, constitutes a world that is Man's "home" even as those blackened or rendered thingly or thinglike and even animallike and monstrous with respect to that world (I explore this in chapter 1) both are not at home in that world and host a kind of utopian potential to unhome or undo the world owing to an insistent refusal of the very world that has been imposed on them and extracts from them, even as that world also refuses them standing.[14] Borrowing from Sigmund Freud, we might call the animacy of such things precisely in their thingliness, in their opacity, in their nontransparency, which is to say, as black(ened) and dark(ened) things, "*uncanny* (*umheimlich*)."[15] They are uncanny things. Strange and estranged, strained, stranded and unhomely, the opacity of dark(ened), black(ened) things is the seized-on backdrop against which Man enacts himself, or "worlds" himself, as a rational Subject or as the measure of the properly human.

Under the rubric of *archē*—the *archē* of racial capitalism as the basis of the modern world system of empire, and also *archē* as a cosmological entry point for investigating how matter itself has come to be imagined or subjected to (anti) blackening—Long was concerned with all of this.[16] I argue that across his oeuvre Long was advancing the proposition that, from its colonial-Enlightenment inception up through the postcolonial, post-Enlightenment reorganization of what Erica Edwards has called "the terror of empire," particularly as Long started taking stock of it beginning in the 1960s (that reorganizing would reach a counter-revolutionary head in 1968 and would set in motion a neoliberal reconfiguration of empire), this *archē* has been the propulsive force of "the culture of empire."[17] Indeed, within the culture of empire, this *archē* was the propulsive force of the university even as the modern university was poised to establish "African American studies" (and similar and related critical "studies" such as women's studies, etc.) within its fold.[18]

Given this, Long's provocation, which across the pages of this book I work to clarify but also extend or poetically think or innovate with, was twofold. On the one hand, his provocation turned on the argument that the nineteenth-century emergence of the scientific study of religion (*Religionswissenschaft*) and its refinement across the twentieth century was at the forefront of empire's new terms of cultural order and knowing. And yet, on the other hand, he invited a consideration of what has been called *black religion* not as fulfilling "a salvific wish" of redemption from racial-colonial terror through uplift or incorporation into and recognition within the terms of order but rather as registering what I underscore as an alternate cosmology, an *an-archic* or unstately and potentially stateless disturbance of the *archē* of religion that in fact establishes the modern world and its terms of order.[19] Understanding this requires coming to terms with black religion's ambivalent relationship, indeed its anarchic relationship, to the very notion of *religion* as one of the world's—the modern world's—keywords.

Before proceeding further, given its central place in my argument, I want to tarry for a moment with this word, *archē*.[20] In this, again, I aim to think with Long, who when he used the term always kept in mind its full semantic range. I have already noted that possible meanings of this Greek term (ἀρχή) are *foundation*, *sovereignty*, or *rule* (and by extension *law*, as in *rule of law*). But there are other meanings as well. *Archē*, Long observes, has the sense of "beginning, starting point, principle, underlying substance as primordial . . . ultimate undemonstrable principle . . . something 'original.'" These senses of *archē* echo inside of such notions as "indigeneity" and "indigenous people" as well as in such colonially deployed terms as *the primitive*, a term built on the shadow concept of civilization and the civilized.[21] Besides these adumbrations of *archē*, there are others that Long had his eye on as part of the religious structuring of the world. There is *archē* as authorial origin or principle of governance (as in mon*archy*, olig*archy*, and poly*archy*); *archē* as a primary, often charismatic or heroic figure (one example of an *archon*, or a primary figure, is a patri*arch*); *archē* as that which provides the essential rules of the game or proposition; *archē* as the foundation or ground of something (as in the grounds of an argument, or even perhaps in a geological sense, *archē* as actual ground and thus as pointing to the matter or material that is a piece of land, if not earth itself). Finally, there is *archē* in its conveyance of the idea of order, the terms of order.[22]

As I demonstrate in chapters 2 and 3, the modern (re)invention of religion (along with its companion concept of *the secular*) contains within it the terms or the *archē* of a fundamental pandemic or catastrophe. Indeed, the word or very idea of *religion* in its present circulation, which was born with and through early modern transatlantic commerce and exchange, condenses what Sylvia Wynter in a recent interview with Katherine McKittrick describes as our species' "unparalleled catastrophe," at the heart of which was a catastrophic cosmology.[23] In chapters 1, 2, and 3, which may be thought of as part I of this book, I tell a story about this unparalleled catastrophe in the modern (re)invention of religion precisely as the religion of antiblackness. More specifically, this is a story about religion's (re)invention as a matter of the organization of matter itself, matter's would-be subjection to the violence of racial capitalist individuation. That individuation, which represents a transubstantiated "reoccupation" (to borrow Wynter's borrowing of Hans Blumenberg's formulation) of certain Latin Christian protocols of medieval (political) theology, is part of the imposition of a totalitarian universality on matter itself.[24] Out of that imposition and as part of its political manifestation, the state as part of a system of states and as a regulatory apparatus emerged. On the one hand, this began codifying formally in the sixteenth century through the Westphalian international order as a structure of sovereignty that further articulated into the idea of "Europe" and then of "the West" in its simultaneous (racial-occidental) difference from "the East" and (racial-colonial) difference through subjugation of a global South. On the other hand, this imposition of a totalitarian universality on matter is the metaphysical backdrop for the accumulation and planetary circulation of commodities and capital and now the emergence of petroculture.[25] In both respects, at stake is an imposed trans-substancing of existence's basic *elementa* or energies. That trans-substancing has happened—or rather, is happening—through processes of extraction. Matter is now cosubstanced with extracted labor, blood now with land dispossessed, screams now sonically with the earth itself.

I am thinking here with Denise Ferreira da Silva, who explains much of what I am trying to get at as an economic structure of "unpayable debt" tied to the symbolic-ethical tools of racial thought and practice as these work to legitimate or justify (precisely within the juridical context of the *archē* of "law and order" and "the rule of law") settler colonial, antiblack, anti-Latinx, and related violences, where the cause of that violence gets attributed not to the way the (colonially racial capitalist) world is organized and structured but to cultural difference, which is to say, to nonwhite or blackened, darkened difference as symbolized by skin color and violently grafted onto flesh as always already registering moral failure and culpability.[26] Ferreira da Silva turns to Octavia Butler's 1979 novel *Kindred* and specifically to Butler's spacetime-jumping protagonist, Dana, to unfold this. In Ferreira da Silva's reading, Dana is an image of "unpayable debt" or of "the wounded captive body in the scene of subjugation."[27] But also, she images an alternate ecology of matter(ing). After Erica Edwards with Terrion Williamson, we might think such mattering as an unprotected maternal ecology that collectively, anti-imperially, and, after Long with Hartman, anarchically preserves sociality even within catastrophe and therefore beyond the constraints of the current order.[28] That this is an issue precisely of how matter is thought and conceived is in many respects at the heart of the matter for Ferreira da Silva and her reading of Butler's Dana. In contemplating her, "[we confront,] on the one hand, the possibility of thinking the *ongoing present* from a 'raw material' (*elemental*) perspective, one that refuses to reduce existence to the forms and functions of the living body or 'social condition'; on the other hand, the recognition that the violence that characterized slavery as a colonial juridico-economic structure has been met with an insistence not to perish, a refusal of the logic of obliteration."[29] This refusal, which ensues from the perspective of "raw material" or of matter as infinite or in unending transition or movement, the perspective, as I examine in chapter 3, that Long spoke of in strikingly similar terms to Ferreira da Silva's as *materia prima*, Ferreira da Silva calls *negativation*, by which she means a "refusal to die, refusal to comply, refusal to give up and give in—to which the mere existence of black persons here/now testifies."[30] This alternate, elemental perspective on or imagination of matter as performed by Butler's Dana, who in *Kindred* images the wounded captive body, "renders the master's tools inoperative," even as a whole range of possibilities for existing otherwise opens up given that inoperability.[31]

Thinking Ferreira da Silva (and black thought in and as black feminist theory) and Long (and the theory of religion and modernity) with and through each other allows me to argue that as a racial capitalist condition of "unpayable debt," modernity is its own type of cosmological imaginary—which is to say, a mode of religion as religio-secularity—whose refusal occurs through that speculative inhabiting of an alternate cosmology, an anarchic imagining of matter. When I speak of (the) blackness (of black religion), precisely in its relatedness to racial hierarchy as part of the knowledge and management systems of a capitalist world but also as referring to what exceeds the identitarian systems of being, knowing, and management, I am speaking to that alternate cosmology of matter's material multiplicity, a cosmology of the crossroads that is often associated in various African and African diasporic cosmologies with the deity Legba.[32] While I speak to this in chapter 5 in relation to Nathaniel Mackey's practice of the poem, for now and as part of this introduction I'll say that in speaking of blackness in this way, as figuring a horizon beyond and in refusal of a colonial, capitalist system of being, knowing, and managing, I am signaling something resonant with what writer Paul Preciado gets at in dislodging the queer, trans condition from the confines of a binary political and epistemological order premised on proper representation (political and otherwise). With recourse to Uranus, the coldest planet in our solar system, and one of the farthest, Preciado moves onto the territory of nonimperial mythology, indeed into cosmology, to articulate a vision of "utopian gender," as Virginie Despentes puts it in the foreword to Preciado's book.[33] "My trans condition," Preciado says, "is a new form of Uranism. I am not a man and I am not a woman and I am not heterosexual I am not homosexual I am not bisexual. I am a dissident of the sex-gender system. I am the multiplicity of the cosmos trapped in a binary political and epistemological system, shouting in front of you. I am a Uranian confined inside the limits of techno-scientific capitalism."[34] The way that I am trying to think about blackness and black religion or the blackness of black religion resonates with this. Indeed, black studies, arguably most evidently in such modes of inquiry as black feminist theoretical practice and experimental poetics (from experimental writing in poetry and the novel to visual arts, music, and the like), has in its own way been reaching for or bringing to some sort of articulacy the open secret of an alternate cosmology, an otherwise imagining of matter and practice of mattering. This alternate cosmology has been in refusal of the ontologization and thus the political theologization of matter, its antiblackening, wherein matter itself was made a scene of extractive subjection precisely by being subjected to ontology in the making of modern, racially gendered subjects (and objects).

Across these pages I analyze the nature of this extractive subjection with specific attention to black racial histories and examples within the violent history of capitalist value and the yet-unfolding history of global raciality. These histories (of value and globality) are matters of matter's blackening. In speaking in this way, I mean to allow my claim about matter's blackening to provide insight into the racialized othering of indigenous and Asian communities, Palestinians and Jews, peoples of the various Eastern bloc nations (something at the forefront of our attention, given the war that rages in Ukraine as I write this), and so on. Specifically, I provide here an argument for how matter's extractive blackening produces a differential structure of racial globality as terror against the earth. Logics and practices of race-ism wherein communities are alienated from land, and more specifically from earth and thereby from each other, come into view as different and yet related, as nonidentical and therefore not collapsible into each other and yet as connected modes of extractive blackening. What I am suggesting here annotates what W. E. B. Du Bois was getting at when he spoke of the color line belting the planet; what Lisa Lowe gets at in her analysis of racism as a global, differential ordering of relations under the rubric of "continental intimacies"; and what Denise Ferreira da Silva gets at in her masterful work on racial globality and more recently on the violent history of value.[35] Among these thinkers, Ferreira da Silva further stands out, as I have already noted, with her attention to the question of matter and individuation, which are central concerns of this book.[36] I join these thinkers, each of whom addresses the terror of modernity as a terroristic materialism by attending to the general blackening of matter and the specific religiosity of that blackening in underwriting the ideologies and institutions of racial capitalism, which itself must be understood as a general socioecological crisis that manifests and operates as a kind of differential network or assemblage of extractive, planetary racialization. Hence, my attention to black racial histories and examples across these pages is never not with an eye on how various modes of differential blackening or racializing operate within the planetary violence of the extractive blackening of matter.

The point that I'm making here accords with what I demonstrate across the first three chapters of this book, namely, that the modern (re)invention of religion through transatlantic commerce and exchange helped configure space and place (that is, the relations among Europeans, Africans, and various indigenous peoples of the Western Hemisphere and eventually across the planet) through an imagination of time as a progressive sequencing from savage benightedness to rational enlightenment. Within the imagination of space-time that in the context of the emergence of transatlantic commerce and exchange is being imposed on the earth and that institutes "globality," a specific anthropological regime—some have called it "Man," others the "patriarch-form," others still simply "the human"—is set forth.[37] In this regime there are those considered moderns or self-possessed, rational subjects and others who, in effect, are locked up or subjected to a kind of temporal incarceration, shunted inside of a premodernity that gets signified as "backward," "medieval," "strange," mystical, heretical, or of "fetish religion," a term that in its emergence was but a synonym for *black*, we might even say *blackened, religion* (see chapter 3).[38] Those subjected to such space-time sequestration are often, at the level of gender, represented through the figure of the wayward woman, the "witch."[39] What is important to note is that while these terms are meant to signify a temporality that lags behind or an anthropology that indexes an unfulfilled or lagging humanity, what they actually are attempting to incarcerate or put on lockdown is an alternate modality of existence, an alternate imagination of matter. Given this, I'm interested in such terms as *strange, mystical, heretical*, and so on not as signifiers of a time lag (unmodern benightedness) but as signifiers of dissonance and dissidence—a dissonant and dissident medievalism, the black medieval with the black baroque, we might say, the *mater* as the matter of a black Lucretianism, a black naturalism—that exceed the terms of order, terms set in motion through the modern (re)invention of religion as bound up with the advent of racial capitalism.

The Black Study of Religion; or, Matter(ing) Otherwise

I tell the story about the modern invention of religion with these specific matters in mind, with the matter of the imagination of matter in mind. The matter of the imagination of matter reverberates in Cornel West's phrase "race *matters*" and is the issue indirectly circled around in the phrase Black Lives *Matter*.[40] In tracing the modern invention of religion, I will be tracking, shall we say, the matter of matter's (anti)blackening. In these chapters particularly, I invite readers to journey with me into this deeper story about the present, into racial capitalism's genealogy within material religion or within religious matter(s). That is, I am inviting readers into a consideration of how we've come to think about matter itself through antiblackness as religion and how the blackening of matter works to organize the world and constitute the political as a structure of antagonism predicated on logics of separability and individuation.

In unfolding this, I link the critical theorizing taking place in black studies with theorizing religion itself. In so doing, I do three things. First, I clarify what religion is, particularly its modern (re)invention, not merely as a matter of its institutional expressions but even more as an orientation to matter with related, material forms of thought. Second, I surface a relationship between the material (re)invention of religion in the context of Atlantic commerce and exchange and the rise of a racial capitalist world and the way "the human" has been imagined as a denizen of "the world" that's been imposed upon the earth. And, finally, I consider how the modern (re)invention of religion is itself bound up, on the one hand, with what Zakiyyah Iman Jackson has identified as the (anti)blackening of matter in association with the (anti)blackening of black(ened) people and, on the other hand, with the practices of property and the enclosure of the earth.[41]

More specifically, across chapters 1, 2, and 3, or what amounts to part I of the book, I attend to the very imagination of religion and the human that has provided the ground, the *archē*, on which the present is built or that animates our current property-informed understanding of "the world." This property-informed understanding of the world premised on atomistic division and imposed on the earth so as to enclose it—it is *this* that is at the ground or the origin, the *archē*, which is to say, the beginning, of our problems. Such is the genesis of things. By giving attention to modern religion, I consider the emergence of a paradigm of the human inflected through race-gender as technologies of separation, the rise of the modern state, and settler colonial violence against the earth. Another way perhaps to say this is to say that I consider the invention of the idea of religious Man (*Homo religiosus*) as bound up with the rise of Man as a specific kind of political entity (*Homo politicus*, or a citizen-subject of the state) and economic entity (*Homo economicus*). Split between what Sylvia Wynter speaks of as "Man 1" (*Homo politicus*) and "Man 2" (*Homo economicus*), *Homo religiosus* is a *Homo racialis* who in his universality is enlightenment philosophy's transparent subject.[42] That transparency is "whiteness," which while being understood in the symbolic-epidermal register of skin color must also, perhaps more primally, be understood as a certain ethical-civilizational form and practice made manifest through symbolic-epidermal inscription.[43] Denise Ferreira da Silva has analyzed this ethical-civilizational form in terms of the "global idea of race" and more recently under the rubric of the "patriarch-form," which I consider in chapter 4.[44] In this respect, "whiteness" is best thought of as a settler colonial and capitalist cosmology that has spawned an accompanying system of "god(s)," including such vaunted (god-)terms as *Civilization, Capitalism, Freedom,* and *Man*. These terms function like "god(s)" because in some fundamental sense they are. They are the mythological gods that ground this world, just as the ancient Greeks, for example, had gods that grounded their world. In our case, the gods of this world—Civilization, Capitalism, Markets, Man, and the like—are bound up with modernity's (re)invention of religion. Marked by a set of god-terms, whiteness, then, is an anthropo-genesis, a cosmo-genesis, an *archē*, a worlding, a keyword of the beginning of this racial capitalist world. Whiteness is of "in the beginning . . . ," which is just to say (again) that whiteness is the enactment of a cosmology. At the heart of this cosmology is an imagination that we might identify, again with Ferreira da Silva in mind, as difference through governed or regulated separability in evisceration of "difference without separability" or otherwise cosmologies predicated on a physics of entanglement or entangled matter(ing).[45]

In this regard, the first question at the heart of this book is simply, *What is religion*? As I hope these introductory remarks are starting to make clear, my aim is to break a certain common sense around religion. Specifically, I aim to clarify religion's invented status within a colonial and capitalist cosmology of separability and how that invented status is bound to the individuated or atomistic (anti)blackening of matter, which is further related both to the violent (anti) blackening of the people who have come to be called *black people* and to the violent enclosure through colonization and settler colonialism of the earth itself. In short, what I bring into view is religion, or more accurately race-religion or even still, if I may, racereligion (these terms are of a piece; to say one is already to be saying the other), as a construct or a technology of enclosing the earth through a brutalizing political-theological and cosmological imagination that alchemizes matter by extractively (anti)blackening it, subjecting it to brutalizing logics and practices of property ownership and (also as) separability. This imagination of matter, again in connection with the invention of religion, is bound up with "the human" that has emerged as religion's complement. A central claim of this book is that animating the multilayered "pandemics" of the COVID-19 virus, the virus of antiblackness, the virus of gun violence, and the virus of the political (including but not limited to neofascist authoritarianisms) that constricts the potentials of sociality or togetherness with each other and with the earth through a statist "we" (the "we" in "We the People") that is constituted through race-gender and through capitalism—animating this is the modern invention of religion and the human. I begin unraveling this problem by engaging in what I call *the black study of religion*, a new mode of the critical study of religion that with this book I want to begin advancing. That is, I subject religion to black study, revealing the modern (re)invention of religion to be an idea of enclosure.

What distinguishes *the black study* of religion from simply religious or theological studies? Well, on the one hand, the black study of religion discloses the anthropological significance of religion's invention. In this regard, it shows religion's invention as bound up with a newly emergent imagination of "the human" as a technology of atomization. The emergence of the Atlantic World of commerce and exchange is ground zero here (see chapters 2 and, especially, 3 of this book). This is where and when "the human" emerges as a religio-political construct or as a construct of political theology meant to cohere or bind certain groups of people together over against others even as the former are in exploitative dependence on the latter. This operation of cohering is a religious one. One important meaning of *religion* (from the Latin verb *religare*, from which derives the word *religio*, a word introduced by Cicero) is "to bind together" and even obligate under law. *Religio* binds together a "we," often over against a "them." Religion, we might then say, emphasizing precisely its verb quality, "we's." It is an activity of we-ing, though that we-ing is premised on a first maneuver of antagonistically separating, atomizing, dividing, or individuating those in right standing (before the law, as citizens before the state, etc.) from those without such standing. And yet that very we-ing, the very constructing of a "we" for those of or within the walled-in polis, the city-state, is always already fraught, always already under duress, suffering a Sturm und Drang from a would-be, threatening outside, often when that outside shows up internally on the inside, thus getting read as a destabilizing threat to the normative We (the People), the state. That is, the we-ing that is an operation of religion and that is also and as such a practice of the political (and here we already see that religion is not just what happens in formal religious institutions, like churches and the like) is always already working against and in light of its own incoherence and instability. I speak of incoherence here in that the imagination of a pure "I" or a pure, as in racially pure, "we" over against a contaminating "them" cannot hold in the face of the entanglement that is the very condition of matter(ing) as such. Here entanglement is at once a matter of the social and of physics. It is a matter of sociophysics. I have in mind contemporary quantum physics coupled with the ancient poetic philosophy and the materially scientific imagination advanced by Lucretius in *On the Nature of Things* (*De rerum natura*), and this further linked with the kind of black feminist *materi*alism we get with Denise Ferreira da Silva and Zakiyyah Iman Jackson. There are additional connections between the rethinking of matter I am exploring here through the black study of religion and the rethinking of matter in feminist science studies, as, for example, in the work of Karen Barad, and the rethinking of matter in terms of flesh that can be found in certain quarters of queer theory and trans studies, as, for example, in the work of C. Riley Snorton, Gayle Salamon, and Paul Preciado, whose work I've already noted.[46] With this series of connections in mind, (socio)physics proves to be (socio)poetics. This is a mysticism of sociality or a poetics of the social in which matter must be understood without time or beyond the time of the (racial capitalist) world insofar as the world is not enough.[47] As a function, then, of black studies, the black study of religion studies this operation of a capitalistic, individuating we-ing as one in which as a feat of violence "Western civilization" works to sustain itself against an outside that it at once extracts from and depends on precisely to produce itself.

Additionally, and on the other hand, the black study of religion reveals religion's early modern invention as having yet-reverberating ecological significance. It shows religion's (re)invention to be bound up with a problematic imagination of matter in which the earth itself, its material stuff-ness or its very thingliness, is believed to be ownable or in which an extractive logic of property governs one's orientation toward the earth. Within this imagination of matter, there are those who believe themselves to be the owners of the right to ownership, and there are others who are on the underside of this believed right to ownership. The latter are in that group of things called *property*.[48] The former are bodies of credit, the latter of debt, figures that are owned and the embodiment of what is owed. This is an adumbration of John Locke's seventeenth-century settler colonial philosophy of property.[49] Locke's got us all locked up. But before Locke, what makes the world of transatlantic commerce and exchange in its fifteenth-century emergence crucial for understanding this problem is that it is where modern religion was invented to grant philosophical, political, and sexuated coherence (though it was always a coherence fraught with incoherence) to this way of conceiving the earth, extracting from it, and operating on it. The effort to cohere or establish a modern, free self—politically, this self has taken the form of the proper citizen of the state; economically, this free self is in the form of the consumer, who more historically has been both a buyer and seller of goods even when those goods have been the enslaved; and, philosophically, this free self has been figured as enlightened, self-possessed, and rational man—is what generates the global idea of race and the religious imagination that sustains it. To be of this (racial capitalist) world is to be within the invention of religion, within this enclosure invented as part of the enclosing of the earth. It is to be within that anthropological enclosure called *Man*, perhaps even *the human*. The secularism that marks us cannot evade this, for, indeed, secularism alas is a function of the Christian invention of religion, its binary complement that disavows its fraternal twin.[50] If anything, it's precisely this secularist belief in a rational overcoming of religion that further fuels the very invention of religion and its internal imagining of matter and (anti)blackening of the earth that I study in this book. As a poet once put it, "I ran from it and was still in it."[51]

The question becomes, Might there be a way "to be *still*—in it"? To ex-ist and sub-sist, to be otherwise—in it, beyond it? To escape, I mean ex-cape—in it? To be ecstatic, in a rupturing rapture—in it? What of the Real, I mean the Surreal—in it? Indeed, what of this *it*? Even more, what of the "loophole of retreat," Harriet

Jacobs might ask, the fugitive fold—within it?[52] These are questions not so much about the it but of the it within the it, what one of the figures in poet Nathaniel Mackey's *Mu* poem calls "the it of it"—in it.[53] It's this other it, this otherwise it, that has my attention. What's the state of that it, the other it spoken of in Mackey's poem as "the it of it"? What of this alternate atmosphere, this existence in crossing, in passage, at the crossroads, this other thinking and knowing, this other writing, this other theorizing, shall we say, that's out of this world because it signals some other relation to Earth, some other way of being with the earth? Could this be "the it of it"?[54] Might "the it of it" be what Mackey has also called "destination out" from within it, an outdoors and an outside to it (maybe that's it), even if that outside of it, that outdoors of it—let's call this other it the mystic it—is on or from the inside of modernity understood as religio-racial enclosure? Might there be some other im/possible, perhaps apophatic orientation of being and knowing beyond racial hierarchy and epistemology that strictly speaking in its mu-sicality, and muse-icality, and mysticality and (rh)ythmology is irreducible to religion but that nevertheless presents itself in relationship to what is now rather commonsensically, rather reflexively spoken of as *religion*? What if this is black religion, what black religion signals?

Black Radicalism's Spiritual Vocation

This brings me to what I take up in chapters 4 and 5, or what amounts to part II of this book. While the black study of religion introduces a new mode of the "critical study of religion," more important, the black study of religion, through its consideration of black religion, suggests an alternate, entangled way of being with the earth and of being always already differentially entangled with each other, some alternate mode of life together. What I'm after here by way of the black study of religion is an otherwise we. This other, nonindividuated we-ness opens onto an alternate imagination of matter(ing), an alternate, black *material*-ity, an erotic metaphysics as erotic cosmology of flesh announced within the poetics of black thought. I'm interested in the apophatic, that is, the unrepresentable that presents itself, the apophatic saying of the unsayable that constantly undoes all saying because there's always more to be said, always more and less. I'm interested in the parareligious (by which I mean the "it of it") that exceeds the marks, the letters, and thus the iconographic regime of the law of religion, and its twin, the law of secularism. In chapters 4 and 5, this is precisely what I take up—a thinking of and from within this alternate matter-ing, where such matter-ing suggests a distinct cosmology of entangled aliveness, of entangled together-ness, that alternative we-ness that we might call *sociality in the flesh, sociality in black*. In this alternate we-ness, existence (or be-*ing*) generatively begins and ends with the generosity of entanglement, not with the presumptive logics and violent practices of individualized separability—the logics and practices that power the cosmology of (racial) capitalism.

To reiterate, (racial) capitalism is premised on a cosmology, indeed on a (rather curtailed or imperially short-circuited) *mythos* or mythology. It enacts an origin myth, an *archē* premised on separability. By contrast, the alternative operates an-archically, in apposition to the *archē* of racially gendered, racially sexuating capitalism. Thus, anarchy as alternative signals other socialities, other solidarities, some other solidness, the potentials of an alternate unfinishable-we, an always incomplete-we, within which any "I" is similarly incomplete and uncompletable, rooted in an alternate cosmology that points to that sprawling, swerving, and untouchable Silence that conditions all touch. This is matter as the rhythm of things. In her arresting book M *Archive: After the End of the World*, poet and self-described love evangelist Alexis Pauline Gumbs speaks of this cosmology in terms of a "black feminist metaphysics," indeed, as an alternate "mythology" that "[re-rhythms] everything" from the celestial to the oceanic, from the cosmic to the quantum, in light of "the infinite face of the deep."[55] Here we move beyond the differentiating rhythm of market value(s), the rhythm of separation for purposes of extractive enclosure, to some other modality of the sacred and the social or the sacrality of the social on the far side of the reigning *archē*, or what Cedric Robinson called "the terms of order" and "authority," to which he counterposed "the principle of incompleteness."[56]

What Robinson referred to as the principle of incompleteness in *The Terms of Order: Political Science and the Myth of Leadership* (1980), he would not long thereafter in *Black Marxism: The Making of the Black Radical Tradition* (1983) align with the cosmological orientations one finds in obeah, in Haitian Voodoo, in hoodoo in parts of the southern United States, in Jamaican myalism, in Trinidadian shango, and the like. These practices drew on the materials of nature (roots, vegetation, etc.) to produce medicines and other concoctions for curing and healing.[57] But even more, these root work practices offered "ritualistic links . . . with the spirit world beyond the shadows and the sacred trees."[58] What Robinson has his finger on is an alternate worlding beyond the racial-colonial idea(l) of "the world as such." Laying this out fittingly in a section of *Black Marxism* titled "The Roots of the Black Radical Tradition"—which in my own thinking I've come to annotate as "The Root Work of the Black Radical Tradition"—Robinson understands this black radical worlding as premised on "a mystical sense of continuity between the living, the dead, and those yet to be born."[59] Here we find, as scholar Lindsey Stewart puts it, a "privileging of the relationship to the dead over our relation to the slave owner or oppressor. . . . The oppressor's authority is demoted in this transaction, for our power resides in proper relation to the spirit inhabiting the *nkisi* [the ritual object]. In this instance, root work offers an independent means of evaluating the world not by reacting to (or directly challenging) the views of the dominant world, but by proactively offering values through the observation of specific forms of piety toward the prior and ongoing religious beliefs of our ancestors."[60] In Robinson's terms, what this points to is the "magic" of social change, where that magic has manifested historically in slave rebellions and marronage. Often vilified in the racial regime of the master class as witchcraft and sorcery because of its threat to their authority and to the king's authority, that is to say (to put it in the terms of this book), because of its would-be anarchism, this magic registers an alternate materiality of the social. It registers other ways of being with the earth and with each other. In this way, this alternate materiality operates at the crossroads and hosts its own crossroads mode of being and knowing. It offers a thinking in passage, a thinking in crossing, wherein passage and crossing, transitioning and the crossroads, are themselves an alternate source and resource (as I elaborate in chapter 5 of this book) of life and aliveness. In short, the crossroads is really a cosmological crosscurrent that operates anterior to and for this reason against the grain of the racial hierarchy and thus the sovereignty of colonial rule.

Both the "anarchy" and the "mystic song" that title this book are of this crossroads *mater*ialism of incompleteness, this otherwise cosmology. They are of the antepolitical alternative. Which is to say, they are of the radically or unstately or surreally antepolitical alternative that is in the tradition of refusal taken up in fugitivity and marronage. Of a piece with each other, anarchy and mysticism are of some other "knowledge of freedom."[61] Indeed, they signal an alternative atmospherics of the uncanny, the nonrepresentable, or what operates outside property's protocols of ownership. Charles Long mobilizes the ellipsis—the dot-dot-dot (. . .) that represents in writing what exceeds representation, the non-punctuating punctuation mark, as Jennifer DeVere Brody has put it—as a figure of such anarchy, indeed, of what is called *black religion*.[62] In this sense, anarchy is mystically elliptical. A figure of the mysticality, the *mater*ialism, or the matter of blackness, ellipsis or anarchy bespeaks a poethics of disordered love beyond the terms or the grammar of order. Which is also to say that the anarchy that I begin elaborating in this book points to the spiritual vocation of the black radical tradition, to the prayer internal to this tradition. Beyond critique, this book is about that vocation.

Speaking of prayer and black radicalism's spiritual vocation, I would like to offer one final example to round out this introduction before offering a general summary of the chapters and thus the road ahead. That example comes from Frantz Fanon. But this is a different Fanon than typically is thought about. I'm interested in Fanon's prayer, for it may be that there's something to be gleaned toward an unstately, a nonstatist postcoloniality, one that is truly decolonial from the horizon of (his) prayer. Maybe with and beyond Fanon himself, we can hear again *Black Skin, White Masks'* concluding words. They are words of apocalypse, an unveiling that reveals the book to have already been an elliptically open prayer that destabilizes phenomenology's (Kantian) idea of the subjective consciousness even as Fanon invokes that very idea in his closing words only to cause the very idea of closed consciousness to creak under the weight of blackness, which is to say, under the weight of incompleteness. By the end of the book, we discover that *Black Skin, White Masks* is a book filled not so much with a set of declarations or predications. Rather, we discover it to have been an open-ended, incomplete meditation of which the last lines are just that, its last but not final words. Those words he calls prayer:

> At the end of this book we would like the reader to feel with us the open dimension of every consciousness.
> My final prayer:
> O my body, always make me a man who questions![63]

These lines suggest that *Black Skin, White Masks* is itself perhaps a prayer book, the last line of it being a final prayer. What's cool and provocative about this is that it suggests, notwithstanding Fanon's humanism or his own sometimes one-dimensional interpretation of blackness that tends to come through as a certain pathologization of blackness, that *Black Skin* has another side to it. That other side announces itself through and as prayer. Figuring himself as one involved in prayer, indeed, figuring his psychoanalytically inflected analysis of the case of blackness within the horizon of prayer understood as a potential orientation outside of racial capitalist ontology, Fanon may be understood as more than the typically received Fanon. This is a Fanon of black religion as I am positing it and studying it in this book. This is a Fanon who prays. Which is to say, this is a Fanon against Fanon, a Fanon who from within the very terms of "the human" produced through antiblackness is dis/oriented toward the open, toward *the it of it*, toward *that within* that exceeds the reigning terms of "the human," even while Fanon directs his prayer to a god-object (what he called "my body" as object of possession) and within a humanist teleology (what Fanon figures as the realization of a certain manhood).[64] What has my attention here is not per se this set of problems, which in another context might be more fully addressed and dealt with. Rather, riveting my attention is the fact of prayer as bound up with the fact of blackness, the case of prayer as part of the case of blackness. What has my attention is that prayer would dare appear within *Black Skin, White Masks*, that Fanon would dare pose *Black Skin, White Masks* as (a) prayer. What could be the possible significance of this?

I propose that if we can think a Fanon in the direction of the black study of prayer, this being an aspect of the black study of religion, indeed of black study, as I am proposing in this book; that is, if we can think prayer in the direction of incompleteness rather than as commerce between hierarchically distinguished sovereign subjects (a "God" who lords or masters over a creature); if we can think prayer as a practice of and toward the open, practice without telos or a regulatory endgame, without sovereignty, as a practice of insovereign incompletion, as improper, anarchic refusal of stateliness, propriety, property, and the proper and thus as registering an alternate imagination of matter as sheer, indeterminate, congregate swerving (something akin to what Lucretius proposed in *De rerum natura*)—if we can go in this direction, which seems to be a subterranean impulse in the Fanonian text, we can then think a Fanon for whom prayer is dis/orientation, indeed, an open set of practices that signals indeterminate *mater*iality, unstately sociality, and disidentification with religion as individuating force. At that point, something like black religion, turned in the direction that I've been suggesting in this introduction and that I more fully adumbrate in the chapters that follow, marks the decolonial text. In short, black religion then shows up, para-Fanon-like, as religion's disidentified, dis/oriented, its queer, uncanny, afro-surreal, its "mad" and "maddening" (in that sense that La Marr Jurelle Bruce talks about), its "atheological" (in that sense that Ashon Crawley but also Georges Bataille talks about), its hoodoo'ed and voodoo'ed, its anguished yet joyous, its limboed yet celebratory outside (as Lindsey Stewart, following Zora Neale Hurston, elaborates).[65] It shows up as black radical, parareligious creativity, as religion's (black) outdoors, as that "collective craft" of poetic living.[66]

Mindful of this, this book, which is perhaps my own sacrilegious prayer book, aims then to release black religion from the byways of the study of church history and denominational or cultic distinctions in order to reveal *black religion* as a term through which to reckon with black radicalism's spiritual, which is to say, its *mater*ial, vocation. That vocation is linked to an alternative imagination of matter and operates as an insurgency at the site of the modern invention of religion itself. So understood, *black religion* anagrammatizes *religion*. This book is about that anagram, that scrambling, that hieroglyph, that "ideogram," as Long once called it, that cosmogram.[67] It's about (the blackness of) black religion in its nonreduction to racial-religious enclosure. It is an invitation into the study of an expansive, alternate cosmology, a cosmopoetic, anarchic "we" that does not need an externalized, individuated, or otherized "them" to establish itself. Indeed, such a "we" exceeds and refuses establishment.

The Road Ahead

There are five chapters in this book. In chapter 1, "Black (Feminist) Anarchy," I think principally with film scholar and queer-of-color theorist Kara Keeling and philosopher and literary theorist Zakiyyah Iman Jackson, while in chapter 2, "The Matter of Anarchy," and chapter 3, "Anarchy and the Fetish," I engage theorist of religion and scholar of black religion Charles Long. Across these three chapters, I explore the problem of the (anti)blackening of matter by way of the black study of religion and in the interest of setting up a consideration of black religion as made up of practices premised on an alternate imagination of matter. My aim is to elaborate black religion as a sociophysics of difference without separability. More specifically, across chapters 1–3, I introduce what I call *the black study of religion* to address antiblackness as religion or as a material cosmology built on the principle (*archē*) of the (anti)blackening of matter. This (anti)blackening, which entails both matter's epidermalization and its transubstantiation into property, is built on the would-be evisceration of black *mater* or the maternal as a generative, erotic depth that imbues matter, giving matter in-finiteness or its capacity to ongoingly regenerate itself as flows of entangled difference out of the cycle of dying and living. This cycle is matter. In chapter 1, I follow Keeling and Jackson in considering how *mater* as matter, as matter's *material* depth, was targeted in matter's (anti)blackening, in the (anti)blackening of now-black(ened) people, and in the making of "this world" or in the establishing of a cosmology of racial capitalism. I am keenly interested in chapter 1 in Keeling's and Jackson's pinpointing of a logic of religion internal to the making of "this world" or the (anti)blackening of matter and, indeed, the (anti)blackening of the earth. In chapters 2 and 3, I think with and build from the work of Charles Long to continue the direction of thinking begun in chapter 1 with Keeling and Jackson. The upshot of these chapters is to offer an account of the modern invention of religion as predicated on enclosing and extracting from the earth, on enclosing and extracting from black *mater* as matter, in short, on eviscerating matter's depth and foreclosing on alternate cosmologies or imaginations of matter(-ing), particularly, those advancing incompleteness.

Chapters 4 ("The Anarchy of Black Religion") and 5 ("Anarchy Is a Poem, Is a Song . . .") may be considered part II of the book and also the book's most speculative and experimental part. Here, beyond the analysis and critique of the cosmology of racial capitalism and the antiblackening of matter as developed in chapters 1–3, I think the alternative of black *mater* as mattering otherwise in incompleteness via what has been called black religion. I argue that what is called black religion is not just a species of religion in blackface. No. What is called black religion is part and parcel of blackness as incompletion and a signal of matter's re-generative indeterminacy. This alternate mattering may be understood, after theologian and scholar of religious ethics Victor Anderson, as predicated on blackness's "divine grotesqueries," that is, on a blackness "beyond ontological Blackness."[68] To understand blackness as an alternative cosmology of matter-ing, to understand it in terms of the black *mater*nal, which as Keeling notes may have a certain relationship to those identified as "black women" but is not simply and reductively equatable with those so designated (see chapter 1), is to understand blackness as more than "a blackness that whiteness created," as Anderson puts it, more than blackness reduced to racial category or within ontology.[69] As a cosmology of entanglement or entangled matter-ing, blackness signals what may be thought of as that spiritual vocation of an alternative we-ness, an alternative sociality with the earth and cosmos and therefore each other.[70] In chapters 4 and 5, I fill this out by thinking again with scholar of black religion Charles Long and poet, novelist, and essayist Nathaniel Mackey.

Specifically, chapter 4 explores the alternative sociality and practice of the sacred talked about above through Long's notion of ellipsis, the dot-dot-dot (. . .), or the punctuation mark that signals when something is left out or indicates that more is to be said though that more exceeds saying. I reflect on ellipsis as a figure of (the blackness of) black religion by attending to the mathematics internal to Long's notion of ellipsis, for ellipse is eclipsed within ellipsis. More specifically, I inquire into black religion in the dark zone, in the void, in the eclipsed (non)space between ellipse and ellipsis. This, then, is a mathopoetics of black religion. It is here that I most fully develop the idea of anarchy (*an-archē*) as a parareligious impulse of elliptical unfinishedness internal to black social life.

Chapter 5 builds on this account of the anarchy of black religion from chapter 4 through a consideration of Nathaniel Mackey's practice of the poem. The claim I advance in this chapter is that Mackey's practice of the poem is an example precisely of the account of black religion that I start to develop through engaging Long's poetics of religion. Might it be that the black experimental arts host the cosmology of mattering otherwise, the understanding of (the blackness of) black religion that in thinking with Long (and others) I am elaborating? Chapter 5 on Mackey's practice of the poem—and indeed this book as a whole—explores an answer of yes to this question. More specifically, with chapter 4 on Long's mathopoetics of ellipsis as a figure of black religion, this chapter on Mackey's practice of the poem advances a poetics of black religion or an exploration of the spiritual as *material* vocation of the black radical tradition as it operates at the site of language. Indeed, between chapters 4 and 5, I bring into view a nonsettler understanding of the holy, of Silence, of the sacred—a kind of black radical sacrality—as bound up with the *material* profaneness, the undergroundedness, the earthly fundament of blackness. This black earthiness that also bespeaks the blueness of ocean and sky, sea and heavens, I explore under the banner of anarchy as constant origination, constant re-generation without origin, unending beginningness. I'm speaking here of the mysticality of blackness or of blackness as a mode of mysticism manifest in the aesthetics of social practice. What has been called black religion is of this aesthetic practice; there is a (para)religiosity to the "aesthetic sociology of Blackness," to "black gathering," in quantum assembly.[71] With Mackey, this book travels the pathway of poetry, culminating in a line of verse, a song. And so this book along with being perhaps a sacrilegious prayer book is also and as such a (prose) poem, a (mystic) song.

When all of this is added up, what I present here is the scaffolding of a new approach to black religion. I use the word *new* haltingly, especially given how the university or the regime of academe is so committed to the new as a species of ownership whereby *Homo academicus* as a species of "the human" establishes academic ownership, possession, and prowess. I'm under no illusions: I'm a part of the academic colonial machine, the religious studies machine even. And yet I see this work as trying to break that machine or at least put a spoke in its wheels through the black study of religion. That is, this work is both more and less than one. "I" may have written this book, but I certainly don't own it. In fact, the writerly "I"—the "author"—is here under pressure. I'm under pressure inasmuch as this book is, I hope, a beautiful mess of entanglements. It is an instance of the very crossroads practices of way making that I am trying to get some traction in thinking about under the sign of blackness and black religion, under the sign of the blackness of black religion. This book, then, is itself a practice of black *mater* as matter's differential performance. This book is a larger conversation, and insofar as that conversation is ongoing and incomplete, so too is this book. Thus, what presents itself here are traces of conversations with many interlocutors—some directly as friends, comrades, and colleagues; others more indirectly through their scholarship and writing—who have helped me think about what here I've shorthanded as *the anarchy of black religion*. In this important sense, I claim no newness at all. I only hope to participate in a renewal of an assembly that racial capitalism from the jump aimed to interdict. In this respect, what I claim is having already been claimed inside of a certain sharing; I claim a certain apprenticeship to a field of study, to black study. And yet what perhaps is new in this book, at least somewhat, is the religious studies sensibility that animates it through a method that I call *the black study of religion*. I bring this method of inquiry to bear on black studies or African diaspora studies to address or bring more explicitly to the fore the spiritual as material vocation of this tradition. In other words, this book brings together black religious studies, on the one hand, and Africana, African diaspora, and African American studies, on the other, within a single theoretical constellation, believing that thinking through the blackness of black religion mutually theorizes black religion and blackness.

Chapter One

Black (Feminist) Anarchy

Although the historical continuity of the identity category "Black women" has been unevenly associated with femininity, the nexus at which Black race meets feminine genders has been significant to the calculus involved in the distribution of property, profit, and power. It is a store of value. The resulting figure, whom we might recognize today as "the Black woman," stitches processes of racialization to those of political economy, and thereby carries a potential to disrupt both.—KARA KEELING, *Queer Times, Black Futures* (2019)

Blackness is not imperviousness to a politics of sex-gender but a site of its profound intensification.—ZAKIYYAH IMAN JACKSON, *Becoming Human* (2020)

[Nalo] Hopkinson's novel [*Brown Girl in the Ring*] recasts the metonymic of literature and blackness precisely by exploiting the equation of blackness, and in particular Africanness, with irrationality and teratology—by troping the trope of African religion.—ZAKIYYAH IMAN JACKSON, *Becoming Human* (2020)

Religion, Blackness, Black Studies

Though they have tended to lurk somewhat unthought in the background, the question and problem, as well as the poetics and possibilities, of religion are becoming a matter of increased attention in assessments of antiblackness and in thinking about black life in antiblackness's wake. With attention on recent black feminist interrogations of the human and of how religion and the sacred increasingly figure into grappling with this problem, my aim in this chapter is to think through or clarify the stakes of the more general shadow concern with religion in contemporary black thought. More specifically, with a focus on black feminist critiques of the human in the making of an antiblack world, this chapter's concern is with how black studies has been involved in a proxy engagement with religion's entanglement with antiblackness, racial capitalism, the issue of the human, and logics of property through which the earth itself becomes imagined as something to be extracted from and owned.

One finds a concern with religion that moves in the directions I am here talking about arguably most prominently in the work of philosopher and cultural theorist Sylvia Wynter. But it is not just in Wynter's work. A lurking or absent presence of issues of religion as they bear on the problem of the human and the imagination of the earth as a propertized or ownable thing courses through the work of writers and poets like Wilson Harris, Édouard Glissant, M. NourbeSe Philip, Ed Roberson, and Nathaniel Mackey. Additionally, one need only consider her 1974 dissertation on black culture and the performative rhetoric of the black sermon or her foundational essay "Mama's Baby, Papa's Maybe: An American Grammar Book" to see that issues of religion and myth (not in the common sense of myth as something simply made up or false in contrast to what's fact or true, but myth in the technical sense of the stories on which cultures establish themselves) to know that issues of religion and myth have been central to Hortense Spillers's intellectual itinerary.[1] Indeed, it is in relation to her assessments of the racially gendered logics of "the human" that her "countermythic" theorizing of black culture must also be understood. I could go on with other examples from black studies of how issues of religion shadow black thought, but my point for now is a simple one: black studies has been engaging as part of its "wake work" not just with the problem of the human. More precisely, I argue that it's been carrying out a proxy engagement with the problem of religion as part of its interrogations of the human.[2]

My two interlocutors in this chapter for thinking through this are film studies and queer-of-color scholar Kara Keeling and literary scholar Zakiyyah Iman Jackson. I'm interested in how their work aids in clarifying religion's operations as an organizing concept of modernity as well as how black life and existence are a locus for beginning to think toward an alternate imagination of religion. Of interest is how their work begins to point toward an understanding of black religion's complex relationship to the very notion of religion, an understanding of black religion perhaps as a poetic detour with respect to the very notion of religion. Adapting Jackson's statement from this chapter's epigraph, I ask, How might we understand that troping of the trope of religion, that poetics of religion, we might say, that's operative as blackness's creative potentials for

disrupting the economy and processes of racialization? How might we understand what Keeling calls the "opacity of black existence" and the queerness of
its "futures," where "'black futures' . . . names what remains unaccountable to
existing instruments of measurement and the interests those measurements
serve?"[3] When Keeling further says that "the ungovernable, anarchic here and
now harbors Black futures," what does this have to do with religion?[4] And stay-
ing with Keeling, how is this all related to the figure of "the black woman" within
the economy and processes of racialization and the potentials to disrupt this
order of things?[5]

These are the questions at the heart of this chapter as I launch into an under-
taking that I have come to call *the black study of religion.*[6] However, given the
general confusion around the term *religion* as well as the general ambivalence
if not outright resistance within black studies and in other adjacent fields of
the critical humanities toward "going there," as the saying goes, I want to pause
here for a slight moment to clarify what I do and do not mean in my use of this
term and thus why "going there" is necessary. By *religion* I do not mean some
universal feature of "consciousness" that spans the totality of human experience
across time. I do not mean religion as the genus under which fall the various species or varieties of religion or religious experience. Or to borrow from scholar of
religion Brent Nongbri, I do not mean religion or faith as "timeless mysterious
things that have always been present," that which is "'simply *there* as an identifiable factor of human experience.'"[7] Viewed in this way, religion and religious
experience are simply an aspect of the being of the human, an aspect of human
being in its evolutionary and phenomenological unfolding across time. Against
this more or less commonsense notion of religion both within and outside of
academe, across these pages, and again purloining from Nongbri, "I use the
phrase 'the modern notion of religion' (or one of several synonymous words and
phrases—'religion,' 'the concept of religion,' etc.) as a kind of shorthand. When
I say [religion], I am not contrasting that phrase with any 'ancient notion' of religion, *for religion is a modern innovation.*"[8] Which is to say, "religion has a history.
It was born out of a mix of Christian disputes about truth, European colonial
exploits, and the formation of nation-states."[9] In these pages, my concern is with
this mix. Particularly, it is with the specific Christianity and European coloniality of (the invention of) religion that powers the definition of the human that
we've been laboring under. I am constantly bearing in mind that that definition
of the human that we've been laboring under is being religiously produced in
relationship to the competition between European-colonial powers out of which
our current imagination of nation-states eventually solidified.[10] In this sense,
my attention is constantly on the religiosity if not the outright religion of state

apparatuses and, from the flip side of the coin, the statism, stateliness, and, finally, the coloniality of religion. My interest is in the overlap of *Homo politicus*, *Homo economicus*, and *Homo religiosus*, though my emphasis is on religion's concurrent production or coproduction with the Western coloniality of the human insofar as religion and the human constitute a singular nexus. This is what has my attention. Indeed, it is on this point that I depart a bit from Nongbri, who at best is thinking at the edges of the problem of the human as coproduced with religion. That is to say, the concern here is with the religious (as secular) production of a global anthropology, or of what Denise Ferreira da Silva has called a "global idea of race."[11] And from the other side, I'm simultaneously concerned with a humanist production of religion or with how that modern innovation called religion helps stand up or enact a particular definition of the human, one "so tangled in separation that it is consistently making our lives incompatible with the planet."[12] These together—religion as the terrain of a certain definition and practice of the human and the human as an anthropology of religion—are the hinges on which the door of globality swings. As one can see, the question of religion is at best only partially addressed when framed through questions of institutional denominationalism or even through interfaith dialogue and the like, for these approaches to religion rest on having made a settlement with or having accepted the Latin (become European and from there Western) Christian coloniality of religion as such and the production and imposition of a certain kind of world on top of the earth that follows from it.

Rather than accept the settlement around religion, I interrogate it. I argue in this chapter that through its rigorous analyses of the modern figure of Man or the human, black feminist theory has started to expose both the specific modernity of Man and the specific modernity of religion in Man's making as these turn on (en)gender(ing) and sexuation. It's in this regard that I want to venture some experimental considerations on how black feminist theory opens, on the one hand, onto the black study of religion and how, on the other, it allows us to bring what is called *black religion* into view as *anarchy* (a compound term with the Greek prefix *an-* and the root word *archē*), which is to say, as varied practices of "stealing away" into a collective interiority. Such anarchic interiority is generative of alternate meanings of life. Christopher Freeburg compellingly calls these alternate meanings both "interior life" and "counterlife."[13] About the latter term, he explains:

> Counterlife unsettles singular narratives, teloses, fixed categories, oppositions, and what it means to be or have a self. The counterlife of slavery has to do with realizing that slaves' lives, across art and media, exceed the explanatory force of the terms that currently define the field. Through

the counterlife lens, when slaves acquire philosophical insights, create art, seize religious meaning, commit acts of violence, or perform historical memory, they prompt simultaneous and multiple points of critical view—a profound irreducibility—which take on their own importance. Reading for counterlife helps us discover how slave texts reveal the "disorderly flux of life" and thinking inside violent oppressive environments to which conventional terms and frames do not fully attend.[14]

Indeed, to read for counterlife is to read under the imperative of the unruly or anarchic opacities of existence as such and not so much as a function of resistance and the supposedly all-determinative force of the dominating order. It is to read for the refusals of the religio-secular terms of order even as, in accordance with the idea of counterlife, one understands stealing away (in the face of having been stolen) as a having been seized by and a seizing of parareligious or anarcho-religious meanings. Here I am fusing anarchy and counterlife, which allows me to develop a distinction between religious meaning (under the presumption of the modern invention of religion) and the opacities of living artistically or para- or anarcho-religiously.

What Freeburg is getting at through the lens of counterlife to grapple with slave social life and slavery's hereafter aids me in articulating what I mean by *anarchy*. By anarchy I do not mean a political program. Rather, by anarchy I mean an other (and not simply another) imagination of freedom as premised on an other (and not merely another) imagination of matter. Which is also to say that by anarchy I mean the refusal of the *archē* of religion as "ground," "foundation," "origin," and "genesis" (all valences of the Greek term *archē*) of the definition, framework, and orientation of the human and the attendant presumptions of agency and subjectivity. Anarchy bespeaks practices of alternative imaginations of matter that are out from that imagination of matter that is ensconced within the modern invention of religion and that informs the imagination of the human. The latter hosts an imagination of matter in which matter is (anti) blackened, made to the measure of individuated units of value that might appear, for example, in double-entry bookkeeping, a banking reconciliation sheet, an accounting log filled with the hieroglyphic markings signifying debits and credits, debt and capital, assets and liabilities, things owned and what's owed; in short, an imagination that transubstantiates matter into property, into atomized units of measure pressed within a logic of ownership (including, first and foremost, owning oneself or being sovereignly self-possessed) and dispossession.

In this chapter I explore these issues via the work of literary and cultural theorist Zakiyyah Iman Jackson in concert with the work of black studies and queer-of-color theorist Kara Keeling. If by the end of this chapter I open up questions of cosmology, then in the last two chapters of this book, I circle back to cosmology to explore it as a spiritual locus of radicalism or, again, what I call anarchy. The ultimate concern I have in this chapter in thinking with Keeling and Jackson is how this duet's dovetailing inquiries into the problem of the human revolve around the racial capitalist dynamics of gendered sexuation and how this registers a crisis of cosmology as a problem of religion and matter, or what Charles Long spoke of as the problem of religious matter(s).

"The Black Woman"

In setting forth this argument, I begin with a passage from Kara Keeling's remarkable *Queer Times, Black Futures*. The passage brings into preliminary focus why black feminist theory can aid in grappling with Long's thought and how it can therefore also aid my own effort here to extend his thought into a theorization of black religion as anarchy (as *anarchē*).[15] Keeling says:

> What we recognize today as Black femininity, regardless of the official sex of the body that expresses it, has been a site of the oftentimes violent suturing of individuals to racial collectives over time. This process, as Cedric Robinson has proven, is entangled with the history of capitalism and European nationalism, wherein capitalism remains inseparable from the historical practice of enslaving Africans as legal forms of property, and nationalism is bound up with questions of sovereignty. Although the historical continuity of the identity category "Black women" has been unevenly associated with femininity, the nexus at which black race meets feminine genders has been significant to the calculus involved in the distribution of property, profit, and power. It is a store of value. The resulting figure, whom we might recognize today as "the Black woman," stitches processes of racialization to those of political economy, and thereby carries the potential to disrupt both.[16]

I want to call attention to Keeling's reading of black femininity and the identity category of "the Black woman" both as a store of value and as a signifying site of suture within the regime of the human. More still, I'm interested in how what Keeling recounts here interestingly sets us up to more deeply understand vital aspects of what theorist of religion Charles Long over a distinguished six decades of intellectual work was saying regarding the emergence of the very notion of religion as we use it—this category being bound up with matter's epidermal and sociocultural (anti)blackening.

Long exerted much intellectual energy in making the case that this blackening occurred at the discursive site of "the fetish" in the Atlantic World of commerce and exchange beginning in the mid-fifteenth century off the coast of West Africa. At the discursive site of the fetish, we witness the emergence of a mode of mattering that posited matter as in itself empty or evacuated of inherent meaning, its irreducible "total value," its life, stolen. Deanimated, supposedly at least, imagined as static, atomized, nonflowing, or nonmoving, matter could be imagined as commoditizable. At the level of imagination, it could be transformed into what was believed to be capable of being owned, transformed in this sense into property or "being for the captor."[17] I know this formulation about ownership—*transformed into what was believed to be capable of being owned*—is cumbersome, but I think it nevertheless necessary to say it this way. I am trying to think about the fetish as both a concept (and thus as a certain protocol of Reason, with a capital *R*) and a structure of belief (and here we verge on religion). As concept and structure, the fetish has material effects; it affects. Indeed, as concept, the fetish indexes a mode of matter(ing) whose value inheres in its capacity, to put this in Keeling's language, to speculatively warehouse or store value. We will consider the problem of the fetish in more detail in chapter 3. For now, I'll simply say that Long shows that in religionizing Africans under the rubric of declaring them animists, fetishists, or practitioners of "African religion"—this procedure itself being the ground zero of (racially) blackening the African so as to produce what Zakiyyah Iman Jackson has called "black(ened) people"—the African was violently *transubstantiated*. Indeed, I here go so far as to say (and this, too, we will examine in an upcoming chapter) that the African was violently *alchemized* into a Negro, plasticized as flesh, made the locus of experimentation for how matter might be denuded of form in the interest of speculatively warehousing value.

What has my attention in the above quote by Keeling is Keeling's sense of this very problem—which is to say, the problem of religion—though her line of sight onto the problem of religious matter is not framed as a problem of religion (the fetish) per se. Keeling keenly observes that matter's blackening takes place as an operation of (en)gendering and sexuation. This (en)gendering and sexuating or this engendered sexuation "stitches processes of racialization to those of political economy" so as to produce and reproduce that enclosure that we might call *the* world of *the* human, *the* world of Man. "Black femininity" has been vital in producing and reproducing that world while also figuring as a certain "monstrous" abjection with respect to *the* world.[18] Herein lies the significance of Keeling's statement regarding "Black women's" uneven association with femininity and positioning as the nexus where "black race meets feminine genders." That nexus or specific locus of evacuated matter is where property (value) (re)produces more property (value) for the (human) captor.

Now Keeling does not herself tie this deanimation of matter, its potential conversion into the commodity forms, to religion, but what she's generally outlined echoes Long's insights as a theorist of religion as the religious (!) production of the commodity. Long's insight is that religion—or, more precisely, a Europeanist discourse on religion as offspring of a Europeanist Christian imagination—is at the origin (*archē*) and provides, shall we say, the principle (*archē*) behind or the ground of (again, *archē*) what I have just described following Keeling.[19] This is an ontotheological qua racial capitalist and political-nationalist, or more simply a statist, organizing of matter that funds the human as a project of "White Being."[20] What Long, however, does not contend with is how as a religious scene of the racial (anti)blackening of matter the fetish is also and as such a scene of the production of the human precisely as an imagination of the species. Moreover, what Long has an inkling of but does not develop is how the fetishistic outlook on matter entails a blackening of matter that, on the one hand, engenders humanistic gender and humanistic sexuation. On the other hand, the fetishistic outlook as a feature of colonial Europeanist discourse posits those declared to be enthralled to fetish objects as a (racialized) "species." From one angle this species is outside the domain of the human; from another, and by virtue of taking human form, shall we say, this species is also within the human domain. Within the human but not of it: this is the contradictory structure of the imagination of matter that is at work here. According to the terms of this imagination, it is the wandering, dissident, and abject orientation toward matter that is associated with the African that is key to the production—indeed, the invention—of an emergent idea of "race."

Let me quickly say, importantly, that I do not read melancholically the wandering, dissidence, and abjection ascribed to Africans as fetish worshippers or as practitioners of improper (read: black[ened]) religion, saddled as they are with an irrationally wayward imagination of matter.[21] That is, driving this analysis is not a wish for black(ened) people to be seen as properly human. It is not an argument for their admittance through recognition into the precincts of the organizing definition of the human. Rather, I read it *an-archically* or against the grain of the (religious) *archē* of Man by which Man stands his (!) ground, erecting himself on top of the earth. The task I've set myself is to begin elaborating the anarchy—by which I mean the *an-archē*—of black religion precisely as deviant, fugitive, and ana-formative dissidence from and improvisation through what has been called religion and the human.

Here I return to Keeling insofar as her observation about racial capitalist exchange and the abjectionality of black femininity "where black race meets feminine genders" obtains precisely on this point about black anarchy as a going astray, a flying away, or as the improvisation of form. The point that I take from Keeling is that transatlantic exchange established a storehouse of value that would have an ongoing multiplier effect (the speculative surplus of exchange value), as well as her further observation that this storehouse of value wherein a violent "mathematics" takes place is associated with a certain pristine even if abjected figural form—to wit, "the Black woman." This figural form points at once to abjection even as it also points to the *an-archē* of abjection or to abjection's anarchic potentials.[22] As figure, "the Black woman" yokes processes of racialization to those of political economy, these both being undergirded by the genocidal and geocidal catastrophe of colonization and enslavement or the ecological devastation of the earth. Taking the point further, given what I've minimally said so far about Charles Long's work, which in short order I will further expand on, "the black woman," too, is a locus of or a portal for questions about the joint production of religion and modernity; "she" yokes the very processes of racialization and political economy of which Keeling speaks to the invention of religion as a regulatory and discursive regime.[23]

Black(female)ness and the Blackening of Matter

It is here that I'd like to introduce Zakiyyah Iman Jackson's work, which in a number of respects I've already been echoing. Jackson's work is relevant for my purposes for at least two reasons. First, her work amplifies Keeling's point regarding "the black woman" as where "black race meets feminine genders." Second, in what amounts to a robust amplification of Keeling's point regarding "the black woman" in the order of modern representation or signification, Jackson attends explicitly to how religion as a distinctively modern innovation factors into matter's antiblackening, which is to say, into the creation of whiteness as a fundamentally religious arrangement, a regime that acts on the basis of an "imperial myth" of grasping, appropriating, and expropriating or extracting and that aims to organize the senses around empirical representation. In short, around property.

I begin with the first point of relevance, namely, Jackson's amplification of Keeling's point regarding "the black woman" as where "black race meets feminine genders." That meeting point, we saw, registers a new imagination of matter wherein "the black woman" serves as a storehouse or a vehicle of value. Jackson's work is significant in expanding on and clarifying Keeling's basic claim and insight. That is to say, Jackson clarifies how black(ened) life and labor are at once drawn upon as part of a process of producing or giving form or shape to the human within an emerging Western imaginary even as blackness is abjected from that form.[24] Jackson names this process "plasticization." We might further call it *liquification*; Jackson at one point calls it *fluidification*. At any rate, Jackson's fundamental claim is that plasticization—not dehumanization—is the principal work of antiblackness. Indeed, (anti)black plasticization is the ur-scene of violence in the making of the modern world between the Janus-faced categories of "the human" and "the animal." Differently put, plasticization is a metaphysical "scene of subjection," the basis of a certain imagination of matter.[25] On the basis of that imagination—modernity's imagination of matter as predicated on black plasticization—the human acquires form. Also on this basis, what we've come to call "world"—*the* world *as such*, the world as a singular thing, as the supposedly only possible world, as produced of and sustained by extraction—is formed.

The centrality in this of gender, sexuality, and maternity is, Jackson tells us, often overlooked in "philosophers' and historians' emphasis on antiblack formulations of African reason and history."[26] Hence, Jackson pays attention to how "black female flesh persistently functions as the limit case of 'the human' and is its matrix-figure," for it is with this figure "that, historically, the delineation between the species has fundamentally hinged."[27] Which is to say, the delineation between the species has hinged on "the question of reproduction." It is by "how the means and scene of birth is interpreted" that "the limit of the human has been determined."[28] All of which is to say that from the vantage point of a Eurocentric humanism, reproduction is not so much for the sake of the racially black(ened) having a place within the species domain of the human. Rather, "Eurocentric humanism needs blackness as . . . prop[erty] in order to erect whiteness," that is, to establish or otherwise figure human being or universal humanity as "White Being."[29] Eurocentric humanism needs a passageway through which to establish the human's difference from "the animal" as defined in both human and nonhuman terms. Jackson's interest is in calling attention to how "black(female)ness" is mobilized in this specific context. In Jackson's words:

> Our task [is] to take seriously the particularization of gender and sexuality in black(ened) people in the context of a humanism that in its desire to universalize, ritualistically posits black(female)ness as opacity, inversion, and limit. In such a context, the black body is characterized by a plasticity, whereby raciality arbitrarily remaps black(ened) gender and sexuality, nonteleologically and nonbinaristically, with fleeting adherence to normativized heteropatriarchal codes. In such a context of paradoxical (un)

gendering, and by gendering I mean humanization, power only takes direction from its own shifting exigencies—a predicament that might be described as chaos. This chaos by design is used to marginalize black(ened) genders and sexualities as the border of the sociological: a condition I refer to as ontologized plasticity. . . . Plasticity is a praxis that seeks to define the essence of a black(ened) thing as infinitely mutable, in antiblack, often paradoxical, sexuating terms as a means of hierarchically delineating sex/gender, reproduction, and states of being more generally.[30]

Again, on plasticity, Jackson says:

New World slavery established a field of demand that tyrannically presumed, as if by will alone, that the enslaved, in their humanity, could function as infinitely malleable lexical and biological matter, at once sub/super/human. What appear as alternating, or serialized, discrete moods of (mis)recognition—sub/super/humanization, animalization/humanization, privation/superfluity—are in fact varying dimensions at once, a simultaneous actualization of the discontinuous and incompatible: everything and nothing at the register of ontology such that form shall not hold. Blackness, in this case, functions not simply as a negative relation but as a plastic fleshly being that stabilizes and gives form to human and animal as categories.[31]

As a way of describing the role black(female)ness serves for humanism, *plasticity* connotes (racial) violence, which is to be distinguished from what is often figured as (racial) exclusion or even (racialized) dehumanization. More specifically, plasticity points to the (middle?) passage that is constantly, violently, made through the enslaved such that they might serve as "infinitely malleable lexical and biological matter" against which the proper, ethical domain of the human, the domain where universal, juridical principles prevail, is established. In this, the enslaved function as "plastic fleshly being," those for whom form does not hold. Which is to say, they are de-formed as part of a process of bringing forth or giving form to or otherwise constructing and ongoingly stabilizing "the human" and "the animal" as formal categories of the understanding or of humanist reason, to employ an idiom derived, of course, from Immanuel Kant's *Critique of Pure Reason*.[32] In this process of categorically establishing "the human" and "the animal" via the "plastic function" that racialization serves, black(ened) people incarnate or represent humanity's abject dimensions.[33] In other words, they are a demonic incarnation (to inject a theological terminology) of that de-formation that facilitates the formation of "the human" and "the animal," indeed, that facilitates

"White Being." Put differently, black(ened) people function as a type of abject chaos—or in Jackson's nomenclature "black(female)ness," figuring as an "Ultimate Chaos." It's not that black(ened) people are not human. Rather, the humanity granted them within the system of universal, liberal humanism is plasticized or formlessly "blank," and for this reason able to serve whatever purpose necessary to and within the humanist terms of order.[34]

Jackson turns to the scene of Paul D's encounter with a red-combed rooster named Mister in Toni Morrison's novel *Beloved* as an example of precisely how plasticization as enforced and "coerced formlessness" works. Through her reading of Paul D and Mister, Jackson figures Morrison as, in fact, philosophizing the very plasticization that upholds humanism and buttresses the order of White Being. Jackson begins her meditation first, however, with attention to how Mr. Garner, the master of the fictional "Sweet Home" plantation that provides much of the setting of *Beloved*, sets the terms of the genre and engendering of the human. He sets those terms via the masculinity of the human that he indexes in the novel. In so doing, he also sets or even is the horizon for Paul D's striving for masculinity and thus his pining, shall we say, to inhabit the human and be recognized as such. But also, Mr. Garner sets the terms or the horizon for Paul D's understanding of that other Mr. of the story, namely, the Mister who is the red-combed rooster and who serves in the story as an apparition for Paul D—at one point, Jackson speaks of Mister as a "demonic apparition"—of a longed-for masculinity that presents itself at the scene of an animal.[35]

What sets Mr. Garner apart in Morrison's story is that he appears "to depart from the generalized principles that characterized slavery as depicted in the text."[36] As those principles would have it, "reciprocal recognition between white and black men would disrupt the natural order of plantation life." Indeed, because "normative modes of gender such as patriarchal authority and filial recognition are the entitlements of manhood in the Oedipal symbolic economies of the US South, slavery's logic insists that there 'ain't no nigger men.'"[37] And yet Morrison's Garner is interesting in that rather than deploying sovereign power to deny manhood to his slaves, he in fact gifts manhood to the men of the plantation. In other words, Garner produces the "Sweet Home man." In a moment that rivals Frederick Douglass's fight with the slave breaker, Mr. Covey, in the famous scene at the chiastic center of the 1845 *Narrative*, Morrison gives us another moment in which we see a slave become a man.[38] Though differently from Douglass, who figures himself as reclaiming a stolen manhood, in the case of the Sweet Home men manhood is conferred. Mr. Garner gifts it, rather than Paul D and the other Sweet Home men seizing or (re)claiming it. What the story attends to is this: if Mr. Garner gifts masculinity to the Sweet Home men and in the process actually shows himself to be (like) God, the *imago dei* of a sovereign Creator who in this capacity creates (the Sweet Home) man in his image and after his likeness, then Morrison's story considers the travails that ensue for the thing created, for Paul D, in his reception of and his being attached or cathected to the "gift" (which is also a certain poisonous curse) of becoming human, of being a Sweet Home man, that is to say, of being a man or rather a "man-not" within the regime of the human.[39]

What Jackson reveals in her exquisite reading of *Beloved* via the question of the status of manhood is that this conferred manhood, which seemingly is to uplift Paul D and the other Sweet Home men, is less about the Sweet Home men and more about how that sovereign conferral is a technology for Mr. Garner's burnishing of his own proper and more perfect and self-perfecting manhood or humanity. As Jackson puts it, "So that he might 'demonstrate . . . what a real Kentuckian was,' Garner consolidated his manhood in the bestowal of abject manhood on the enslaved in the figure of the 'Sweet Home man.'"[40] He transgressed the protocols of the master-slave relation, transmogrifying by sovereign fiat the slave into a man, not out of any "recognition of the injustice of denied intersubjectivity but as performance of his dominance. . . . Thus, by inviting the slave to transgress slavery's limitations, he displays the arbitrariness of his power. . . . Garner's 'superior' manhood rests on the arbitrariness of his power."[41] Such is Paul D's "plastic function" for Mr. Garner. Such is the work his incorporation into the precincts of manhood serves.

But the contortions of the making of the "Sweet Home man" do not stop here. Morrison works hard to elaborate the psychic straits, shall we say, dare I say, the mind-fuck, that Garner's conferral of manhood puts Paul D into as he attaches himself to the illusion of heteropatriarchal manhood and its sovereign "I." Jackson is a sharp reader of and a reliable guide to what Morrison is working out on this point. Paul D wants to believe (and *believe* is, indeed, the vital term here) in the manhood that Mr. Garner providentially (another vital term: *providence*) confers on the Sweet Home men. He "wants to believe that he is a fully autonomous man, coherent, and whole."[42] However, the more Paul D attaches himself to said manhood, the more he works to live into it, to perform it, the more he has doubts about it. That is, "he wonders if his manhood rests entirely on the word of a white man, stirring within him a nascent question: Is his sense of manhood the product of a 'wonderful lie'?"[43] Indeed, "ironically, the more Paul D clings to rugged expressions of masculinity—curtailed emotion, mastery over bodily sensation, and killing if need be—the more he is boxed into not simply animality but plasticity: he can be manipulated and poured into a mold designed by Garner, and later by Beloved—acting as an avatar of slavery. For Paul D, masculinity is a symbol of his *presence* as a human."[44]

Paul D's doubts crescendo in his encounter with Mister, a rooster on the Sweet Home plantation. With his hands tied behind his back and hobbled low to the ground, animal to animal, Paul D meets Mister, who struts about, with the red comb (as the mythic phallic sign of a certain masculinity) on full display atop his head as he commands the respect of all of the other yard birds of the plantation. In that encounter Paul D's own sense of manhood, which was tenuous at best, is more fully destabilized as he encounters Mister and witnesses Mister's animal humanity, his humanimalized masculinity. In a sense, Mister is Paul D's doppelgänger, his mirror stage. But it's deeper than that: "When Paul D comes face-to-face, eye to eye, [we might even say, I to I], male to male with Mister"—this animal who from Paul D's perspective fully embodies the very sovereign manhood he is so invested in, so wants to realize in himself, but that he also doubts whether he's in full possession of—"he is compelled to confront [the fact that] the state of his manhood is not one of coherence, unification, and integrity but is, rather, riven, circumscribed, and indefinite."[45] Hence, it's not that in Mister, Paul D meets an apparition of himself. Rather, he is made to confront his own masculine incoherence, his nonattainment of a conferred masculinity, which is to say, a conferred humanity. In the face of this, what's to be done? That is to say, if, in Mr. Garner's eyes, "Paul D is not decisively and symmetrically 'man' but is, instead, an occasion for the theater of sovereign power and manipulated matter"—that is to say, he is "plastic"—then Paul D's "encounter with Mister sets in motion the inter-related processes of *relinquishing* his identification as a 'Sweet Home man' and redefining his gender and being in improvisational terms rather than in fidelity to those inherited from slavery."[46]

Jackson's use of the word *relinquish* here is quite interesting, not because it seemingly echoes the idea of "letting be" (*Gelassenheit*) as Martin Heidegger uses this term within his philosophical arsenal, but rather because of the term's deeper lineage within dissident mysticisms of the West, particularly the mysticism of Meister Eckhart and, even more important, behind Eckhart, the beguine mysticism of Marguerite Porete.[47] Burned at the inquisitor's stake in 1310 in a public square in Paris as a condemned heretic for her nonconformist spirituality (ultimately, she's in a tradition of those deemed witches, including William Shakespeare's Sycorax in *The Tempest*), Porete was given the epithet "pseudo-woman" (*pseudomulier*) for her mysticism of apophatic "unsaying." Developed in her *Mirror of Simple Souls*, which is believed to have been written somewhere between 1296 and 1306, Porete's mysticism unsays a substantialist deity. Following this, her mysticism unsays gender essentialism. She does away with a stable idea of the human just on the cusp of its modernist, racial capitalist congealing. As she burns away opposites and distinctions of separability—and in this echoes, as it were, an anoriginal love that posits no distinctions through separability—church authorities, invested as they were in hierarchies or orders of separability, turn her over to the secular arm of the polis for burning at the stake. There are two modes of relinquishing at play here. The former is Porete's relinquishing, which Meister Eckhart will take up and make more well known in his sermons and the like. Here the mysticism of relinquishment points to a precreative condition of existing without separability. The latter relinquishing is that enacted by the ecclesial authorities who turned Porete over to the state, as it were, who then relinquished her or killed her by burning her at the stake in order to ensure or otherwise shore up the terms of order.[48]

With these two modes of relinquishment in mind (and having bypassed Heidegger's taking up of Eckhart by emphasizing Porete's dissident, de-formative pseudo-woman mysticism), I come back to Jackson's claim that Paul D's "encounter with Mister sets in motion the inter-related processes of *relinquishing* his identification as a 'Sweet Home man' and redefining his gender and being in improvisational terms rather than in fidelity to those inherited from slavery." I want to route Jackson's statement in a Poretean-Eckhartian direction, which I further want to stage as a kind of proto-black religious direction, the direction of a kind of black mysticism.[49] Paul D must confront a loss of, or rather he must enter on a relinquishing of, perhaps even an annihilating of, a plasticized humanity and genre of manhood that was conferred on him but was never properly his nor strictly speaking for him. In fact, what must be annihilated is the identification itself with the genre of manhood that grants Paul D a (plasticized) humanity that props up (Mr. Garner's) humanism as such. Here annihilated identification may be akin to the "disidentification" of which José Esteban Muñoz speaks.[50] This disidentification with Sweet Home manhood, the rupturing of a problematic jouissance, is in the improvisational interest of the blackness of blackness, in the interest of black(female)ness, or, finally, in the interest of what Hortense Spillers speaks of as the "female within."[51]

We are now getting close to answering the question of what, ultimately, this scene between Paul D and Mister, against the backdrop of Mr. Garner's calculated conferral of manhood, says about black anarchy as black religious *anarchē*. What are we to take from a story in which the masculinist kingship and sovereignty Paul D so desires and has seemingly had conferred on him is manifest in an animal whose sovereign masculinity seems so intact ("Mister is 'king'"; "Mister was allowed to be and stay what he was," Paul D says), while Paul D's conferred masculinity is so hobbled or unstable ("But I wasn't allowed to *be* and *stay* what I was . . .")?[52] More still, does not the man-to-man confrontation between Paul D and Mister acquire another level of intensity once one factors in that Paul D functions like a surrogate mama to Mister? After all (and this, too, is something to which Jackson calls attention), it was Paul D who took Mister out of his shell after the mother "hen walked on off with all the hatched peeps trailing behind her," leaving Mister behind as an unhatched, leftover egg that "looked like a blank"?[53] Paul D tells us that he's the one who tapped the egg open, and "here come Mister, bad feet and all." In his unstable or plasticized masculinity, Paul D gives birth to the rooster; he mothers into being Mister's roostered-as-achieved masculinity, and yet desires what he sees in Mister as his filial offspring, as it were. He desires Mister's perceived-to-be-stable masculinity, for the birth of which Paul D himself is the surrogate vehicle.

Having pointed out these issues—Garner's conferral of masculinity and thus his plasticized en-gendering of the human onto Paul D; Paul D's own psychic ambivalence toward that masculinity; the crescendoing of the ambivalence in the face of the animal; and, finally, Paul D's own plasticized slippage between the masculine and the mother—Jackson raises the crucial question of ontology: "What is the *being* of blackness?" The response is worth quoting at length, for in it she crystallizes the stakes of plasticity while also making evident how her meditation on plasticized, black(ened) masculinity turns us back to questions of matter, as *mater*. She turns us back to questions of mat(t)er's "generative function." To the question, "So, what [then] is the *being* of blackness?" Jackson responds:

> Ultimately, (anti)blackness appears to be a matrix: a mold, a womb, a binding substance, a network of intersections, functioning as an encoder or decoder. It is an essential enabling condition for something of, but distinguishable from, its source—and therefore, it performs a kind of natality, performing a generative function rather than serving as an identity.
>
> If (anti)blackness is a matrix, then the normative of "the human" and the entire set of arrangements Sweet Home allegorizes have their source in abject blackness. In the process of distinguishing itself from blackness, normative humanity nevertheless bears the shadowy traces of blackness's abject generativity. As "the defined" rather than the "definers," the enslaved's abjection places blackness under the sign of the feminine, the object, matter, and the animal regardless of sex.[54]

Under the sign of the feminine as transmogrifiable, transubstantiatable matter, as matter subject to alchemic processes, within the regime of slavery blackness is subjected to a type of violence that is not the same as mere labor exploitation, though that is certainly occurring within the violence of enslavement. Rather, "as *Beloved* depicts it, the slave's body is always subjected to something else, to forms of domination that are in excess of forced labor."[55] This excess may be thought of as "a form of engineering" wherein "'the slave' is paradigmatically that which shall be appropriated by emergent demands of the reigning order as needed, with no regard for the potential irreparable effects of ontological slippage. Arguably, plasticization is the fundamental violation of enslavement: not any one particular form of violence—animalization or objectification, for instance—but rather coerced formlessness as a mode of domination and the *Unheimlich* (uncanny) existence that is its result."[56] This coerced formlessness locates "not as sociological subjectivity or identity but as a matrix for forms of modern subjecthood and subjectivity," as "infinitely malleable lexical and biological matter," in short, as "a plastic upon which projects of humanization *and* animalization rest."[57]

And yet Mister's animal perspective is a destabilizing point in which something else irrupts blindingly into view for Paul D as in a flash. The near nullification of his gendered-sexual being as a crisis of sovereignty within the signifying system of the human (this is what Mister brings into relief for Paul D) signals a possible rupture of and vertiginous rapture beyond the grammar of "the human" as a semiosis or a system of signification in which plasticization is its grounding technology. He is made to confront the beguiling fiction of the human and the violence that sustains it even as he is invited onto the mystic, fugitive pathway of the beguine, the pathway of the felonious monks and nuns, the no-ones who are not one and the no-bodies of sentient flesh. This is a path, as Jackson elaborates it thinking between Morrison and Fred Moten, of invention, indeed of improvisation, which is to say, "movement without predetermined terminus but nevertheless in an insistent direction."[58] Such improvisatory invention suggests "a 'deviance of form' that always 'operates as a kind of foreshadowing, if not prophetic, description' as well as a 'trace of another organization' and 'extemporaneous formation and deformation of rules, rather than the following of them.'"[59] Invention and improvisation here are the movement of (not simply the being of) black(female)ness, of black *mater* as matter, as waywardly opaque (Saidiya Hartman might call them "occult," as might Jayna Brown) practices of mattering otherwise.[60] Such practices are trace elements of another organization. The condition of earthiness and earthliness, of being earth. Some other sociality.

The Black Study of Religion

The relinquishment that I have considered here with assistance from Jackson's reading of Morrison and my own further amplification of her reading of Morrison takes us to the threshold of (what has been called) black religion as something at once related to but, in the end, parasemiotically out from religion and the human. In the next two chapters—chapter 2, on the question of matter itself as a question of anarchy, and chapter 3, on what might be called the Europeanist production of the Afro-Atlantic fetish as the ground of the modern invention of religion—I want to give intensified consideration to the specific religiosity of antiblackness or world blackening as a matter of material religion. This is precisely where Jackson leads us, where she leaves us, namely, to how plasticization as central to the making of black(ened) people and an antiblack world is fundamentally a religious operation of matter predicated on a certain imagination of the sacred or a mythic envisioning of the gods and their people. Indeed, it is an operation, Jackson ever so briefly but quite rightly argues, of the fetish. Here "the African mask," interpreted within nineteenth-century anthropology as fetish object, was taken as a sign of African atavism, a sign of African "disordered being" inasmuch as the African mask, necklace, stone carving, amulet, or what have you exceeded what the object represented, was more than the thing itself. In this, "the fetishized mask is perceived as the synechdochic-embodiment of the African's purported stonelike atemporal opacity and disordered metaphysics more generally, such that African masks and people are not merely correlates but appear interchangeable. Whereas for Heidegger, the hand is the synecdoche for thought, which is the synecdoche for world-making rich in spirit, historically in the West, the fetishized mask is the synecdoche of Hegel's Africa or the spiritless impoverishment of thought and world."[61]

What Jackson calls attention to here is how nonrepresentationalist modes of existing are both indicted and, as it were, invaded so as to erect or stand up that representationalist schema or form of the properly, rationally, and universally human. Religion, however, qua bad religion, religion qua nonrepresentationalist religion qua black religion, qua blackness, is the locus of the indictment and colonial invasion. Indeed, religion, "cast in the racialized terms of a teratology, [with] the so-called fetish [as] its signal anxiety," is the site of it all.[62] What Jackson has her finger on is the fact that this very characterization and categorization of African religions qua *religion* as bad religion, of African religions as "black religion," is an ontoepistemic imposition. It is what I, with Denise Ferreira da Silva and R. A. Judy in mind, would characterize as an "engulfment" into a Euro-Atlantic "semiosis."[63]

Given religion's emergence as a protocol of blackening, a serious task confronted Europeans, both their merchants and eventually their philosophers and other intellectuals: namely, how to bring proper reason out of the shadow of (black) religion, how to rationalize religion, how to bring forth pure reason, and thus how to bring forth the properly human. The scientific or critical study of religion, which consolidates in the nineteenth century, and anthropology, or the scientific or critical study of Man (Kant said his entire philosophy came down to the question *Was ist der Mensch?* [What is man?]), are white science.[64] Premised on a disavowal of its own affectability, its own relationship of entangled and absolute dependence on Africa, on things called black, indeed on black religion, white science (of which anthropology and the critical study of religion, historically, are a part, are its ground zero) is an ontoepistemic effort to establish an incoherent, antiblack purity of subjectivity that would purify religion. (Kant called such purified religion "rational religion" by which he meant religion unmarked by "fetish faith."[65]) Such religion would eventually be able on the basis (or *archē*) of pure reason to disavow itself precisely as religion. The name of that disavowal is what we now commonly called secularity or the secular. Such is the problem of religion and the human as these are bound up with the blackening of matter and the making of an antiblack world.

Meanwhile, even as all of this is the case as a task confronting Europeans regarding reason and subjectivity and regarding religion and the human, there is also the question of how to think what is called black religion as practices of opacity that are irreducible to the semiosis of what I've called here white sciences of purity and that Keeling has helped us see as bound up with racial capitalist commodification in "the black woman" figured as a store of value and that Keeling also links with the problem of individuation, as did I in the introduction. I propose that Charles Long is uniquely positioned to aid us in building on Keeling's and Jackson's insights as I've engaged them in this chapter to further confront these issues of religion and the human. Indeed, over the course of six decades as a historian of religion and a scholar of black religion and culture, he insisted that the epidermalizing or the racial blackening of the African took place fundamentally through that modern innovation or technology called *religion*. I want to consider Long's analysis of this problem.

My approach to him will be a bit different from how he tends to be engaged, when he is engaged, in black religious studies. While Long is often taken up, and not without good reason, as someone who provides us tools to take seriously the varieties of black religious experience, I will not engage him in this direction. Rather, backing up from here, my concern in the following two chapters will be to think black religion ironically. Which is to say, I want to think black religion as otherwise than religion while doing so from within the category of religion. Put differently, I want to unhinge black religion from the category of religion that, in fact, on one level generated it while also thinking black religion as more and less than the category of religion. My effort to think black religion in this way is part and parcel of the need to understand blackness as more and less than, as irreducibly anterior to, racial categorization, as irreducible to the human. In this regard, as blackness exceeds racial categories, so too does what is called black religion (and perhaps with a certain reworking what has been called "black theology" too . . . perhaps) exceed religio-theological categories. The gamble and ethical stakes of thinking with Long in this way, in thinking with him as a critical theorist, are to enact a thinking of black religion that is ani*mater*ially and thus anarchically "in the break" of religion and the human and the terms of matter, meaning, value, and signification these inventions set in motion.[66] This will constitute "a thinking [of black religion] in disorder," a thinking in anarchy (*an-archē*)—a thinking without the Principle, the Ground, or the Being of Rule that emerges in modernity as a project of ontology and of the human.[67] To think that improvisational *beyond*, that anarchy, which as *an-archē* is irreducible to any *archē* or Being of Rule, is the task of theorizing black religion and the spiritual vocation of black sociality.

And so, now to Charles Long and the black study of religion.

Chapter Two

The Matter of Anarchy

New World slavery established a field of demand that tyrannically presumed, as if by will alone, that the enslaved . . . could function as infinitely malleable lexical and biological matter, at once sub/super/human . . . [as] everything and nothing at the register of ontology such that form shall not hold.—ZAKIYYAH IMAN JACKSON, *Becoming Human* (2020)

Metallurgy [and alchemy] thus [take] on the character of obstetrics . . . unfolding of subterranean embryology. . . . To collaborate in the work of Nature, to help her to produce at an ever-increasing tempo, to change the modalities of matter—here, in our view, lies one of the key sources of alchemical ideology.—MIRCEA ELIADE, *The Forge and the Crucible* (1979)

"Bringer of Problems"

In the introduction and then again at the end of the previous chapter, I gave a sense of the approach I here take to Charles Long and to his engagement with the problem of "the imagination of matter," where matter signals the stuff of existence and even nonexistence, which remains a mode of existence, a function of the differential unity of life. Moreover, in the previous chapter I drew on this phrase—*the imagination of matter*—as part of elaborating Zakiyyah Iman Jackson's engagement with matter as bound up with the problem of religion. The approach I took goes against the grain of a certain common sense that sees religion as nonmaterial or as concerning things "spiritual," where, again within this mistaken common sense, spirit figures as opposed to matter. The presumption is that there is no materiality to or of spirit. Kara Keeling and Jackson intuit this not to be the case, while Long from within the field of religious studies displays precisely why and how this is not the case. Before the buzz around "material religion," before the chatter within the fields of religious studies and the anthropology of religion about "lived religion," Long was calling attention to religious materiality as central to the rise of the Atlantic World, to the making of an antiblack world, and to racial capitalist reason and its logics of individuation and socioecological catastrophe.

In this chapter I think more intently with Long about religion's invention as hosting a mode of mattering through extracting from life and land, an imagination of matter premised on separability. Exploring the nexus of matter and imagination, or what Long called "the imagination of matter," was his way into the entanglements of religion, racial capitalism, and now late-liberal reasoning and extractivism. Indeed, this chapter proceeds as a kind of exegesis of the Longian phrase, *the imagination of matter*, as itself a meditation on these matters. I am interested in Long's taking up of the issue of matter from one of his teachers and how in taking it up he works both within and against his disciplinary home base, the "history of religions" as a subfield of the critical study of religion (*Religionswissenschaft*). By the end of this chapter, I hope that I will have clarified how Long as a "bringer of problems," to purloin Corey Walker's beautifully provocative phrase, problematized the field of religious studies and opened up a new horizon of religious inquiry within black studies and the theorizing of black culture by giving attention to the question of matter as a question of religion's (re)invention.[1] As a bringer of problems, Long worked within the terms of the field of religious studies generally and within the terms of the history of religions to disclose how a certain blackening of matter lay at the root of the (re)invention of religion and is within the deep structure of the critical study of religion and the rise of modern capitalism as a devastating socioecological, extractivist practice. This chapter tracks Long's lifting off the ground what I call the *black study of religion*, while in the next chapter I extend the argument begun here to a consideration of Long's account of the rise of Atlantic World commerce and exchange as a religious event of the (anti)blackening of matter vis-à-vis the European production of (the idea of) the Afro-Atlantic fetish.

The journey in this investigation all begins for Long in the late 1950s when he arrived from Little Rock, Arkansas, to the University of Chicago Divinity School. It is in light of his time there as a graduate student and eventually as a faculty member that he forged the phrase *the imagination of matter*. Indeed, he forged it in thinking with one of his teachers, later to become a faculty colleague. This is the French-Romanian historian of religions Mircea Eliade. In an essay titled "Mircea Eliade and the Imagination of Matter," Long engages two of Eliade's works: *The Forge and the Crucible: The Origins and Structures of Alchemy* (1956; English trans. 1962) and *Patterns in Comparative Religion* (1958). The bulk of this chapter is given over to a reading of Long's engagement with these two texts in his essay on his teacher, Mircea Eliade.

I won't bury the lede: I argue that Long subjects Eliade, and by extension the general field of religious studies, to black study. That is, he reads Eliade in such a way as to develop an understanding of matter inflected by black (religious) studies. He will learn from Eliade, bending his insights, breaching them, as it were, and redirecting them toward a religious studies interpretation of matter's (anti)blackening in the rise of Atlantic World commerce and exchange, which is to say, in the rise of extractive Western capitalism, and with this in the rise of the United States and the Americas as religious matter(s). What will become clear by the time Long is done, and by the time this and the next chapter are concluded, is that what is needed is what Zakiyyah Iman Jackson, in her reading of Nalo Hopkinson's *Brown Girl in the Ring*, has called a "troping of the trope of African religion."[2] Such parareligious troping of religion is at the heart of those constellations of practices that have been called black religion and, more generally still, black faith understood as arts of creative endurance. The matter of black religion or, perhaps better, the matter of black faith understood as a "troping of the trope of African religion" and as the arts of creative endurance connotes matter not in terms of the individuation that drives Western capitalism, its racial world, and finally its quest for salvation or to preserve itself at all costs. Rather, it connotes matter as that haptic weave of multiplicity, matter as the generative, collective, and confluent open field of always possible and often present-at-hand alternatives.

Long begins his essay "Mircea Eliade and the Imagination of Matter" with a consideration of Eliade's *Patterns in Comparative Religion*, noting the irritation that this work roused among anthropologists and others in the critical humanities when it first appeared on the scene. "It reminds them too much," says Long, "of James George Frazier's *The Golden Bough* or of lesser popular texts of exotic oddities that purport to describe the customs of primitive cultures."[3] At the crux of the angst around this text was this feeling that *Patterns* "represents the kind of work that cannot, at least, should not be undertaken, for it appears to rest on a naïveté lacking in scholarly sophistication regarding the relationship of religion, behavior, and social structure."[4] While not making an excuse for the residual talk about the "primitive" in a number of Eliade's formulations throughout the book, Long nevertheless sees something else at stake that scholars were either ignoring or disciplined into not seeing about Eliade's work. Long argues that Eliade was, in fact, "presenting a systematic text, attempting to address the issue of religion as a specific mode of being" and thus as indexing a specific *material* understanding of the world, a certain *material* orientation in the world, and, finally, a particular *material* practice of worlding.[5] However, what Eliade was doing in this respect was lost to view, Long charges, due to certain habits of thought in the critical humanities at the time of *Patterns'* publication. Long calls these habits of thought an "imperialism of method," which has led various disciplines to "reduce the forms of religion to those human dimensions more consonant with the ideologies and existential situations of a nonreligious [read: a Western, methodologically secular] modernity."[6] It is this epistemic imperialism that has made Eliade's intervention, Long contends, either misunderstood or virtually illegible.

The task Long sets for himself in "Mircea Eliade and the Imagination of Matter" is to set the record straight by suggesting that Eliade's *Patterns in Comparative Religion* is, in fact, "a most fruitful text for raising the issue of religious epistemology. In this text Eliade attempts to account for the inner structure of the consciousness of *Homo religiosus* from an examination of the sacred symbols of archaic cultures."[7] More specifically, key for my concerns here is Long's claim that "Eliade's work shows how the forms of matter (nature) evoke modes of consciousness and experience."[8]

THE MATTER OF RELIGION

I will not here reproduce Long's careful analysis of the intricacies of Eliade's argument, for what concerns me is what Long wants to take away from Eliade. On this Long is direct: in all that Eliade says in *Patterns*,

> [he] is speaking of a primary and primordial intuition of matter. In other words, he is approaching the issue of religious experiences in a twofold manner. The specific intuition of human consciousness is always correlated within an a priori form of the world. It is the universality of matter itself in all of its several forms, rather than simply the inner workings of human consciousness epistemologically or psychologically which is the source of the religious consciousness. . . . For Eliade the very structure of the religious consciousness is predicated on a form of the world which is present as a concrete form [we might annotate here and say, a concrete imagination] of matter.[9]

More still, "while it is the case that the religious consciousness is always capable of recognizing the distinction between the sacred and the profane, this is merely the most general formulation of the religious dialectic. Every religious person and community recognizes this distinction in a precise and specific manner, and the archaic source of these specificities is the *a priori* concrete forms of matter."[10]

What Long is calling attention to in these statements is not merely Eliade's account of a "religious dialectic" structured between the sacred and the profane. Rather, of deeper interest to him is what that dialectic hopes to explain. What the religious dialectic is mobilized to explain is the "religious person's" or, even more, a community's presuppositions about matter or material existence. Those presuppositions, which Eliade frames as structured by a religious dialect, are a kind of societal operating system by which those of the community live and move and have being. In this way, they exhibit an orientation to matter or material existence. With Eliade, Long sees this outlook on matter—or the stuff of the world and how persons see themselves related to and as of that stuff—as an a priori or as a kind of regulative ideal, to use a Kantian language. Finally, for Eliade as Long interprets him, the outlook or imagination of matter that structures consciousness within the community or the socius comes to be signified within a semiosis in which material elements such as the sun, the moon, water, wind, stones, and the like—precisely as particular expressions of matter—constitute a symbology through which persons within the society can understand their place terrestrially and within the cosmos as a vault of being. In this sense, as Long explains, "a primary imaginative religious structure" operates in symbolic relationship to matter or to the material elements of the world.[11] "These imaginary modes of matter hold exemplary places in Eliade's thought" about archaic man, such that, for example, "the waxing and waning of the moon is the archetype of *real human* time. This time, [Eliade] explains, should be distinguished from astronomical time (rationalized time) which comes later. Here we are dealing with time in the *concrete* sense," that is to say, as immanent to matter qua matter or as stuff.[12] "The rhythms of the moon measure and synthesize the various modes of *concrete* time."[13] Long provides more examples—particularly around the sun and around water—within Eliade's *Patterns in Comparative Religion* to illustrate what is emerging about the imagination of matter.

What Long wants to draw from Eliade is emerging clearly enough: he wants to draw attention to "the meaning of matter as a constitutive ingredient in the formulation of the archaic consciousness in Eliade's thought."[14] The religious consciousness in archaic societies is not antimaterial. To the contrary, it is rigorously material. Indeed, it is earthly and earthy, bound up with the very elements of earth and of existence as such. That is to say, Long sees Eliade as revealing with the tools of the history of religions as a subfield within the modern critical study of religion that "the basic human discoveries about matter were made by [what have been called] archaic societies. . . . [The] techniques that form the basis of [such societies]" rested on understanding the primal elements of life (i.e., the sun, moon, stars, stones, water, plants, wind, fire, and the like) as part of a "magical experience" in which matter itself is understood as enspirited, deeply animated, or marked by a more-than that is operative on varied vibrational frequencies.[15] Such an understanding of matter as vibrationally animated, indeed as vibration, requires an understanding of the senses as capacitated or capable of being rhythmically attuned to this fuller sense of matter and the elements by virtue of the participation of the senses within matter's movement, its flow. The senses are vibrational too. They are material, of matter. They matter.

But there is something further that Long wants to draw out regarding the theme of an imagination of matter in Eliade that will inform what he later does with it. For this, Long shifts from a consideration of Eliade's *Patterns in Comparative Religion* to a consideration of one of Eliade's lesser considered texts, *The Forge and the Crucible: The Origins and Structures of Alchemy*. In this text "Eliade undertakes an analysis of alchemy—a technique present in the traditional citied traditions, but forming a continuity with archaic metallurgy."[16] Further specifying alchemy's basis, in a way that resonates with my engagement with Zakiyyah Iman Jackson's notion of black *mater* as matter in the prior chapter, Long quotes Eliade as saying:

> Mineral substances shared in the sacredness attaching to the Earth-Mother. Very early on we are confronted with the notion that ores "grow" in the belly of the earth after the manner of embryos. Metallurgy thus takes on the character of obstetrics. Miner and metalworker intervene in the unfolding of subterranean embryology: they accelerate the rhythm of the growth of ores, they collaborate in the work of Nature and assist it to give birth more rapidly. In a word, man, with his various techniques, gradually takes the place of Time: his labours replace the work of Time.
>
> To collaborate in the work of Nature, to help her to produce at an ever-increasing tempo, to change the modalities of matter—here, in our view, lies one of the key sources of alchemical ideology.[17]

This is a quite stunning statement, having about it several moving parts. Central, however, is the idea that as an ancient technique alchemy is premised on the idea of the aliveness and sacrality of minerals as "'living' substances."[18] More than this, alchemy is premised on the idea that minerals, stones, ores, and the like are, in fact, alive, just as an embryo in utero potentiates aliveness, gestating in the womb that is the "belly of the earth." Here the earth is *terra mater*, "Mother-Earth," the matrix from which in due time after "growing ripe" in the suspension of "telluric darkness" precious stones, metals, and the like come forth after a "'gynecomorphic' birth."[19] Thus, in answer to the question, "Who is the alchemist?" or further still to the question, "What is it that the ancient smelter, smith, and alchemist do?" the answer returns that they are involved in a kind of "obstetrics" and "subterranean embryology."[20] Collaborating with Nature, the smelter, smith, and alchemist are, on Eliade's reading of alchemy, gynecological obstetricians of sorts. They assist—Eliade's word is *collaborate*, a word that I shall problematize in short order—in a geological birthing process. Standing in the place of time, "in their labours" the ancient smelter, smith, and alchemist assist Nature, which is in a long, temporal reproductive labor process as it gives birth from within itself or shapes further what comes from within the earth. Thus, the ancient smelter and smith, for example, in forging a sword from extracted ore, or the ancient alchemist, in employing techniques to transform some extracted metal into gold, are each in their own way "[pursuing] the transformation of matter, its perfection and its transmutation."[21] In thus dealing extractively with the geological or subterranean strata of life, these technicians of matter, whose techniques are premised on matter's fecundity, work in lockstep with the potentiating capacities of *terra mater*. In collaborating in this way with *mater* as matter, alchemists prove to be matter's technicians and in their own way technicians of the sacred too. They are involved in a process of "alchemical soteriology" precisely by "[changing] the modalities of matter."[22] Putting it in his own terms, Long says that in all of this what Eliade clarifies is that "the alchemists through magico-religious techniques attempted the transmutation of . . . base metals into gold . . . [not because] they were mere gold-seekers or counterfeiters." Rather, "they had probably discovered and/or retained an [even] older conception of the Earth-Mother, bearer of embryos" wherein matter as such was *mater*, imbued with all manner of generative potentials.[23]

Gynecology and the Imagination of Matter

Before considering further what Long pulls from Eliade's analysis to inform his own understanding of the rise of the world of transatlantic commerce and exchange as a religio-magical and a soteriological or salvational event (for that is where this is headed), it is worth tarrying a bit more with the power of Eliade's imagining of ancient alchemy through the metaphor of modern gynecology-obstetrics. With this metaphor the gendered logics of extraction as bound up with matter and religion, or the matter of religion, comes clearly into view. More still, in taking up this aspect of the question of the imagination of matter, I also here aim, as mentioned earlier, to put some pressure on the notion of *collaboration* that Eliade deploys inside of this very metaphor to clarify how alchemy works as a materially engendering technology, whose legacy through transatlantic commerce and exchange remains operative in vital ways. After a conversation with Morgan Barbre, a graduate student I've worked with and whose work as a practicing doula informs her religious studies research into race and white womanhood, both the power of and the problems with Eliade's use of gynecology-obstetrics as a metaphor of alchemy became even clearer. Barbre introduced me to the field of the anthropology of birthing, which has helped me understand on a level that before engaging with her was quite beyond me how misplaced Eliade's deployment of the notion of collaboration inside of the metaphor of obstetrics is for talking about alchemy as a technology of matter and what problems this notion (re)produces.[24] By inserting collaboration into the metaphor of obstetrics to elaborate on the "cooperation" with Nature he sees metalworkers and the like engaged in, Eliade somewhat undermines the depths of his own insight into the power of technocratic obstetrics as a metaphor to talk about alchemy and the earth extraction that he is describing. This will prove to matter significantly for an understanding of what alchemy has to do with the (anti)blackening of the earth that is at play with the rise of a transatlantic world of commerce and exchange, indeed, with the slave ship and its wake.[25]

Suggesting a medicalized relationship to matter, obstetrics as a mode of Western technocratic medicine posits the doctor or a similarly positioned practitioner as the authority of knowing in the birthing process rather than, as is the case in various other cultural birthing systems, the birthing or laboring person. Differently put, within the regime of obstetric medicine, the birthing person is positioned as somewhere between nonagential and agential, but if agential, secondarily so at best, insofar as the birthing person is subordinated to the agentiality and knowing of the figural "man of science," that is, the "doctor" as *Homo scientificus* and thus the figure of medical-scientific authority in the activity of birthing. Inserting forceps into the womb to extract from it, the obstetrician-gynecologist (OB-GYN) is agential in this model of the birth process. What I want to zero in on is the image that guides the imagination here. That image is not so much of the birthing person actually giving birth as it is of the figural man of science, through inserting the forceps into the womb and extracting from it, giving birth. Moreover, as Barbre has said, summarizing the work of Susan Bordo, a leading feminist theorist in this area of inquiry, what this mode of "medical industrial hegemony fashions [is] a 'fetal super-subject,'" plasticized from "a relatively *unseen* (at least before the routinization of the sonogram and other monitoring technologies) fetus." This fashioning or plasticization occurs at the site of the pregnant person, who is figured as a "maternal incubator."[26] In this model of birthing, if there is collaboration between doctor and laboring person, it is asymmetrical, which of course begs the question then of collaboration.[27] The power of Eliade's recourse to medical obstetrics lies in the fittingness of the model of authority, being, and knowing within this field for describing ancient alchemy practices. It, too, as Eliade shows, operates invasively and extractively. Like the OB-GYN who reaches into the womb of the laboring person to bring forth a "super-subject" from a "maternal incubator," so too does the type of alchemist Eliade describes extractively reach into the Mother-Earth, into *mater*.

In the end, what Eliade misses but that his own recourse to gynecology and obstetrics actually makes available to him is precisely the ambivalence of alchemy. On the one hand, it is premised on the insight into the fundamental generativity of matter as *mater*. As *mater*, matter is an invaginatively expansive or open field of forms generating more forms through an ongoing cycle of dying and living, living and dying. On the other hand, however, alchemy as Eliade describes has also been a scene of invasion and extraction structured around gender protocols. Eliade does not address any of this, though there are traces of these issues throughout his powerful analysis of ancient and medieval alchemy. My point here is that due to a lack of gender analysis, Eliade does not reckon with the implications of the obstetric metaphor he mobilizes to unfold the history of alchemy. With this metaphor he figures the ancient alchemist, smelter, and smith as advancing techniques of extraction from the earth, figured as a kind of womb. And yet, there is something more than metaphorically obstetrical at stake here. It is precisely this "more than metaphor" that eludes Eliade, though the history he unfolds actually provides a way to understand this more than.

I can imagine a possible retort to the criticism I've just leveled to the effect that Eliade is only being descriptive in what he's saying. As a historian, he is only describing how various ancient alchemists, smiths, and smelters describe what they do. He should, therefore, be held to the standard of the adequacy of his historical description. Yes, that's fair enough. But another way to appreciate what I am calling attention to is that notwithstanding the power of Eliade's use of obstetrics, which I think in itself is quite fitting for what he's historically describing, the metaphor is not historically neutral. Eliade was working on *The Forge and the Crucible: The Origins and Structures of Alchemy* at a time that one might consider the apex of technocratic obstetrics in the United States. That is to say, his thinking through the history of alchemy is occurring in lockstep with a transformation that is taking place in the technology of birthing in the West generally and in the United States specifically. (Immigrating from France, Eliade took up his teaching post at the University of Chicago in 1957.) This is a time when most people giving birth (in hospitals) were etherized—euphemistically referred to as "Twilight Sleep"—and effectively rendered animallike, often being tied down and restrained. This was thought to be a more humane way to handle labor pain, the thinking being along the lines of "she won't remember it." But remember what? Well . . . the procedure of extraction.

All of this is to say that Eliade's recourse to gynecological obstetrics as a metaphor to explain the history of alchemy is neither neutral nor innocent. It is, indeed, of Eliade's own moment. What is fascinating, given this, is that the very metaphor of gynecological obstetrics carries traces of the history of alchemy that the metaphor is mobilized to aid in explaining. Which means we are dealing with a metaphor that is more than metamorphic. It's, shall we say, a *real* metaphor that brings modernity and the imagination of matter on which it rests into view as gyneco-obstetric. This in a significant sense is lost on Eliade, notwithstanding his recourse to obstetrics as a metaphor to brilliantly describe ancient alchemy. That is, lacking in Eliade is a sense of how, or even that, as a matter of history the gendered and extractive logics of alchemy have exerted an imaginative and practical force in the birthing (pun intended) of modernity and its project of ontology through Atlantic commerce and exchange and even on the tools of thought he deploys as a historian of religion.

Alchemy and the Maternal Ecology of Blackness

Against this backdrop we can even more appreciate Long as a close reader of Eliade but also why I am reading Long too (and thereby black religion) with black feminist theory. I want to suggest that in thinking with Eliade, Long in fact is setting up a consideration of modernity; the emergence of Atlantic World contact, commerce, and exchange; and the eventual political-economic formation called "the West" as informed by the terms of ancient alchemy as this informs the (re)invention of religion. Indeed, via his reading of Eliade, Long, too, finds in the alchemist a sacred metalworker, a matter-worker, who extracts from the incubating womb of *terra mater* precious ores, minerals, and metals. But extending Eliade (and here's the move of the black study of religion), Long in effect posits that the alchemist and "his" gyneco-obstetric as socio-extractive maneuvers have not gone away. Modern alchemists, shall we say, as matter-workers have imposed on matter a new imagination. Out of that imagination a new "thing" or "fetal super-subject" has emerged. That thing is the commodity. But in this framework who are the modern alchemists? A Longian reading of Eliade leads us to answer that they were the enslaving colonial merchants and their economic heirs, along with their philosophical heirs who elaborated the ontological and epistemic frameworks of value that were internal to the gyneco-obstetric and socio-extractive affair of modernity. These figures—from colonial merchants, missionaries, and priests to jurists, theologians, philosophers, and economists—are characters in a dramaturgy of modernity as a ritualized and extractive scene of an obscene obstetrics. Which also means that each of these figures of modernity is an alchemist of a certain sort. Indeed, to stay more immediately with colonial merchants as practitioners of the modern world's founding logistics, as Stefano Harney and Fred Moten help us understand, they are technicians of matter, insofar as they, too, were involved in what we might call a process of transatlantic alchemy on *mater*, that from which something is extracted.[28] That something is the commodity as vessel for exchange, holder of surplus value, and as that around which "the human" constitutes itself and acquires orientation. But the production or bringing forth of the commodity form and around it "the human," as Jackson helps us understand, is premised on *mater* or "the fleshly being of blackness," which in the modern scene is "experimented with as if it were infinitely malleable indexical matter and biological matter, such that blackness is produced as sub/super/human at once, a form where form shall not hold: potentially 'everything and nothing' at the register of ontology."[29]

What I am suggesting here can be broadened further. In *Poetics of Relation* Édouard Glissant spoke of "the belly of the slave ship," figuring that belly as an abyss into which Africans were thrown.[30] This "belly of the boat," he says, "dissolves you, precipitates you into a non-world from which you cry out. This boat is a womb, a womb abyss. This boat: pregnant."[31] Not only must Glissant's framing of the Middle Passage be understood, as Omise'eke Natasha Tinsley insightfully argues, as part of modernity's "sexual geography" and of Caribbean discourse's wide-ranging and not-uncomplicated response to that geography, but such language is resonant with the Eliadean discourse on alchemy that Long seizes on.[32] Another example is "The Belly of the World: A Note on Black Women's Labors," Saidiya Hartman's beautiful essay that titularly picks up on Glissant's language. Hartman develops the gendered and gynecological significance of Glissant's language, linking it to a discourse of property:

> The slave ship is a womb/abyss. The plantation is the belly of the world. *Partus sequitur ventrem*—the child follows the belly. The master dreams of future increase. The modern world follows the belly. Gestational language has been key to describing the world-making and world-breaking capacities of racial slavery. What it created and what it destroyed has been explicated by way of gendered figures of conception, birth, parturition, and severed or negated maternity. To be a slave is to be "excluded from the prerogatives of birth." The mother's only claim—to transfer her dispossession to the child. The material relations of sexuality and reproduction

defined black women's historical experiences as laborers and shaped the character of their refusal of and resistance to slavery. The theft, regulation and destruction of black women's sexual and reproductive capacities would also define the afterlife of slavery.

Most often when the productive labor of the slave comes into view, it is as a category absent gender and sexual differentiation.[33]

Hartman here is on the terrain of alchemy as well, though beyond Glissant (and Long too) she attends to issues of gender and sexuation. That is, she picks up on the gendered and sexuating themes within alchemy as these relate to issues of "the material relations of sexuality and reproduction" within "black women's historical experiences." Historian Jennifer L. Morgan rigorously elaborates on just these issues in her research into the "reproductive potential . . . [and] possibilities of [black women's] wombs" as this figured into the history of New World slavery. The extractive potential of the womb figured into "the cost-benefit calculations colonial slaveowners [made regarding] the speculative value of a reproducing labor force," thus making the modern world a material and symbolic zone of what Jennifer Nash has more recently called "obstetric violence."[34] What is of significance here is that these insights about the womb, from Hartman to Morgan to Nash, and about the black(ened) womb as a site of extractive, reproductive potential, shall we say, function against the backdrop of alchemy and its extension into the (re)invention of religion. Indeed, the strand of black feminist theorization that I am here engaging with may be understood as thinking insurgently with black life in its otherwise everydayness, an everydayness, that is, in which black life creatively counteralchemizes against, though from within, the very "alchemy of race" that marks modernity as constituted through extraction.

The creative counteralchemizing that happens at the level of the alternative or the alter-everyday of surreally surviving, of surreally sur-thriving, the catastrophes of empire as a violently imposed imagination of matter premised on racial capitalist logics of extractive separability and individuation is forcefully evident in poet Alexis Pauline Gumbs's *M Archive: After the End of the World*, where with Gumbs's poetic guidance the reader is "periodically . . . confronted with [chemistry's] periodic table of elements."[35] Gumbs has in mind M. Jacqui Alexander's *Pedagogies of Crossing*, which Gumbs summarizes as clarifying that "the middle passage of the transatlantic slave trade [operated] as an act of violence that continues to impact the entire planet through the indivisibility of the water, wind, earth, and fire that surround and constitute our world. [Alexander] also suggests that the crossing was not only a geographic transfer of millions of people but also a movement of energies and elements into a relationship that persists, a material and conceptual relationship with the potential and compelled crossings we make in each moment."[36] Gumbs reshuffles, even conjures with, those material elements and with that ongoing movement of energies to creatively and speculatively advance "[possibilities] of being . . . after and with the consequences of fracking past peak oil . . . after and with a multitude of other small and large present apocalypses. After the end of the world as we know it. After the ways we have been knowing the world."[37] This reshuffling of material and chemical elements of water, wind, earth, and fire is nothing less than the enactment of an alternative imagination of matter premised on nonseparability or "difference without separability." Or, as I develop it later in chapters 4 and 5 of this book, this *mater*-ial reshuffling is a feat of poetics, the art and artistry of black faith, a troping of the trope of (African) religion. More precisely still, it is a feat of "poethics" where the poethical, after Denise Ferreira da Silva though in duended communion with Long, Glissant, and R. A. Judy, concerns living artistically or in the "blacklight" of opacity.[38] Such artistic or socio-aesthetic living cuts to the quick of what I have been calling in these pages *the blackness of black religion* approached through *the black study of religion*. The blackness of black religion signals that socioecological movement, as Gumbs might put it, of "what we cannot know from here."[39]

One further finds the kind of counteralchemizing that I am talking about in the work of poet M. NourbeSe Philip, whose poem *Zong!* emerges in relationship to the late eighteenth-century incident on board the slave ship *Zong* in which the ship's captain threw overboard upward of 150 Africans in a calculated decision to collect insurance proceeds against them. Philip imagines as a "word store" and a "matrix" the five hundred–plus words that make up the summary legal judgment of the lawsuit (known as *Gregson v. Gilbert*).[40] From this matrix or word store, the poet produces or conjures the poem. Or is it that the poem conjures itself through the medium of the poet? Or is it both at the same time and thus apart from the regime of time that has come into play with capitalist-extractive reason? In this way, the poem *Zong!* is a vessel of another sort—a vessel for the ongoing aliveness of the dead.[41] More still, as a poet, and more precisely as a figure of "Sycorax," Philip may be thought of as counteralchemizing with black *mater*, that unrepresentable mode of matter(ing) beyond capitalist reason that figures the African as that humanimalized commodity that as property props up the properly human.[42]

While a notion of alchemy and counteralchemizing is afoot in the examples I've here adduced, it is Zakiyyah Jackson who in fact gives us the alchemical terminology of *mater* as black *mater*.[43] Locating antiblackness specifically on the terrain of alchemy, she offers a further point of resonance beyond her general concern with the question of matter with Long's meditation on Eliade's meditations on alchemy. In this way, black studies converges with religious studies on the question and problem of "Man" as the name of a specific world orientation; black study becomes the black study of religion regarding this problem. That is, approached with Jackson in mind, the human or "Man" is precisely he who as a kind of alchemist experimentalizes with so as to enact a white science on the earth through his extractive use of the elements, his extractive use of *mater*. Specifically, from black *mater* the commodity form or the property mode of matter(ing) is extracted even as in this very process the hu/Man produces himself as a self-possessed, propertied subject in the very reaching into the womb of black *mater* to bring forth the commodity form. This is in keeping with what Eliade says about the alchemist: "The alchemist takes up and perfects the work of Nature, *while at the same time working to 'make' himself*."[44] Indeed, in participating in an "'experimental' manner" "in the complex and dramatic Life of Matter," the alchemist "partakes in the mysteries of the transmutation of man" through a descent into the death and resurrection of matter, into and out of the Earth-Mother (*terra mater*).[45] Interestingly, Long quotes this very passage in his essay on Eliade. He notes the Earth-Mother language in Eliade but does not linger with it. As for Eliade himself, speaking of the alchemist as applying a technique of descending into and bringing some new form of matter out of *mater*, Eliade presents alchemy as achieving "transmutation . . . by causing matter to pass through four phases, named, from the colours taken on by the ingredients: *melansis* (black), leukosis (white), xanthosis (yellow), and iosis (red). . . . With innumerable variations, the four (or five) [color] phases are retained throughout the whole history of Arabian Western alchemy" with "black (the *nigredo* of medieval writers)" or blackening as descent into *mater* "[symbolizing] death."[46] What Eliade is at pains to clarify is that through what he calls a "regression *ad uterum*" or to the "fluid state of matter," or on the cosmological plane to "chaos," to the *massa confusa* of the *abyssus*; into *materia prima* as the primordial state of matter; in short, through a black(ened) descent into *mater*, the alchemist subjects mineral substances to "suffering" and, indeed, "death," so that they may be "'reborne' to another mode of being" or "transmuted."[47]

Finally, Eliade notes that "Western alchemists integrated their symbolism into Christian theology. The death of matter was sanctified by the death of Christ who assured its redemption."[48] In the next chapter, I argue, following Long and what I have been pointing to here, that this death of matter as matter's blackening and as an alchemical working on black *mater* warrants us in speaking not only of Transatlantic Alchemy (as I've started doing here) but of a Transatlantic Transubstantiation. More still, it will require us to imagine a counteralchemical as an extraceremonial practice beyond the rituals of the racially gendered and sexuating blackening. This extraceremonial practice operates in relationship to racial blackening while also being parasemiotically irreducible to racial blackening, as R. A. Judy with Kevin Quashie helps us think about. Here Blackness is marked by open-ended, revisable practices of living artistically, practices of poetic, poethical life.[49] It refers to black *mater* as the locus of an entangled and *an-archic massa confusa* that is utterly off the timeline of "the human" or the mode of matter(ing) attendant on this figure. For now, my point is simply to say that in his reading of Eliade's *The Forge and the Crucible*, Long is himself considering the Atlantic World as a crucible of racial alchemy that is operative within the emergent capitalist mode of mattering that is hidden to view through the imposition of something called "African religion" as black(ened) religion, as fetish religion, on the African.

Indeed, Long closes his meditation on Eliade, matter, and alchemy with a statement that provides a window into or anticipates where he will take the question of matter in the wake of what he's culled from Eliade's *Patterns in Comparative Religion* and *The Forge and the Crucible: The Origins and Structures of Alchemy*. In this, he anticipates significant currents of present-day black studies theorization. There is the suggestion in Long's "Mircea Eliade and the Imagination of Matter" that with the rise of (racial) capitalism as harboring a new *archē* or Principle of Being and Rule emergent through transatlantic commerce, contact, and exchange and through its chief invention, the commodity, "the inner structure of matter as the basis for cosmic order [has changed]. . . . Through these changes [the] Life and integrity of matter became skewered, infantilized, trivialized, and disenchanted. *There is nevertheless the possibility for the rediscovery of the life of matter as a religious phenomenon—an equal and sometimes alternate structure in the face of the dehumanizing and terroristic meaning of history.*"[50] Long here suggests the real stakes of why he's taken the reader (and why I've taken you, dear reader, in my tracking with Long) through an engagement with Eliade and the innards of the field of religious studies, generally, and the history of religions subfield, particularly. This was not just a reading of Eliade for Eliade's sake, Long wants us to know. Rather, this was an engagement with the history of religions aimed at reorienting religious studies around the question of matter through a consideration of the Atlantic World of commerce, contact, and exchanges with these Eliadean themes in mind. Eliade's work brings the question of matter and/as the question of the meaning of religion into critical relief. Indeed, Long's claim is that Eliade understood "primitive cultures" as creative thinkers of matter and that such thinking was central to them understanding their place in the sacred cosmos and thus to them organizing their worlds. They help us understand that matter is not inert but animate; that matter flows and, indeed, is flow, is movement at every level, cosmic and quantum; that matter even precedes and is without space-time.[51] In this, Eliade did crucial ground-clearing work, after which

Long positions himself as taking further steps. The latter's takeoff point from the former entails contending with the change that has occurred with respect to the imagination of matter via the emergence of the Atlantic World. Long's contention is that "the life and integrity of matter" has been compromised by way of a new *archē* of meaning and imagination that has been extracted from it. That extraction, which is a kind of obstetric invasion of and extraction from matter, has instituted what is called "reality" and the hegemony of the empirical or what Jackson has called "*the* world as such."[52] Something that advances itself as "real" has interdicted the matter of the surreal assembly. The change that has occurred revolves around the new structures of matter(ing) that obtained with the rise of the Atlantic World or with what Long speaks of at the end of his meditation on Eliade as "the dehumanizing and terroristic meaning of history." The task then is to understand the perils of the reigning *archē* and imagination of matter and meaning, as well as to elaborate possible reimaginings, surreal reimaginings, of matter in the face of as well as beyond or in refusal of "the dehumanizing and terroristic meaning of history."

The Afro-Surreal

Surreal reimaginings: this is what is practiced under the sign of black religion and the blackness thereof. Such surreal reimaginings are practices of blackness as anarchic insurgency. To slightly annotate Long from the above quote, they signal what might be called "the nevertheless possibility." Chapters 4 and 5 ahead consider this parareligious nevertheless. That is, they consider the faith that animates blackness, which I understand as the physics of radical creativity. That creativity Long thinks about with recourse to the geometric mathematics of the ellipse and its grammatical extension into the punctuation mark of the ellipsis (see chapter 4), while Nathaniel Mackey's practice of the poem, as I will engage with it, is an instance of that parareligious nevertheless, that aesthetic insistence, that insurgent persistence, that marks blackness and that Long thinks about under the sign of black religion (see chapter 5). But before we get to that, there is the next chapter's furthering of where I've left off in this chapter. In the next chapter, I extend the analysis of the rise of racial capitalism as a kind of alchemical, transubstantiational happening that occurred in relationship to Atlantic commerce and exchange. It was through such commerce and exchange that under the sign of the fetish Western capitalism arose as a religious event of matter. In examining this, we will extend our engagement with Long and the black study of religion.

Chapter Three

Anarchy and the Fetish

The power of juxtaposing market rationality to fetish religion was realized through a long history of rendering black religion as the quintessential manifestation of superstition, delusion, and savagery, properties that coalesced into the racial constitution of the heathen. . . . Guinea Africa became the most potent and widely circulated hieroglyph [in European and eventually Enlightenment thought] for describing the religion of primitives as a racializing exercise.—SYLVESTER JOHNSON, *African American Religions* (2015)

The Matter of the World

This epigraph by scholar of African American studies and religious studies Sylvester Johnson in its own way points to a chief concern of this chapter: to wit, how the Negro was transubstantiated or religionized into existence and how that religionization must be understood in relationship to the market rationalities and reasons of state that obtained in fifteenth- and sixteenth-century Atlantic commerce and exchange. In thinking about the Atlantic World as a locus of matter's fundamental transubstantiation through market logics of property, I consider these issues under the rubric "transatlantic transubstantiation" to further consider the imagination of matter that has taken hold. On this Charles Long continues to be someone I want to think with in this chapter.

In this chapter I unfold this line of argumentation by attending to how the discourse of *the fetish* within the Atlantic commercial theater is for Long a key site of the antiblack epidermalizing of matter, the racial blackening of matter precisely at the originary scene of primitive accumulation, the *archē*, in which the African is blackened or transubstantiated into the Negro. What I want to show is that antiblackness, or more precisely the (anti)blackening of matter and the making of the Negro, is an operation of religion such that racialization is a feat of religionization; it occurs through the invention of what is called religion. I carry out this argument by tracking Long's account of this in his essay "Indigenous People, Materialities, and Religion: Outline for a New Orientation to Religious Meaning" (2004). To be sure, Long is engaging this theme through much of his corpus of writings. Indeed, I bring on board some of this other material while making this argument. But because of its lucidity and its approach to the history of the Atlantic as a scene of religion and theology, Long's "Indigenous People, Materialities, and Religion" essay offers one of the most compelling sites of the black study of religion with racialization as religionization as its topic of concern. Hence, I begin there.

Scattered throughout Long's writings, particularly those published after his signature work *Significations: Signs, Symbols, and Images in the Interpretation of Religion* (1986), is a consistent and, I'd dare say, insistent line of argumentation about a new imagination of matter that has been inaugurated with the emergence of Atlantic World commerce and exchange. Internal to this imagination of matter is a new *archē* of being (human). I summarize Long's general claim about this *archē*, this imagination of matter, as follows: Atlantic commerce and exchange in the Age of Discovery and Conquest were a genesis, a "beginning, starting point," the natal occasion of a "new orientation" toward the substance and stuff, in short, the matter, of the world. Indeed, it was the natal occasion of a new orientation to "*the* world as such," to use Zakiyyah Iman Jackson's nomenclature, toward what Long spoke of as its "underlying substance as primordial and ultimate undemonstrable principal."[1] This new orientation toward matter was bound up with practices of property and the instantiation of the European as the measure of the hu/Man. Long sees Mircea Eliade as setting up a consideration of this, though Eliade himself does not take it up.

In this chapter I track Long's concern with the (religious) mattering that took place in the Atlantic theater, the violence against *mater* that I considered in the previous chapter. Here we enter a core concern of the black study of religion. That core concern is the study of the problematic orientation toward matter that organizes the modern world and that has been propped up by a certain vision of the gods or of what is deemed ultimate or of ultimate concern. This problem of matter—the problem, I contend, that in some fundamental sense is being attended to in the movement named Black Lives Matter—is the background against which to understand what I will interpret as Long's reading of black religion as exceeding or as more expansive than the notion of religion. That excess or more-than, which is the more-than that is the blackness of black religion, turns on Long's nascent discourse on or theorization of anarchy (*an-archē*). Such anarchy (*an-archē*)—the anarchy of an an-archic blackness and, further still, of an anarchic or unstately faithfulness to the entanglement of all things, a devotion that orients the spiritual vocation of black radicalism—points to what has been called "the groundedness of an uncontainable outside."[2] That groundedness hosts alternate socialities that have been spoken of as socialities of entangled "incompleteness."[3] Within the terms of the argument I am developing here, such socialities may be thought of as premised on an alternative imagination of matter—black *mater* as mattering otherwise. The praxis of this otherwise mattering, which is to say, the praxis of other genres of existence, suggests thinking blackness in its irreducibility to racial categories and thus as an alternative, dissident alchemizing, an alter-alchemy, a para-alchemy, which is precisely what Charles Long at the end of "Mircea Eliade and the Imagination of Matter" seems to be reaching for in his formulations. Such a praxis of reimagining matter takes place as practices of living and aliveness beyond the very binary of Life and Death as these have been racially parceled out (whiteness as the horizon of Life and thus as that which must be defended against blackness as the horizon of Death) and that which organizes the reigning *archē* or metaphysics of matter(ing).[4]

Transatlantic Transubstantiation

Long begins by announcing that his intent is to outline a new orientation to religious meaning by probing the question of the *archai*. This is a term that he situates within a family of terms that include the terms *indigenous* and *primal.* There is an ambiguity around these terms and especially around the notion of the *archē* and the *archaic.* Long asks, "Is the archaic, primal, or indigenous at the beginning of human existence, at the beginnings of the modern west, or does the archaic refer to 'a beginning' as a structure of consciousness?"[5] He answers by raising another question, aimed at pressing us to break with both a certain scholarly and popular common sense: "Why . . . in the modern period of the West has so much concern and attention on the scholarly as well as the popular level been related to cultures and peoples who have been classified as archaic, primal, or indigenous?" He goes on to say, "It is very clear that these terms did not originate in the cultures and peoples designated by them. They are terms of the modern West's classification and nomenclature of global cultural reality. And in a strange and complex way they represent specific constitutive elements in the creation of the modern West's understanding of itself; in this manner the indigenous are necessary aspects of any mode of modernity."[6] From here Long argues that to understand the notions of the archaic, primal, or indigenous, one must get at what's concealed within these terms.

Take the term *indigenous*. "To be sure, if you take one of the meanings of [this] term—the original or the first—it is clear that there must be indigenous cultures in all parts of the world, West and non-West. While this is true, the West during the modern period created another term to express its new formation; this was the term *civilization*," which as a term "carried a valuational and normative meaning regarding the nature and status of various human societies."[7] After World War II, the

> meaning of civilization, on both the popular and academic levels, emerged as part of a stadial evolutionary history of humankind with the primitives being at the earliest or lowest stages of human evolution. From this perspective the latest or most advanced—and by advanced one always sets forth the notae of technology, science and rational thinking—should have the prestige of embodying the epitome of "civilization." In many respects, the term *indigenous* was adopted as a "politically correct" way of referring to what had before been called the primitives, or tribal peoples, these names now falling into disgrace. "Indigenous" proved also to be an acceptable term for members of those cultures which had previously been designated by the former terms.[8]

After this brief but important journey through the mutations of meaning regarding the term *indigenous*, Long turns to his true concerns: to query the "arche of modernity" as a query into "matter, exchanges, and the gods." "The modern Western world created its own *archē* among the people it took over through imperialism and within the organization of knowledge or the disciplinary order of human sciences. In the one sense these archaic cultures were equated with the early beginnings of human life on the face of the earth, and from this academic stylization, contemporary cultures of the peoples of Africa, North and South America, Oceania, Australia, and other non-Western areas of the world thus became populated by the several 'backward' cultures of the world." Such non-Western cultures were forcibly, violently, brought onto the timeline of the human by being temporally distanced from the West even as this temporal distantiation "was translated into a distantiation in space."[9] The latter distantiation marks a "space defined by the distance of these contemporary cultures from the Western metropoles."[10] Here we see the metaphysics of separability in action through the production of an imaginary of space and time as sequentiality and, again, separability.[11] But also, it is precisely at this point that Long moves to clarify that at issue here are questions of matter and religion, or the question of religious matter(s), operative in the structure of distantiation or of space-time as just described. He says that "missing in discussions and popularization of these topics are the actual relationships and entanglements of cultures that took place during the imperial and colonial ventures of the modem West. For Europeans and Euro-Americans the cultures of the so-called archaic, primitive, and backward peoples of the world became simultaneously the raw materials for the technological manufacturing industry of the West and the ideological basis for various notions of cultural evolution as well as the necessary substantiation for their notion of civilization."[12] Already here Long is signaling a religious language that's all bound up with matter in his very description of what is missing but presupposed in popular discourses as well as in the academic discourses of the human sciences. This is a language of eucharistic transubstantiation inasmuch as the so-called archaic peoples are the raw materials, the sacred (as in sacrificed) stuff, that have undergone violent consumption in the very making of the West. In another place Long speaks of this process by saying that the so-called archaic peoples are "those who have lived as the *materia prima* (raw materials, I think, is the economic way of expressing this)" and who in Silence—not passive silence as in having been silenced but active Silence, which here I have capitalized to try to mark out this difference—kept open, Long says, "the ontological dimension," or, as Cedric Robinson might say, "the ontological totality."[13] That open dimension is one of "incompleteness," to stay with Robinson, that signals other imaginaries of existence, which, pace Jayna Brown, is not the same as other genres of the human.[14] This language of "raw materials" and then "materia prima" takes us back to the prior chapter's consideration of Long's taking up of alchemy via Eliade's *The Forge and the Crucible: The Origins and Structures of Alchemy.* There Eliade says that "in [pursuing] the reduction of substances to their pre-cosmogonic state," the alchemist "[seeks] the *materia prima*," the cosmic night of a descent into *terra mater*.[15] This *terra mater* is akin to Jackson's black *mater*, and both of these are akin to Roman poet-philosopher Lucretius's understanding of matter as *mater* as figured around the feminine mythological goddess Venus.[16] In his account of alchemy, Eliade, however, says that the ancient smelter invades *mater* in order to do a white work or a "work in white." He calls this work "*leukosis*," or that of extracting from *mater*, pulling forth from *mater* as matter value-laden substances (such as gold).[17] The difference now, beyond the argument of "Mircea Eliade and the Imagination of Matter" that we considered earlier, is that Long brings this squarely into the context of the rise of the Atlantic World. Further still, the quote above intermingles or mixes the language of alchemy (*materia prima*) and an implicit or absent presence of *terra mater*/black *mater* as that through which a new mattering as extraction and ingestion is happening. Long says that the West invades and, in this way, ingests the "so-called archaic, primitive, and backward peoples of the world."[18] Through that ingestion, which is a kind of in-gestating, the West extracts from "primitive" peoples and in so doing also brings forth or creates itself precisely as the Western world. There is a fundamental violence against ecology here (where ecology is to be understood in the broadest possible sense as that entangled sociality that is matter) in the name of producing a Western economy (*oikonomia*). What has my attention is how Long interprets this violence wherein ecology is ingested even if it is not fully digestible so as to produce capitalist economy. He uses a language of ingestion as a symbolically eucharistic language to get at or express this.

I will bolster this claim more as I proceed, but my preliminary point is that Long claims here that the "primitives" are those who have been cannibalized and subjected to a process of metabolization through consumption, through being eaten. They have been and continue to be those whom the West eats in order that the West might be ontologically (tran)substantiated as Western civilization. Thus, as raw material that undergoes blackened consumption, the non-West connotes a (middle) passage that helps effect "the transubstantiation of a white," as W. E. B. Du Bois put it in *Black Reconstruction in America, 1860–1880*.[19] This is the making of "the white West," its veritable invention.[20] The "primitive" is the locus of an "accumulation," conscripted into a process that effects an alchemic transsubstancing whose yield is what now travels under the name *civilization*, even as this very term, this god-term, conceals a devastating violence. What is called "the West"—also, what is called "America" as reductively aligned with the United States—is the yield of, a creation out of, this process of extractive violence that occurs through a protocol of invasive ingestion of others, indeed, of earth ecology.

To be even clearer, my claim here is that the consumption of the so-called primitives, the colonized, those rendered "indigenous," happens on the model of the Eucharist. Those who consume this *materia prima* are in this process transsubstanced as the surreality that shadows the "real presence" of the properly human. What I have here called a shadowing reflects something that Kara Keeling after James Snead reminds us of, namely, that "'the Black' in Western philosophical thought [and practice] is . . . 'always there already' before, within, after, and beyond 'the human.'"[21] Insofar as this occurs by way of contacts and exchanges in the Atlantic theater, indeed, insofar as it occurs through violent machinations toward those deemed "indigenous," those who are imagined as savagely backward or as benighted "originals" and who because of their, as it were, backward benightedness are subject to extraction or what Denise Ferreira da Silva calls "engulfment"—insofar as this is the case, we have a way of further understanding how the blackening of matter, of *mater*, places us squarely within modernity as a problem of (meta)physics that is not only specific to racially black subjects.[22] Differently put, we have a way of understanding what Afro-pessimist Frank Wilderson has called the Savage and the Slave as situated differently within global raciality without remaining caught within these very ontologizing ideations, these ontotheologizing god-terms.[23] This is what becomes available for thought, I propose, when thinking with Long about modernity as a specific type of atomistic or individuating physics of separability, a modality of mattering that takes effect through Eucharistic-cannibalizing processes of consumption or engulfment processes that connote a commodity economics or rather a commodity theo-economics (a theological *oikonomia*) of *transatlantic transubstantiation*.

The Fetish; Or, The Racial Capitalist Invention of Religion

What makes historically displaying this claim tricky, though still quite doable, is this: while Long certainly understands that matter(ing) in the transatlantic theater is eucharistic and thus religious, he also understands that how (the imagination of) matter flows through the different nodal points of the Atlantic triangle is quite complex. That complexity concerns a twofold struggle that is at once distinct and also braided as regards Western Christian matter(ing).

One side of the struggle over matter takes place within Europe's metropoles. These concern the Protestant Reformation battles (and subsequently the Roman Catholic Counter-Reformation battles) about the Eucharist in the sixteenth and seventeenth centuries. At issue was whether the bread and wine or the elementals of sacred matter are trans-substanced into Christ's actual body and blood, whether they are his "real presence."[24] This was basically the position of those now identified as Roman Catholic, who were principally in the nations of imperial southern Europe (Portugal, Spain, etc.). The other, Protestant approach to matter was different. For them it was one in which the bread and wine are imagined as evacuated of an animating Christological presence, though the elements can symbolize Christ. While this summary surely leaves out much detail and nuance on the positions of various theologians in the debates, it more or less heuristically is useful in describing what was at play in the metropolitan discussions about Christian materiality vis-à-vis the Eucharist as they were taking place in the European metropolitan centers during the Age of Discovery and Conquest.

This said, in "Indigenous People, Materialities, and Religion," Long pays specific attention to the Protestant reformer John Calvin by way of a brief but quite interesting engagement with Benjamin Nelson's book on Calvin and the "origin" of capitalism.[25] It is here with Calvin in mind that Long discerns "a specific religious orientation of modern European Christianity" on matter.[26] Long concludes that Nelson "has presented . . . a cogent argument for the relationship between Protestantism and the beginnings of capitalism."[27] In pointing out "Calvin's desacralization of the world and Christian worship," Long (reading Nelson) notes that an "ensuing change in the realm of the exchanges between God and the world and within the human community" was afoot.[28] "By tracing through the theology of exchanges (usury and idolatry), Nelson is able to show how Calvin's theology led not only to a new theory of exchange but equally to a new understanding of the 'things' exchanged in the communities created in the exchange."[29]

Meanwhile, and at the same time that the reformers are in the metropoles effecting "a new understanding of the 'things' exchanged," this very question of the meaning of matter is in negotiation in the practices of Europe's Atlantic merchants who are exchanging "commodities" in commerce. These enslaving, missionary-merchants are trying to make sense of the approaches to matter they are encountering in other cultures. Particularly, in cultures off the western coast of Africa, Portuguese merchants are encountering approaches to matter and material objects that both remind them of themselves as Catholics, and that thus harbor an attraction for them, while at the same time they are repulsed, as these approaches to matter strike fear in that they are not fully incorporable into the merchants' semiosis, their structures of meaning-making and signification. In one sense, the modes of mattering and thus the genres of existence they are encountering are a *mysterium fascinosum*; in another, they connote a *mysterium tremendum*. As *mysterium tremendum et fascinosum*, these cultures present an Otherness that is at once an immanent and transcendent mystery. The question is, What do they do in the face of this mysterious Otherness given in the cultures with which they are engaging and exchanging?

Long argues, thinking with anthropologist William Pietz, that the European, starting with the Portuguese, merchant contrived the notion of *the fetish* to describe an essential African difference. With this term they charged those they were encountering off the sub-Saharan western coast of Africa, with whom they were engaging in all manner of exchange and trade, with overvaluing matter by understanding matter and material objects not through logics of individuation but imbued with multiple presences and thus copresences. This is a charge of animism.[30] The claim was that this was a nonrational approach to matter, manifest as bad religion, where *bad religion* here means African religion. It means *fetish religion*.[31] However, behind the imposition of the charge of the fetish on the

African is the hiding of a new *archē* of matter(ing), a new Principle of Being, a project of ontology, in justification of the commodity form. Via the fetish, there is a consumption of or a descent into the mystery, the *mater*, of the Other even as that mystery qua mystery remains indigestible to the new *archē* and exchange structure, the semiosis, within which the European merchants are operating. The symbolic structure is at once Eucharistic *and* alchemical. By this operation of consumption of and descent into *materia prima*, a new mode of humanity, the universal subject of Hegelian History (with a capital *H*), is being created. This new mode of humanity is figured as a self-possessed, sovereign "I" whose self-ownership or whose having a grasp or grip on the self as a free agent without dependence on matter is conditioned by a disavowed (colonial and enslaving) grasping after ownership or the right to own things, including the ground or the earth itself.

Explaining this, Long draws on a series of articles written by William Pietz between 1985 and 1988, the period that saw the publication of *Significations* (1986). With these articles Pietz injected new blood into the study of the fetish. What seized Long's attention about Pietz's articles is their revelation "that one of the major theories concerning the origin of religion was the notion of the 'fetish' and fetishism" and that "this origin was identified with Africans and Africa."[32] In other essays Long cuts to the quick about the significance of Pietz's work for coming to terms with the new *archē* of modernity as this concerns the emergence of a new imagination of matter. At one point Long recounts a story that Pietz himself tells to capture the issues in play as Europeans transacted off the coast of West Africa and had to reckon with the very different approach to material objects as they sought gold, on the one hand, and functioned as ambassadors of the Christian faith, on the other. This context, where trade, religion, and eroticism all come together at the focal point of matter and material objects, brings forth the notion of the fetish as a prime means by which the European merchants distinguished themselves as superior to those with whom they were trading. Here's the story Long recounts:

> A common story told regarding this interrelation [among trade, religion, and eroticism] goes like this. When the Portuguese trader asked about the god of the inhabitants of these islands, they were often told that their god was a talisman that they wore around their necks or somewhere on their person. This object was made of gold. The Portuguese, while being able to accept that they worship a false god, were taken aback when they found that these inhabitants were willing to trade or barter their "god" for any other object that the Portuguese presented for trade. What fascinated the writers about

fetishism was this constellation of a god formed from a precious form of matter (gold), its portability, and its use as an object of exchange.[33]

Stories such as this one recount the basis on which European discourses built a definition of the earliest form of religion. They did this by deploying the fetish idea to connote the religion of the blacks. Sometimes they called this religion "fetish religion"—*fetish* from the Portuguese *feitiço*, meaning "manufactured" or "fabricated"—or even "Guinea religion."[34] Pietz unfolds the history of this term—born in the specific context of Atlantic contact, commerce, and exchange— beginning with this context and tracing its development back into the European metropoles with the emergence of the field of history of religions (with Friedrich Max Müller) and eventually into writings on political economy (Karl Marx) and theories of sexuality (Sigmund Freud). While the history has a number of twists and turns, what Long picks up from Pietz is this: the notion of fetish is less about producing an accurate description of the practices of the people that European merchants encountered and more about establishing the terms of a differential essence between peoples based on claims about approaches to material objects. Rather than seeing what they called *fetish* as a hosting a "material philosophy" or a philosophy of matter as entanglement and nonseparability, as W. E. B. Du Bois later would, European merchants with this term rendered the judgment that what they called *the fetish* bore witness to Africans' overdetermination of matter.[35] More still, this judgment entailed the further one that the reason for this overdetermination of matter was this "idolatrous," "ethnike religion," to use the language of Samuel Purchas (1577–1626), an English cleric and corporate propagandist who linked a discourse about Africans as fetish worshippers of material objects as "gods" to what Purchas elaborated as "the natural religion in Guinea Africa absent or apart from Christian, Jewish, and Muslim influences."[36] Relying on Portuguese and Dutch narratives about the fetish, Purchas, as Sylvester Johnson observes, "amplified this notion of religious difference in Guinea Africa by inscribing meanings about racial Blackness through the discourse of the fetish."[37]

But, most important for my purposes, what the discourse of the fetish did was help advance a claim that in the manufacturing or making of "gods" at will and as material objects, the "ethnike religion of the Blacks" or fetishism indexes irrationality and a deformed approach to matter. Irrationality and deformation here are comparative. Fetishism as hosting a deformed approach to matter contrasts with the mode of mattering at work in the market rationalities that were coming into their own in the Atlantic World and that in due course intellectuals back in the metropolitan centers would theorize in terms of the sovereign, transparent, self-possessed, and free subject over against those, such as the Africans, who in their affectability are mired in matter. That is to say, "fetishism as a theory about the origin of religion in Africa was in one movement applied to the enslaved Africans themselves as a false religion and in another" worked to buttress a new "notion of matter and materiality, this time to African bodies," as disenchanted or transubstantiated into now-ownable flesh ("being for the captor").[38] So manufactured, such flesh, converted into a now-degraded, ownable body, became a locus of a new modality of matter in the form of chattel, which is to say, property. Hence, on the one hand, "one is able to see how African slaves in North America could be treated as chattel, not persons," while on the other, one can see as well "how all material forms of the world and one's relationship to them could be disenchanted into commodities" or into a modern world system of materiality.[39] All of this has its genesis, its *archē*, in the originary moment in which the African and the fetish converge and yet are dissimulated in the language of the commodity, which is to say, in the language of property, even as the very process of dissimulation is entirely internal to the emergence of a new modality of the human premised on this archaic moment of separability through differential essence as it operated in Atlantic contact, commerce, and exchange.[40] Indeed, as Long puts it at the end of one of his many discussions about Pietz and the fetish more generally, what the European discourse of the Africanist fetish actually obscured or sought to quell was a situation of "intense heterogeneity, even of *anarchy*," in which "these coastal enclaves were inhabited by all sorts of persons—Christians, Muslims, Africans, Jews, and every admixture among and between them."[41] That is, what the fetish emerged to interdict was entangled assembly as anarchic heterogeneity.

"Even of Anarchy . . ."

This *anarchic* heterogeneity, what European discourse could not digest, with *the fetish* operating as a sign of the indigestible and of the West's indigestion, suggests a cross-cultural "doubleness," a multiplicity given in the indivisibility of a mode of mattering or material existence in which there is a becoming-in-common, and in incompleteness.[42] Alexis Pauline Gumbs's collective-poet of *M Archive: After the End of the World* speaks of this becoming-in-common as "the black simultaneity of the universe," which I read in connection with Jackson's black *mater* in which the nonrepresentable "dark feminine" signals an alternate, quantum sociality or we-ness that is always already an-archically "flying away from" the *archē*.[43] It was this materially given anarchic we-ness—the "primitive we" of a "primitive thingliness" in which one finds some other ~~metaphysics~~ of matter(ing); Gumbs calls it "black feminist metaphysics"—that, again, under the sign *the fetish* and the commodity form was decidedly refused in the emergent practices of the human and the concomitant philosophical project of ontology and its varied sciences of the human.[44] The task, then, is to think the anarchy (*anarchē*) of this alternative *materiality*. This is precisely the task of the final two chapters of this book, in which I elaborate the anarchy of black religion.

Chapter Four

The Anarchy of Black Religion

For Charles Long

The elliptical mode demonstrates the creative capacities that are possible . . .
—CHARLES H. LONG, *Ellipsis* . . . (2018)

Blackness is the old-new math.
—FRED MOTEN, "Blackness" (2018)

Anarchy

Across this book a claim has been accruing around black religion and the human, around blackness and anarchy, around the blackness of anarchy, and toward the black religiosity of anarchy. With Charles Long, still far too unknown in black studies circles, as interlocutor, I've argued that the black study of religion is the study of a specific type of anarchy. I've been arguing that the black study of religion, as a function of black study, studies this anarchy, its practices. It studies that wayward or parareligious as parahuman relationship of what has sometimes inadequately been called *the black subject* both to the antiblack category of "religion," understood as a distinctly modern invention, and to the imagination or version of the human brought online, as it were, through that invention. In light of this, this book's other task has been to renew the question or try to ask anew, *What is black religion?* My interest is in the black in *black religion*, in the blackness thereof.

I've taken up this task by calling for a shift in how we think about (what has been called) black religion precisely by thinking about it anarchically. By *the anarchy of black religion*, I mean the movement of black *mater* as matter. I mean blackness as materialism—I won't call it a "new materialism," though there are no doubt certain resonances—as an alternative imagination of matter in which matter as *mater* is to be understood not as movement set in motion by an ex nihilo "unmoved mover" but as the condition of an anoriginal swerve, an always already being-in-uncapturable-flight (some have called this *fugitivity*) from the terms of statism, which Cedric Robinson called the "terms of order."[1] What I have been out to show in this book is that those terms of statism as terms of order are terms of sovereignty. Indeed, they are terms, on the one hand, of religion (where, as shown in previous chapters, religion is born as a term of racialized, specifically blackened, un-Reason; the negative term in a dialectic meant to establish the positivity of proper, which is to say, European, Reason and Rationality, both with capital *R*s) and, on the other hand, of the human (another positivist term that, as Sylvia Wynter among others has helped us understand through her account of Man, establishes itself in opposition to those imagined as the homunculi of the world or, with Frantz Fanon, "the wretched of the earth," namely, the so-called Savage and, finally, the Negro).[2] As categories underwriting an imperialist and racial capitalist order of being and knowing, religion and the human, certainly the versions or genres that emerged to regulate contact and commerce in the Atlantic World and that came to set the terms of globality, are burial grounds (again, one of the meanings of the Greek term *archē* is *ground*). They are loci of ruin, fragmentation, and loss, the underlying principle or rationality (two other meanings of the Greek word *archē*) of our present catastrophe. The question is, What is blackness's relationship to this archaic catastrophe, which in this book I have insisted on understanding as an ontotheological or religious catastrophe, a catastrophe of ontology and metaphysics, indeed, as a loss or violence inflicted through the imposition of logics of property, including the atomistic or individuated "I" and its related, exclusionary "we," all made planetary as an imposed "global idea of race"?[3] More still, what is (what is so inadequately called) *black religion* in the face of propertied globality? How might we think black religion's parareligious, its paratheological, or better still, its Georges Bataille–like atheological poetics? How might we think the unstateliness of black religion as aesthetic or poetic practice, as a moving well differentially together, and this as the earth moving well with itself, given that black *mater* as matter, given that black *mater*-ialism, or the materialism of blackness, suggests a radical naturalism in which, as a function of matter's fundamental oneness (a oneness that requires careful specification), difference or Otherness operates nonatomistically, nonindividualistically, and thus differently? What is the mathematics of this sociality, this moving well differentially together?

I want to say that this chapter answers these questions, but that, in fact, would not be the best way to understand this chapter's aspirations. A better way to put what this chapter aspires to is as follows: notwithstanding the fact that in what follows I do advance some predications, I do not offer anything like answers or final solutions to the above questions. If anything, I aspire to sharpen the questions. More specifically, this chapter, like this book, as noted from the start, is written in the spirit of an essay. It is an attempt, operating somewhere in the zone between philosophy and poetics or as a philosophical poetics. It is a quest, a questing, a questioning; an exploration and an experiment. It is experimental; maybe it's one long poem in its own right (in writing it, I increasingly imagined it to be so . . .), though it is a poem of the sort Fanon spoke of when in quoting Paul Valéry he spoke of "language as the god gone astray in the flesh."[4] As an essay, this chapter is an exercise in going astray or in being taken astray or moving astray, in the fray, caught up in(to) the flesh. As such, it is an effort at dwelling and lingering with, and thereby an effort at breaching or, more precisely, inhabiting the breach, the creaking, that is always already there in religion and the human as mutually reinforcing language systems supportive of the terms of a racial capitalist organizing of the planet. Out of this explorative essaying, I advance my most theoretically speculative claims about (what is called) black religion and the anarchic blackness thereof. More specifically, here I begin laying out the scaffolding for a more in-depth study of black radical cosmology and sacrality, if I may put it this way, and thus for an understanding of what might be called the spiritual as material vocation, which is an ecological vocation, of black radicalism.[5]

In this chapter and the next (together they are a unit), I propose an argument about what is called black religion, generally, and blackness's aesthetic-material vocation, which I understand simultaneously as its spiritual-poetic vocation. In this, I propose an argument about what I mean by anarchy as the convergent meeting point of the material spirituality of black radicalism. Specifically, I propose that what is called *black religion* is not just "the black version" of what is often thought of as a sui generis and thus a natural or general phenomenon called *religion*. In other words, black religion is not an instance of the practices of a certain type of racialized or black(ened) *Homo religiosus*. Rather, black religion is at once a contending with the "unparalleled catastrophe" of the racial-religious capitalism that has been imposed on the earth and an open set of practices that operate out of a different orientation to matter and thus a different orientation to the earth and cosmos. As an earthly and earthy orientation, what has been called black religion—which just as well might be thought of as black spirituality or as the spirit(uality) of blackness or perhaps even the matter of black spirit in its inexhaustibly dark churchical, its "aesthetic sociality," as Laura Harris has put it—is a method of thinking, a mode of studied praxis, carried both in formal religious institutions (like, for instance, in the black church or in black Islam, etc.) and in formally nonreligious institutions and spaces.[6] Considered through an expansive understanding of faith, where such faith, black faith, is more a poetic orientation than a creedal, doctrinal, or church-confessional stance, I consider what is called black religion, or, better, I consider black radicalism's spiritual vocation as akin to what Erica Edwards says after a beautiful meditation on Toni Cade Bambara's novel *The Salt Eaters*: "Black women's literature gives us an unromantic picture of endurance amid the continuing onslaught."[7] This aesthetic endurance, which entails an aesthetic sociality, bespeaks what Christopher Freeburg has called a "readiness for a new mode of living amid an accumulation of horror—'living into it' in spite of them."[8] What has been called black religion is part of this anti-imperial, anteconfessional grammar of faith, this ungrammatical, this antegrammatical blackness. It is of that repertoire, that artistic oeuvre whose overture is a constant invitation; of an insistent questing, a creative becoming and "quest(ion)ing," as Denise Ferreira da Silva proposes in her inquiry into "the quest(ion) of blackness toward the end of the world."[9] It is, in short, "prayer" in that sense that Kevin Quashie has helped us think about it, where prayer here points to an expressiveness that need not have a god as its object or horizon but rather suggests "the wild copiousness of the interior."[10] I mean the anteriority of a black interior. Prayer is of that anterior, expressing "a kind of inexpressible expressiveness [in] pursuit of that which cannot be fully revealed" inasmuch as the revelation, the apocalypse, of the not fully revealable points to existence in incompletion or as in-finite.[11] The expressed revelation of the inexpressible is fugitive. I used to think that blackness is apocalyptic, that it signals something of an unveiling or revealing of alternatives in the midst of catastrophe, amid ruin. I actually still think that, but I also now think that it's deeper than that. Blackness, indeed, is apocalypse, it is a blackalyptic unveiling. But this is a peculiar unveiling in that blackness is also an eclipse, a receding. Blackness, including the blackness of black religion, is apoc-eclipse. Blackness constitutes practices that constantly renew and revise themselves, a materially fugitive, an *in*finite, even *trans*finite, withdrawal, matter's fugitive refusal of capture. This is a statement about the *matter*, the specific reality and *mater*iality of blackness and thus a statement about matter's fugitivity, its indivisible swerving, where that swerving registers blackness as a locus of high density and intensity, a sociality of saturation or entanglement.[12] It's a statement about movement(s), that is, about the movement(s) of blackness, about black movement(s). More still, this registers the curious relationship among blackness, poetry, and prayer, or of blackness "(not) in between" poetry and prayer, each of these terms being significations of incompletion, each being "all incomplete," each being indeterminately entangled in incompletion.[13] In making this case, I will begin with a meditation on incompletion meant to set up the concern of the rest of the chapter with Charles Long's mobilization of a mathopoetic imagination centered on the geometry of the ellipse and a grammatico-poetic imagination centered on the punctuation mark or the literary device of ellipsis (. . .). Between ellipse and ellipsis, I explicate a poetics of black religion rooted in and expressive of the anarchy of blackness as such. With this argument in place, I will be set for the final chapter of this book, where I engage National Book Award–winning poet, novelist, and essayist Nathaniel Mackey's practice of the poem as an aesthetic instance of black religion in its swerve with respect to the very notion of religion. In short, between this chapter and the next, I call attention to the spiritual vocation of black radicalism more generally.

Apocalyptic Incompletion

In an earlier chapter, I considered the work of philosopher and literary theorist Zakiyyah Iman Jackson to begin to bring into view this wild copiousness in the face of plasticizing ruination or the extractivism of antiblackening. I tracked Jackson's rigorous engagement with our current catastrophe, her careful explaining of that catastrophe as bound up with violence against black *mater* or against the *mater* of matter, against its internal texture, force, and depth, the imposition of "*the* world as such" on top of the earth. With and after Jackson and in light of the work of Charles Long on the theme of alchemy or the transformation of matter and the very invention of "religion" with the emergence of the Atlantic World, I underscored that our unparalleled catastrophe has involved the appropriation of the power of *mater* as matter, of *mater* as its fundamental blackness. The appropriation of *mater* is nothing less than the extractive appropriation of the power of birth, the power of generativity, the power of creation, the would-be theft of *poiēsis* as the power to make, to craft, to give rise to something new, the would-be seizure of the swerve, the power of emergent flow. Such theft, in order to establish regimes of property, is nothing less than the violent attempt to freeze or arrest ecologies or socialities of the earth, transforming them into extracted fodder for capitalist economy. Matter becomes imagined as property and thus as ownable or (dis)possessable, a structure now of circulating credit and debt under the stately management of markets and policy. This I called *transatlantic transubstantiation*, wherein the depth or the texture of things, matter as such or as that which exceeds things as their very condition of possibility, is both refused and yet seized, disavowed in being extractively appropriated.

There is a connection in what I'm saying here to the work of Denise Ferreira da Silva, whom I mentioned a moment ago. I am thinking about her account of the imposition of what she calls the "patriarch-form" as stasis on matter. The patriarch-form, which resonating with Long's notion of *archē* Ferreira da Silva calls "an *archē-form* of the subject," forecloses on blackness, where blackness is to be understood not so much as a category (of race) but as, in fact, "[referring] to rare and obsolete definitions of matter" that connote "another mode of existing in the world."[14] "As both a movement and a call to respond to everyday events of racial violence (the killing of unarmed black persons by police) that rehearse the ethical syntax that works through/as the liberal democratic state," Black Lives Matter (BLM), Ferreira da Silva suggests, may better be understood as a movement that moves within nature's movement, within its differentially unified, swerving flow.[15] At stake here are a peculiar ontology and ethics of motion that allow BLM to be understood as a movement moving within the motion, the flow, the sociopoetic force of an alternate way of existing. This alternate is unstately, *mater*-ially outside of the state apparatus as a circulatory structure of social debt, credit, and exchange. As the name of this movement suggests when interpreted not as a plea for either "black life" or individuated "black lives" to matter to or be recognized by the state, BLM "signals a political subject emerging in the scene of obliteration through a sentence *without a (self-determined) subject*."[16] In short, BLM may be read as a movement whose moving is in refusal of theopolitical as statist transcendence. This is what the black(ness) in the name Black Lives Matter and the Matter of this same name can be understood as suggesting inasmuch as in its irreducibility to the logic of the state, blackness exceeds "the scientific and historical ways [which, as I've been arguing throughout this book, are rooted in a newly emergent religious-as-racial-capitalist way] of knowing that produced it in the first place."[17] The task, given this, is how to think, and, as Ferreira da Silva otherwise puts it, how to "activate," "Blackness's creative capacity," how "to release that which in Blackness has the capacity to disclose another horizon of existence, with its attendant accounts of existence."[18] My claim is that what is called black religion is a complex of practices that comport toward this other horizon of being and knowing, an open set of expanding practices predicated on an alternative, kinetic imagination of matter.

I want to elaborate this claim by arguing that black religion be understood as a praxis of some other orientation of being and knowing in flight from property but at the scene of property, that is, at the scene of the racial-colonial catastrophe, the catastrophe that Ferreira da Silva has called "engulfment" and "obliteration."[19] But because this engulfment and obliteration, as I have been demonstrating, has to do with the modern instantiation of religion as racial capitalism's or this world's ground or foundation or first principle or *archē*, what is called black religion has to be understood paradoxically, indeed, parasemiotically. It shows up as "disorder," summoning us to "think in disorder." Which is to say, with R. A. Judy in mind, what is called black religion in fact registers a different semiosis such that the term *religion* in the phrase *black religion* must be understood poetically inasmuch as it cannot mean and thus does not indicate the black(ened) version, shall we say, of the thing called *religion*. The *black* juxtaposed to the *religion* in the phrase *black religion* fundamentally destabilizes religion. It amplifies the breach, the break, the creaking that is already present in the word, in the modern invention of religion as a threshold concept between the medieval and the modern and in its emergence to ground and stabilize a world anthropologically structured around those conceptualized as primitive and those who conceptualize themselves as rationally self-possessed, self-owned, individuated minds. In this chapter and continuing into the next, I argue that *black religion* might be better understood as a parasemiotic catch term for practices that reveal or unveil a hidden but open secret, a *gnosis* of submerged but imaginatively available, buried (but) alive, and thus lived alternatives beyond what Cedric Robinson once called "the terms of order."[20] More specifically, as an angle through which to talk about blackness in its relatedness to but, more important, its nonreduction to racial category, and thus as a flash point for raising cosmological, mythological, and philosophical questions about the universe (which itself, as contemporary physics makes clear, is unfinished) and indeed about matter, what is called *black religion* involves practices of the ongoing unveiling or revelation of the im/possible as rooted in an alternative imagination of matter as the material generativity of kinetic uncertainty or indeterminacy.[21] Indeed, *apocalypse* (from the Greek word *apocalupsis*), from which *revelation* as an idea is derived, means "uncovering" and "disclosure," which following feminist theologian Catherine Keller may be further annotated to mean "dis-en-closure."[22] Apocalypse, then, entails revelatory practices of disclosure of alternatives precisely at the site of and yet beyond the catastrophe of dispossessive (en)closure. What apocalypse dis-en-closes is the fact that property is always already stealing itself (away) from having been stolen. There is a theft, an antetheft, anterior to the fact that property is theft. What this discloses—and this is the apocalypse—is that theft is not first. And for that matter, neither is property. Beyond property, beyond settlement, beyond an unmoved mover, movement is. Apocalypse entails practices that host and, in this way, unveil "moving well together" based in nonsettler, nonpossessive existing, in be-ing nonpossessively, this itself being the disclosure of ecologies of a lush, black universe, ecologies of dying and living well wherein such dying and living are not subjected to violent economies of self-possession or the dividing up of things.[23] I am talking about black *mater* as matter, the black *mater*-nal as *mater*-ial "*jus* generativity," as Stefano Harney and Fred Moten have put it, "the quality and capacity to give" or of "generosity," as Ferreira da Silva annotating Harney and Moten put it, "not in the context of an economy (as the managing of scarcity) but as generosity (as in the abundance of the rain forest)."[24] This is a generosity that makes sense within an understanding of matter as in-finite, non-individuated flow or as swerving, even kinked and kinky, unpredictable movement.[25] As swerving or kinky flow, matter within this understanding connotes what Ferreira da Silva has called "difference without separability." Producing a neologism, Harney and Moten invite a consideration of matter in this instance, the mat(t)er of blackness, as the movement of a collective, undercommon, ec-static "diffunity," a "sociality not based on the individual."[26] This is a unity, or better a sociality, or better still a black sociality, of differential, diffused, diffracted gathering. Sharing.[27] In putting it this way, I invoke at once the sense of matter advanced by ancient Roman poet-philosopher Lucretius, who arguably offered the first and yet enduring but only now being seriously reckoned with critique of the atomism or the violent, statist logic of the individual that drives the West; the approaches to matter that quantum physics offers with notions of entanglement, uncertainty, indeterminacy, nonlocality, entropy, and diffraction; and, finally, the black *mater* as the black matter of things as taken up in black study or in relationship to black radicalism.

This is all to say, what I am beginning to put forth here and will extend in the subsequent parts of this chapter when I engage Charles Long on ellipse and ellipsis is a kind of Black Lucretianism to articulate the mystery of matter with a view to theorizing in its light what is called black religion.[28] I locate black religion within this material, this black maternal horizon of diffunity or generosity. Indeed, the blackness of black religion, like the blackness of blackness, points to a material ecology of swerving, undercommon diffunity. The otherness of this ecology is suggestive of an Other-ness that scrambles the terms of order, the god-terms, which are also Man-terms, often in and anchored by discourses of religion. However, in the case of black religion as in the case of blackness (and this is the scrambling), what we are dealing with in contrast to religion is a nonstatic, a kinetically flowing Otherness, an other or otherwise Otherness, in which difference is a function of diffused, differential unity, a function of diffunity. Here matter is nothing less than swerving, sensual, nonseparable difference. "The black gods of the metropolis," to borrow that cool phrase of sociologist Arthur Huff Fauset that he deployed to talk about the varieties of black religion in Philadelphia, and that novelist Onaje Woodbine more recently picked up on, riffing on it as "black gods of the asphalt" to write about religion, hip-hop, and street basketball in Boston, are tied to black performance insofar as it points to a non-atomistic materialism, one that poeticizes being (of and with the) earth.[29] Blackness reveals this alternative imagination of matter, this in-finite naturalism, we might say. Matter's wandering, its gathered escape, its constant ongoingness, its uncapturable migrancy, its moving-on-ness, expresses itself in and as the blackness of black religion. In this sense, as noted earlier, blackness is apocalypse. It uncovers or discloses a haptic, a materially sensual understanding of matter in which matter constantly, differentially touches itself, affects itself, in and as and through sentient flesh and nonsentient nature. At the same time, blackness is not apocalypse, if by apocalypse one means, shall we say, *full* disclosure. What we are dealing with here is the disclosure of an open secret, the revelation of incomprehensible incompletion, of the apophatically un/sayable.[30] As apocalyptic apophasis or as a poetics of performative unsaying, blackness is also (an) eclipse—a receding, a withholding of what can be held but not had, of what, as Sarah Jane Cervenak has said, is "ungiven" because unseizable, because not a part of the give and take of world economy, of gift and giver, of the circulation of credit and debt.[31] That is to say, if when it comes to blackness as black *mater*, apocalypse is a disclosure that conceals, then like an ellipse whose constant is more and less than one, "blackalypse" is (an) eclipse.[32] Theory of black religion, or, more precisely, theory of the blackness of black religion, is theory of *mater*-ial eclipse. It's a blackalyptic apoc-eclipse.

My consideration of Long (in this chapter) and Mackey (in chapter 5) is about the parareligiosity of the blackness of black religion, the parareligiosity of this black religious apoc-eclipse. As for Long, what rivets my attention is his mobilization of geometry and grammatology in the figures of the ellipse and the ellipsis. With the ellipse he presents us with a mathopoetics meant to unfold what is meant by black religion in its specific blackness. That is to say, Long offers the ellipse as a mathopoetic figuration of diffunified sociality, premised on an alternate imagination of matter. With the ellipsis and its dot-dot-dot (. . .), he extends his mathopoetic figuring of the blackness of black religion into a grammatical poetic figuring of black religion in its specific blackness. In this, Long's mathopoetics and grammatical poetics of black religion together signal a cosmopoetics that resonates with the cosmopoetics of dispersed (black) gathering that Sarah Jane Cervenak has recently advanced.[33] Held within an ever-expanding openness, the dot-dot-dot of the ellipsis is at once a diffusion and a gathering of dots. They are a clearing of congregate dots. Ellipsis is congregational. In its congregationality, its churchicality, as the Rastafarians might put it, the ellipsis witnesses to a *jus* generativity, a law of generosity, a fulsome "silence." A figure of where words break off and break down, where words fracture, fragment, and trail off into an unspeakable surplus, ellipsis signals improper political speech. Such broken speech Aristotle long ago in his theory of the polis and of proper politics ascribed to the barbarian or to those who were outside of the domain of the polis properly speaking, though as slaves, women, and those who were the spoils of war, they were exclusionary included within the polis to provide the material labor that in many ways made the polis into a space where luxurious living was possible. With the ellipse and ellipsis, Long "crawls back" into the history of the Atlantic World and its antiblackening of matter to offer what might be called a blackpoetic as "barbaric" imagination of matter that eclipses the polis and that as an eclipse presents the burning outlines of the blackness of black religion and of black religion in its radical unstateliness. Vital here is the movement from the mathopoetics of ellipse to the grammatical poetics of ellipsis. That movement happens by way of blackness as practices of eclipse, indeed as practices of apoc-eclipse, in which in an eclipse darkness becomes visible in the sun's fugitive disappearance that makes a sudden blank in the day. Eclipse exposes black light. Though eclipse is not explicitly theorized by Long, that's OK, because his own intellectual practice, his very theorizing of black religion, in fact performs it. His practice performs the fact that, sharing the same Greek root (-*leipsis*), *ellipse*, *eclipse*, and *ellipsis* are of a poetic piece in the theorization of blackness or, in Long's work specifically, in the theorization of the blackness of black religion. The material flow that makes ellipse, eclipse, and ellipsis of a piece brings into eclipsed view an alternate imagination of matter at the scene of black religion.

Long's significance for black studies comes to the fore precisely here, that is to say, due to his attention to blackness as a curious mode of religion, for how he engages in the black study of religion by subjecting religion to the elliptical thinking of a black radical poetics. As we are about to see, ellipsis, for Long, is a figure at once of blackness and of black religion. It is a figure of the blackness of black religion insofar as black religion references the nonrepresentable even though as a discursive concept religion is born for the purposes of representing and organizing difference. In this sense, black religion signals an unrepresentable, ecstatic disturbance internal to the very concept of religion as born in transatlantic commerce and exchange. The notion of the fetish is invented to stand in for black religion as bad religion. That is to say, within the order of racial capitalism the fetish is invented to stand in for African ways of being, knowing, and aliveness (see chapter 3). And yet, in its irreducibility to the order of racial capitalism, black religion (as the bad religion that fetish names) signals the unrepresentable. Indeed, precisely as a way of talking about blackness's spiritual vocation, black religion operates according to an apophatic logic that undoes representation by reframing and unsaying it. Black religion is the internal creaking or unsaying of the very concept of religion insofar as (the blackness of) black religion is internally heterogeneous, incomplete, or open. This openness or incompletion allows for joining or connection with other forms of social existence. In other words, it allows for assemblage. It is this that Long mobilizes ellipsis to signify.

There is one more point about ellipsis as a figure of apocalyptic incompletion worth making. It is a point that will also serve as a preliminary statement about Mackey and that will suggest Mackey as an eclipsed, elliptical presence in my discussion of Long in the remainder of this chapter. This is a point about the importance of seriality, indeed the seriality of ellipsis, the dot-dot-dot, constituting what Jennifer DeVere Brody has called the ambivalence of this nonpunctuating punctuation mark, this mark that "belabors the point."[34] The seriality of the ellipsis, the fact that it is represented by repeating dots, is of *implied*, by which I mean un- or not formally thematized, concern for Long. Later in this chapter, I will show this to be the case in Long's dealing with the mathematics or the geometry of the ellipse as this lies behind or on some level remains operative even if eclipsed within the figure of the ellipsis as (anti)punctuation mark on the terrain of grammar. The dot-dot-dot of the ellipsis is itself a nonidentical repetition just as the points on the curve of an ellipse nonidentically repeat. What the ellipsis adds to this repetition is the idea that the repetition operates as serial extension. The extension points to nonidenticalness in repetition such that elliptical repetition is differential all the way down. Each dot in the dot-dot-dot differs from the other dots and even from itself.[35] This nonidentical repetition, this circularity that returns neither to the same place, as it were, nor in the same way is of implicit concern in Long's understanding of black religion and, indeed, of blackness. But what is implied regarding seriality as nonidentical repetition, and by extension in Long's theorizing of black opacity as signaled by ellipsis, is of explicit concern in Mackey's theory and practice of the poem as cross-cultural artistry. Hence, it is Mackey's practice of the poem that will have my formal attention in the next chapter. That said, it is worth noting in the context of this chapter that Mackey's practice of the poem shadows the reading I advance in this one on Long on ellipsis. The former's practice of the poem helps me suss out Long's anarchic poetics of ellipse and ellipsis as figures of black religion, even as Long's account of black religion helps me make a statement about the mystic, dare I say, the black religious intensity of Mackey's practice of the poem and by (serial) extension what might be termed the spiritual vocation of black radical aesthetics.

Regarding Mackey, I begin by noting that since the 1970s he has been writing two long poems: *Song of the Andoumboulou* and *Mu*. The sixth of the *Song of the Andoumboulou* poems shifts form to become a letter written to a friend named "Angel of Dust." Over time, a series of poem-letters follow. They will be collected to become a novel with the general title *From a Broken Bottle Traces of Perfume Still Emanate*. At present that novel has five volumes or installments to it. Thus, the novel, composed of letters, which are themselves a kind of poetry, is a figure of ongoingness or, in Long's terms, ellipsis. In the next chapter, I offer a close reading of the poem-letter that is "Song of the Andoumboulou: 6." What's worth saying now as part of these introductory remarks on Mackey is this: central to Mackey's work is the long form of experimental writing, the long poem, by which I mean their numeric piling up. As of this writing, *Song of the Andoumboulou* has over 260 poems making it up, and *Mu* over 200—and they are still going, still being written. Additionally, Mackey sees the two poem series as woven together, refusing to stay in separate lanes. This, too, is a function of their seriality. "Braided together," as he puts it, the two poem series are "each the other's understudy. Each is the other, each is both . . . each is the other's twin or contagion, each entwines the other's crabbed advance."[36] As "two and the same," the poems are a cross-cultural, unending song, a cosmogonic imaginary, the mythography of an-other world, a field of openings manifest even at the level of form. The song, by which is meant the poems, is a music sung under catastrophic, funerary conditions. Indeed, "Song of the Andoumboulou: 1," and thus the poem that inaugurates the poem series, speaks to this issue of a music that is made from/within catastrophe but that yet exceeds that catastrophe, that "natal occasion."[37] "Song of the Andoumboulou: 1" begins with the statement "The song says the / dead will not / ascend without song."[38] The poems are about loss and the dead. But the song, the poems, is also about ascension, what we might imaginatively call *rapture*. Here rapturous ascension is of the mystery of song, is mystic song. Which is to say, the poem advances as a reaching for connection in brokenness—broken connection, connection in severance. This is "wounded kinship," a crabbed yet erotically advancing, a cramped yet sensuously capacious, reaching for another imagination of connection.[39] In this sacrally erotic reaching for connection in severance, in brokenness, Mackey's serial poems interrogate the version of the human that we are operating under while also, and in my view more importantly, opening the imagination, indeed "the soul," to use a language Mackey himself employed in an interview, to aesthetically experimentalize other versions of existence, some other andoumboulouous praxis of being ~~human~~.[40] This Mackeyan practice of the poem, carrier of a poetics of broken, cross-cultural connection imagined in unending "ungivenness," which is to say, in an unending ritual of renewal and nonidentical extension, I want to read here as resonant with Long's notion of ellipsis as a figure of blackness and of black religion, and thus as a figure of the anarchy of black religion.[41] Additionally, and in reverse, Mackey's practice of the poem and the "aesthetic sociality" it performs I want to read as a figure of black religious anarchy, indeed, as an example of the experimental return to myth and as a praxis of the "troping of the trope of black religion" that Zakiyyah Jackson sees as central to much of the praxis of black radical creativity.[42]

The claim, then, that I here advance is that Long's notion of ellipsis and Mackey's poetics, as manifest in his practice of the poem, move us from the literal to the imaginal. They move us to *poiēsis*. *Poiēsis* in black entails flight from the *archē* of an imperial myth at the heart of which is a proper reason/improper religion (as in blackened un-reason, blackened religion) binary, which is also a secular-religion binary. This binary imposition is bound up with the antiblackening of matter in the birth of the Atlantic World as discussed in prior chapters. Between this and the next chapter, I listen to the alternative as opened up in the Long-Mackey, Mackey-Long duet. In Mackey, I hear the poetics, even more the poem, of black religion. Black religion comes into view as a function of blackness and/as poetry. With Long, we are given a theoretical vantage from which to think the religiosity, indeed the spiritual vocation, of the black radical tradition. The Long-Mackey, Mackey-Long duet sings a music whose bass notes, by which I mean base notes, are driven by an underworldly "re: Source," to borrow a keyword from Mackey's "Song of the Andoumboulou: 6," which I consider at length in the next chapter. That "re: Source" is poetry, of which the poem is a prime but not the only instance. Mackey's practice of the poem participates or moves in the eddies of this "re: Source" even as Long's notion of ellipsis theorizes out of it. As practitioners of poetry, both are involved in imaginal way making. Both are concerned with the continual making of worlds by virtue of the "unfinished genesis of the imagination," as Caribbean writer Wilson Harris, whose influence on Mackey is tremendous and is worthy of study in its own right, might say.[43] That "unfinished genesis," another name for which, again, is *poetry*, also names the ellipsis of black social life or what, in elliptically extending Long's work, I'm calling the *anarchy of black religion*.

Now to the immediate matter of this chapter: Charles Long's elliptical poetics . . .

Mathopoetics; Or, Ellipse

Key in understanding the anarchy of black religion is coming to terms with how black religion relates to but is irreducible to that modern innovation that is called religion. Black religion is in but not of, both more and less than, the semiosis of religion. It operates in the noise-filled silence of the signifying system called religion, in the break in the order of signs, symbols, and representational images and icons that have emerged with the invention of religion as central to the birth of the Atlantic World and thereby the Western modernity of the world. With *ellipsis* as a figure of black poetics and ultimately of what is meant by black religion, this noise-filled silence is precisely Long's concern, and it is what scholar of African American literature and religion Carolyn Jones Medine has in a riveting way elaborated in her unpacking of the Longian notion of ellipsis. So crisp and provocative is her reading that I want to think with her on ellipsis as a platform from which to fill out the notion of black (religious) anarchy or the anarchy of black religion.

Earlier in this chapter I provided a basic sense of the meaning of ellipsis. But as we start this part of the chapter, it is worth having Long's own words in mind from the introduction to his *Ellipsis . . . : The Collected Writings of Charles H. Long,* which is where he elaborates the idea. It is important to note where Long begins his elaboration of ellipsis and why he alights on this figure as illustrative of black religion. He begins not with the grammatical figure of the ellipsis as the book's title announces. Rather, he begins with what's behind the ellipsis, what's eclipsed within it, namely, the mathematical-geometric figure of the ellipse. I want to make a case here for Long as offering a poetics of black religion by way of the mathematics of the ellipse. This is a mathopoetics of black religion that's tied to his approach to the ellipse and its eclipsed but grammatical extension into the dot-dot-dot of the ellipsis. Ellipse-eclipse-ellipsis. Ellipsis through an eclipse becomes illustrative of the ellipse.

I borrow the idea of "mathopoetics" from mathematician-philosopher Fernando Zalamea, who in his compelling *Synthetic Philosophy of Contemporary Mathematics* offers an understanding of mathematics, following approaches to mathematics in the twentieth century such as Kurt Gödel's, premised on "fundamental incompleteness" and thus not as representationally modeling through its symbols and formulae proper, discreetly individuated, or set objects.[44] As Barry Esson and Bryony McIntyre put it in their wonderful summation of Zalamea's work, while "mathematical theorems and models prove nothing outside of their mathematical context" (and so an ellipse, in one sense, tells us nothing outside of the ellipse that's being talked about or modeled), Zalamea nevertheless "furnishes a way to use [mathematical theorems, models, and contexts] allegorically, helping us read the world in more complex ways," specifically, through incompletion.[45] More specifically, Esson and McIntyre summarize that according to Zalamea's *Synthetic Philosophy* "the principle [*sic*] limitations of a philosophy of mathematics" are that they are under the sway of an analytic philosophy that is "'perniciously influenced' by classical logic and set theory, and their inability to engage with 'certain inherently vague environments, certain penumbral zones,' where 'complex mixtures emerge that resist every sort of strict decomposition.'"

For this reason, Zalamea argues, the philosophy of mathematics *"has turned its back on* and has abandoned high mathematical creativity, be it geometrical, topological, differential, algebraic or combinatorial, thereby estranging itself from the real center of the discipline that helped [the discipline] to emerge."[46] In response to this, "the philosophy of mathematics should . . . turn back to examine, without prejudices and without taking pre-established theoretical positions, the *phenomenological spectrum of mathematical activity,*" including the emergence of "mathematical creativity."[47] This "turning back" that Zalamea calls for—perhaps after Long, whose context is the black study of religion, we can call it a "crawling back"—is for the purposes of opening up mathematical thinking beyond the limits of analytic epistemology (and, arguably, beyond an adjacent ontotheology) that has tended to encumber the philosophy of mathematics.[48] Beyond an epistemology derived from an analytic tradition, Zalamea calls for a "synthetic," comparative epistemology that is in keeping with the indeterminacy and incompleteness that are at the heart of contemporary mathematical philosophy and that, for that matter, are surrealistically at the heart of the real, at the heart of matter, that is *mater.* Such an epistemology, Zalamea says, "pivots on the analytic difficulty in confronting certain inherently vague environments, certain *penumbral zones* [having to do with the "sinuous, nonlinear" dynamics of "mathematical creativity"], certain 'outposts of the obscure' . . . certain elastic places of 'spatial negativity', certain 'hinge-horizons' where complex mixtures emerge that *resist* every sort of strict decomposition."[49] These penumbral zones in mathematics are in fact spatially negative, hinge zones marked by a "dialectic of the obscure and the luminous" or by what in a Longian register we might call the luminosity of opacity. These zones, which are internal to mathematical practice and which in fact propel the discipline as its condition of possibility, register the *poiēsis* that drives mathematics, the poetics that animates it. Zalamea's work, in short, calls attention to mathematics' mathopoetic interior. That interior is topographical or more like a differentially unified or a socially diffunified neighborhood. It is not of the singular individuated point. Rather, mathopoetics points to the aesthetically anterior creativity that flows through mathematics and that renders mathematical formulae, geometric figures, theorems, and the like incomplete or as singular instantiations of an open set.

I have said all of this to say that Long's attention to the geometric figure of the ellipse functions as a mathopoetic anterior to the ellipsis, which for him is itself illustrative of (the blackness of) black religion, where black religion is to be understood outside of the terms of the modern invention of religion as itself a kind of individuating theory of the complete set. What we are being invited to consider via Long is the mathopoetics of black religion. Indeed, reading

Long's attention to the ellipse that is eclipsed within ellipsis mathopoetically allows an approach to black religion under the aspect of incompletion wherein on the far side of dogma black religion emerges as "an entangled social field" of nonindividuation that in its parareligious refusal of religion as *archē* of racial capitalism "stands outside of and critiques possessive individualism and the violent processes that individuate communities."[50] If from our earlier consideration of the fetish (chapter 3) we learned anything, it is that the fetish, which is to say, modern religion as the ground (*archē*) of primitive accumulation, emerges in Atlantic commerce and exchange as the primal technology of a primitive individuation (the emergence of the propertied self that in claiming property in a self individuates things to claim them as property) and thereby exploitation. Modern religious individuation as an operation of capitalist individuation operates through "[mechanisms] by which power arbitrates on who is included under its protection" and whom it exclusionarily includes by "[exposing them] to techniques of exploitation: slavery, extraction, criminalization, torture, debt."[51] Long both has a read on this and advances an account of black religion in relationship to it. By way of the geometry of the ellipse not as a Euclidean object of stasis but as the host of mathematical and topographical creativity and by way of the ellipse's illustrative extension as ellipsis, Long opens a way of understanding black religion as premised on blackness or black sociality as an entangled social field of an alternative, nonindividuated understanding of matter.

Let's turn to Long directly. Reproducing the geometric and mathematical form of the ellipse as part of his explanation of what ellipsis means, Long explains why he's alighted on *Ellipsis . . .* as the title of his book and as a figure under which he gathers a host of essays written since the publication of his most well-known work, his magnum opus, *Significations* (1986). In *Ellipsis*'s introduction, Long says, "I have titled my text, ELLIPSIS. Ellipsis is a grammatical and literary term derived from the geometrical figure of the ellipse. See the geometric and mathematical form of the ellipse below."[52] He then produces an image of an ellipse that is like the one produced as figure 4.1.

Following the image of an ellipse that he produces, Long comments on the specific mathematics of this geometric shape before then speaking to how the ellipse as a geometric shape or mathematical form relates to its literary-grammatical offshoot, the ellipsis or the dot-dot-dot (. . .) that on the plane of writing functions to present the nonrepresentable, to present what defies representation, what exceeds words insofar as they are understood problematically as representational signs. I'll get to Long's specific account of ellipsis in a moment, but let's tarry for a bit over the geometrics or the mathematics of the ellipse and how it differs from that other, more well-known mathematical and geometric

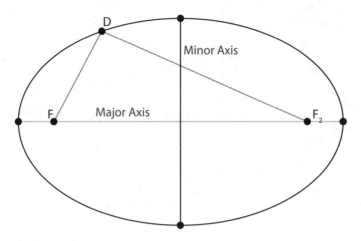

FIGURE 4.1. Ellipsis. *Source*: Author produced.

shape, the circle. For the mathematics of the ellipse shadows the ellipsis as well as informing Long's thinking about blackness and black thought generally and black religion more specifically.

According to the *Oxford English Dictionary* (OED), an ellipse is "a plane closed curve (in popular language a regular oval), which may be defined in various ways." More specifically, it is "(a) . . . the figure produced when a cone is cut obliquely by a plane." The notion of obliquity, that which diverges from verticality and horizontality and which is not of the straight line, is crucial to the geometry of the ellipse. The oblique cut in a cone is what makes the curve or oval shape that is the ellipse. This brings us to the next part of the OED's definition. An ellipse is "(b) a curve in which the sum of the distances of any point from the two foci is a constant quantity." The above diagram (figure 4.1) helps us with the second part of this definition. Point D on figure 4.1 is a point on the curve identified by the sum of the distance from that point to Focus 1 (marked as F on the major axis) and from that point as well to Focus 2 (marked as F₂, again on the major axis). Point D can be defined as the sum of these two distances. One can do this for any point or position on the curve and thus define any point on the curve. Finally, and importantly, the OED says that an ellipse can also be defined as "(c) a curve in which the focal distance of any point bears to its distance from the directrix a constant ratio smaller than unity."[53] As if the mathematics of the ellipse were not complicated enough, this third way of defining an ellipse perhaps bends the mind the most, though arguably it's the most important of the definitions for grappling with what Long is doing. To aid in contending with its significance, I have produced a second image of an ellipse (see figure 4.2), this one, however,

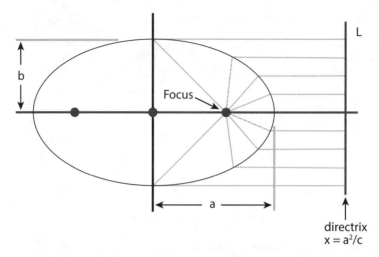

FIGURE 4.2. Ellipsis with directrix. *Source*: Author produced.

having a distinct line that is outside of the ellipse but to which each point on the curve making up the ellipse relates. That is, each point on the curve of the ellipse relates immanently to an outside that's out from the inside-outside and the outside-inside of the ellipse as such. This line (labeled *L* in figure 4.2), or other mode of an outside, mathematicians have called the *directrix*.

In this third definition, an ellipse is the locus of a point that moves such that its distance from a fixed point (the Focus in the diagram) bears a fixed ratio (in geometry, this fixed ratio is referred to as *eccentric*) to its distance from a fixed line (the directrix). What makes the ratio eccentric is that that ratio is constant, always more than 0 but less than 1. In the language of the OED, relative to some outside (the directrix), an ellipse is a figure of geometric eccentricity in that the points of its curve signal a strange, we might even say a queer, unity in that it consists in a movement that is "a constant ratio smaller than unity." I interpret this (and I think Long does too) to mean that the ellipse signals a unity that is less than, smaller than, the unity of identity. It is important to say that this does not mean that it is not a "unity" or gathering of some sort. Eccentric in character, the ellipse is a shape of nonidentical or not self-identical unity. Difference does not converge on or comport toward a "multicultural" unity of the same. Instead, difference here is, indeed, differential, or, in geometric terms, "eccentric." Ecstatic, it is out (*ek-*) from any stabilizing center (*centric*), other than the mono-unity of the One (and the Many as a function of the One).

What I've tracked here from the OED's definition of the ellipse comports with what Long says as well. Commenting on the image of the ellipse that he produces in his text (like figure 4.1 and my extension of it, following certain mathematical conventions, in figure 4.2) while also connecting the geometric shape that is the ellipse to the grammatical-literary figure of ellipsis, Long explains:

> An ellipse is a smooth closed curve that is symmetric about its horizontal and vertical axes. The distances between antipodal points on the ellipse are pairs whose midpoint is at the center of the ellipse, it is maximum along the major axis or traverse diameter. The ellipse contains two foci that define the locus of a point that moves so that the ratio of the distance from a fixed point *is always a constant less than one*. Ellipsis is derivative from this geometric shape. . . . [More specifically] the grammatical and literary derivative from the ellipse, the ellipsis, are [*sic*] three dots with space on each side, that connote that something has been left out. This "something left out" is assumed to be known though in some cases this [assumption of knowing what's been left out] is problematic. [The left-out element that the ellipsis, the dot-dot-dot, signals] is that part of the formula of the ellipse that emphasizes, "the constant less than one."[54]

We see Long here explaining the significance of the mathematics of the ellipse and how the ellipsis illustrates this significance. He highlights that in contrast to a circle, which has one center point, the ellipse has two off-center foci around which there is movement on an outer or peripheral curve and in relationship to an outside that is out from, in apposition to and anterior to, the inside-outside, center-periphery binary. Because with a circle there is one center point, the distance between the center and any given point on the peripheral curve is equivalent to that of any other point. With a circle all distance on the curve is equidistance. Shortly, I will provide a more nuanced, nonbinaristic way of understanding the difference between circle and ellipsis, one that is more in keeping with mathopoetics and that for that reason does not set up the circle as something of a straw man that must take the fall in order to valorize the ellipse. For now, though, let's remain with the contrast between these two geometric shapes and how the ellipse is not the circle. Because, with respect to the ellipse, movement on the outer curve is around two off-center foci, the distance any point has to the foci will always be different from that of any other point. In fact, any given point on the curve will be constituted by the very difference it has with respect to the two foci. In other words, a constant internal differing constitutes any given point on the curve as such. By internal differing, I mean that any given point on the elliptical curve is always doubly constituted through its two foci. That constant differing is precisely what is constant, precisely what internally constitutes any point on the curve.

But difference works in another way, too, with respect to a point on the curve of an ellipse. Not only is each point on the curve of an ellipse internally differing from itself because it's always related to two foci and not one center point, but each point on the curve differs from every other point on the curve in their differing from themselves. Which is to say, difference does not only internally constitute any given point on an elliptical curve. At the very same time, every point on the curve is constituted differentially with respect to every other point on the curve even as each point on the curve is internally nonidentical or differs within itself. Each point differs from itself in differing from the others. That is to say, no point on an elliptical curve duplicates the ratio of any other point. In short, with an ellipse, difference differs from and within itself while also being a site in which all of that difference is differentially entangled.

A major point that I want to draw from this is that on this reading of an ellipse as a figure of reality, the very notion of a self, of an "I" that might be imagined like a mathematical point as identical to itself at any point within space and time, does not work here. It falls away. The two foci of an ellipse are to be understood less as stable center points or as coherent, individuated points that constitute two centers. Rather, just as the outer peripheral points on the curve are shot through with multiplicity, so too in fact is each focus. Arguably, the foci are but metastable congealings of debris. They, again, may be understood as a certain metastable constellation of matter, a movement of matter that I've been narrating here by highlighting the periphery or the edge of the ellipse in relationship to its two foci points. I've been making a case that the periphery, the edge of the ellipse, is fractal, multiply constituted as a constant less than one, that refuses the hegemony of the one, that refuses being one. What I am now adding is this: the center point also (albeit two of them in the case of the ellipse) is equally a moving, topographical constellation. When all of this is put together, we are in position to say that what the ellipse bears witness to is that the notion of a coherent, singular point, peripheral or center (and regarding the center even if that point is doubled, as is the case with the ellipse, in contrast to the circle with its singular point), is something of a ruse that in the face of a mathopoetic imagination, in the face of mathematics as a feat of creativity, perhaps even of aesthetic sociality in incompletion, cannot stand. This is precisely Zalamea's point in calling for a kind of diffunified, *synthetic* philosophy of mathematics. And it is the point, in a similar vein, so I am here suggesting, that Long is making in turning to a mathopoetics to theoretically elaborate (the blackness of) black religion. The point is this: the point is always already exploded, blown up, inverted, turned inside out and outside in by virtue of a creative imagination that defies any and all atomism. In this respect, each point, be it the points at the ellipse's peripheral edge or the two foci within (making those double foci more like a Du Boisian "double consciousness"), or be it the (non)point of black religion, is more like a topographical singularity and less like an enclosed, atomized nodule. As Fred Moten puts it in a conversation with Zalamea that's relevant to this point that I'm trying to make about the mathematical point:

> The discovery of a way of approaching topology has made it possible for me to renew something of my own approach to black culture, to black life, because . . . when you get close up, the point broadens out into the neighborhood. All of a sudden, you start to see the complexity of the thing. . . . All of a sudden, I get close up, and it broadens out, and it spreads out, and more detail comes into play, and I realize what I'm interested in is the unruliness of a neighborhood rather than the circumscription of a point. And that is the mathematics, so to speak. That is the problematic of the approach of the topographical, of the approach to, at least a humble approach, to the topographical nature of black social life.[55]

Even when Long contrasts the ellipse to the circle, that contrast must not be made into a hard-and-fast contrast, into a binary opposition between the ellipse and the circle in favor of the former. On one level, there is a difference to be appreciated between the ellipse and the circle. Moving around a singular rather than a doubled center point, the ratio of each point on the circle's curve is equivalent to the ratio of every other point on the curve. This means that the circle is a structure of sheer equivalence. Equivalence and equidistance are what is constant with a circle. With a circle, many-ness functions as a sameness, as a many-sided equivalence, we might say. That equivalence is represented by the number one, while philosophically or ideationally, it is represented by the idea of the One understood as singular principle or origin, as the *archē* or the genesis of all things. Hence, even when the circle produces a Many (which indeed it does, for, after all, there are many points on the circle's curve), that is, when the circle is understood as a figure of "difference" (which, again, it must), the Many that it produces is a function and dispersal of the One as or in the Many.[56]

Things are much different, by which I mean difference is different, with the ellipse. The ellipse hosts a different kind of difference in that, with it, difference differing from itself is what is constant, we might say, what is shared. Long captures this in his crisp formulation: "The ellipse contains two foci that define the locus of a point [on the ellipse's curve] that moves so that the ratio of the distance from a fixed point *is always a constant less than one.*" The "one" in this formulation connotes equivalence, where each point on the curve would be equivalent to any other point because they are equidistant from the center point. To say that with the ellipse the constant is less than one is simply a way of explaining how an ellipse is not a circle. More specifically, it is a statement of how the ellipse is a figure of difference as such insofar as it is a figure of constant or ongoing differing, constant and ongoing deferring and even refusal or falling short of being one.

What is deceptive about contrasting the ellipse and the circle in this way is that it risks continuing to think in an analytically reductive way. That is, it risks letting the force of mathopoetic thinking slip away. What must be reckoned with is this: neither the two foci of the ellipse nor the one of the circle is in a Longian mathematical imagination, which is a poetic imagination, understood in a strictly numerical sense. The ellipse and the circle within a Zalamean-Longian framework are not ideal, platonic forms that stand opposed to each other. The two (foci of the ellipse) are not opposed to the one (center point of the circle). We are not here working within a strictly Euclidean or Platonic framework of the One versus the Many. Thinking nonanalytically and nonrepresentationally, which is to say, thinking mathopoetically, the one center point of the circle and the two foci of the ellipse mutually explicate the indivisibility of nature or matter. Which is to say, if the circle is understood as an instance of the ellipse, then the one or the center point of the circle may be understood as concentrating the foci and thus the multiplicity of the ellipse. This is akin to how, within musical performance, the soloist may be understood as a focal point that concentrates the ensemble. The numerics that I am unfolding here and that I have caught sight of in thinking with Long is a function of a mathopoetics of blackness and thereby of black religion. Stated differently, I am here suggesting a nonopposition of the circle and the ellipse, where the latter explicates the former and where the former is internal to the latter insofar as within an alternative imagination of matter, an imagination premised on matter as nonseparable and nonatomistic, we have moved from an outlook of Epicurean atomism, which continues to inform our imaginations of space and time within Western capitalism, to what might be thought of as a mathematics of kinetic materialism, the *mater*-ialism of blackness.

Poetics of a Punctuation Mark; Or, Ellipsis . . .

Such is the mathematics, broadly speaking, of the ellipse as Long poetically takes it up. Notwithstanding all that I've said, Long's interest is not so much or merely with the mathematics of the matter. All of this is eclipsed inside of, even as it shines through, his real interest, which is in how the literary-grammatical sign of the ellipsis, the dot-dot-dot that indicates that something's been left out in the scene of writing, follows from or transposes the mathematical figure of the ellipse. Indeed, this is precisely where the difference between the circle and the ellipse matters, for, as he puts it, "what seems to be implied by the 'left out' nature connoted by the ellipsis is the geometric figure of the circle."[57] It is the circle, as the sign of the knowable and fully representable—"with its 360 degrees, its unitary focus, and its equal radii, the circle more often than not has been used to symbolize the perfect container, as well as a sign of authority and order"— that the ellipse has no truck with.[58] Indeed, the ellipse, along with the ellipsis, which transposes onto the literary-grammatical plane the emphasis on what is "less than one," emphasizes, as Carolyn Jones Medine highlights after Long, *mystery* as itself an alternate mode of meaning-making that is bound up with what is constantly open or refuses closure notwithstanding the violence of enclosure or dispossession. Mystery here concerns some other mode of matter-ing, an otherwise animacy, due on the one hand to a quality of inherent unfinishedness and on the other to some other sociality of connection, some other we-ness, given in and as entangled differentiation.

The point that I am making here regarding ellipsis as the mystery of another mode of mattering, one that defies regimes of representation and equivalence, one that bespeaks some fugitive equation and that across the pages of this book I have been adumbrating as anarchy (*an-archē* as "the groundedness of an uncontainable outside," as refusal of property's origin with a lordly "I Am"), starts to come through in Medine's on-point elaboration of Long on ellipsis as a figure of thought and a stylistics and rhythmics of existence.[59] After rehearsing the basic understanding of ellipsis as grammatically indicating that something has been left out and as signaling a break or hiatus, Medine drills down on this issue of ellipsis as signaling that something's been left out, yoking the thing left out to the notion of mystery. "The three dots" of the ellipsis, she says both under the provocation of Long and with aspects of continental philosophy in mind,

> also suggest something mysterious, unfinished, or suspended. In "Blanchot . . . Writing . . . Ellipsis," Michael Naas turns to Derrida's essay, "Ellipsis," which addresses Maurice Blanchot. Using Blanchot's *Thomas the Obscure*, Naas comments on Derrida's reading, arguing that the ellipsis suggests either implicit understanding or "the place of a forgetting or a reserve, [marking] a moment of repression or reticence." It is an *aposiopesis*, a breaking off that suggests that something cannot be expressed—or will not be expressed, I would add—but that, nevertheless, conveys a coded meaning.
>
> In oratory, the ellipsis requires a pause. For Long, the ellipsis marks and is a gap that may suggest *a hiatus*, the opening of a space for refiguring identity itself. The Greek ἔ suggests an omission, therefore, but also a lack—that, as Jean-Luc Nancy puts it in his discussion of Derrida, "falls

short of being identical, and more precisely, [which] falls short of being circular." It is the "circle that misses itself."[60]

There is a rich adumbration of ellipsis here. Ellipsis is "the place of a forgetting" that itself indicates repressed nonknowledge. Such nonknowledge is itself a gnosis or a locus of unknowing, a locus that undoes knowing. Ellipsis, in this regard, is an alternate knowing. Also coming through in this passage is ellipsis as the locus of a "reserve" that gives pause, that causes hesitation ("reticence"), that in marking speech breaks off speech (*aposiopesis*), that breaches the order of signification. Hence, ellipsis is not unlike Victor Turner's notion of threshold or liminality, or Deana Lawson's portal, or Hortense Spillers's notion of vestibularity.[61] Ellipsis, in this respect, carries one into the break. "In the break," as Moten helps us understand, there is some other experience of time, a timeless space-time.[62] There is what Jackson speaks of as some other sense of and feel for things.[63] Feel me?

Additionally, in thinking with and after Long, Medine in this passage invites us to think about ellipsis as a kind of refusal, indeed, as a kind of silence in which perhaps "something cannot be expressed" but more notably, she says, "will not be [and thus refuses] to be expressed." On this score or as a practice of refusal, ellipsis signals not a being silenced but what might be thought of in that M. NourbeSe Philip way of thinking about it, as an active, untouchable as in ungraspable Silence (I use a capital S here to mark the difference).[64] This is a Silence, a "reserve" that I want to think of as a reservoir, that indicates an eso- and an exo-tericism, an interiority and exteriority, that is out from the binary of inside and outside. This is a mystery of otherwise existence, by which I mean an alternate matter-ing or animacy. Let's call it an ecstatics of base matter(-ing). And, finally, Medine emphasizes ellipsis as Gap or Event. Ellipsis is the Event that opens identity precisely by breaching any sense of identity as some coherent, self-contained, singular thing. In other words, as Event, ellipsis short-circuits the "I." It short-circuits identity as self-identical. It short-circuits the circularity of the One (and the same). In short, the mystery of ellipsis inheres in ellipsis as a practice of the open, of the Outside, as a practice of beginning (which is different from foundational discourses of "*the* beginning" or of origins). As such or as hiatus, ellipsis points to something like an open-field poetics, a poetics of the wild, "wilderness" and "wandering."[65]

After this elaboration of Long on these varied dimensions of ellipsis, Medine drills down further on ellipsis as hiatus or event in order to reach further into ellipsis as mystery. For this, she borrows Jean-Luc Nancy's notion of an "elliptical sense," thinking it with Long's notion of ellipsis. The key point is this: with the ellipse, circularity itself collapses; the circle fails to close the loop of its own peripheral movement of equidistant perfection around a single center. In the collapse of circularity, the notion of a singular center itself gives way, bifurcating into the imperfection of two foci. Medine explains that it is just that imperfection with respect to a single center that Long fundamentally seizes on in taking up the figure of the ellipse and its grammatical and literary extension as the ellipsis. For him, we might say what distinguishes the circle (of the modern invention of race-religion) from the ellipse and the ellipsis (of the blackness of black religion) is just this hiatus or breach of circularity. As a failed or compressed circle, a circle squashed down the way a limbo dancer suffers contortion so as to move spider-like, Ananse-like, in a sideways kind of way so as to maneuver in a tight space or from within constraint, this itself being an image of black religion's relationship to the modern invention of religion, the ellipse does not connote a "repetition that is identical to itself, but a doubling and displacement that opens possibility."[66] Or to put this in Derrida's and Nancy's terms (as Medine, quoting them, does), "in the 'suspense of the interval,' the return is 'of an *elliptical essence*. Something invisible is missing in the grammar of this repetition'—nothing has 'budged,' but meaning is altered and the 'ring no longer has exactly the same center.' What Derrida seeks, Nancy argues, is not the origin [or the *archē*], but to recover 'the condition of possibility of the origin,' origin thinking 'anew,' which for Derrida is *différance*, the repetition of meaning, Nancy argues, 'that does not consist in its duplication.'"[67] That condition of possibility is nothing less than the hiatus itself, that which cannot be enclosed and that thus reveals every regime of enclosure, every regime of the sentence, to be in fact internally creaking, internally unstable and unsettled. To recover that condition, to think from it, to dwell with it as praxis, is to abide not with the *archē* or an origin per se but with *an-archē*, with hiatus that is always already rupturing the origin. The mystery of ellipsis as the hiatus of anarchy is practice of the Outside. It is Black Outdoors. Ellipsis is mystery. Mysterious *ressourcement* at the wound, in loss, from dispossession, in rapture from the sovereignty of property.

But what might the resourcing of anarchy or anarchy as an-originary resource mean? To resource anarchy (*an-archē*) means operating out of a different orientation toward materiality, beyond the reigning regime of sense. Here matter is not a function of what in Christian theology has been called the "order of creation" and what I would further call the "order of religion(s)" as bound up with the ontotheological order of Men. Such order, as we saw in earlier chapters, has its basis, its origin (*archē*), with the European-produced discourse of the fetish that came to be imposed on Africa and that was key in producing the Negro as the irrational and negative anchor of *Homo capitalisticus* with his practices of commerce and exchange. To resource anarchy is to operate otherwise with respect to matter. It is to imagine matter otherwise. It is to imagine it beyond a Eurocentric "sacralization of order"—from the order of creation to the order of religion(s) to the order of Men imagined as "lords of all the world."[68] Resourcing anarchy entails refusing every imagination of founding origins, including the Western Christian imagination's discourse of a founding origin in God's sovereign Word as expression of a lordly "I Am" that figures a He-Creator as Lord or sovereign property owner over a subordinate, figured as feminized and always potentially unruly, Creation.[69] Rather, resourcing anarchy involves an ellipsical and elliptical approach to matter. Here *mater* as matter or as mat(t)er comes into view as matrix, as an-original "gathering space" that potentiates becomings of entangled difference or "difference without separability."[70] Here difference is precisely our shared commons. It is precisely what is shared. And yet, what is shared here is not a substantial whatness. It is not an isolable or possessable or propertied quiddity that is transferred or otherwise given to pregiven subjects. Rather, as the clearing for existence in all of its manifestations, in all of its entangled becomings and possible assemblages—in short, as a horizon of belonging through heterogeneity—matter is always already a horizon of entanglement and sharing that yields differences, proliferates form, and generates earth as a point within or a vector of cosmos. As should be clear, then, when I speak of *mater* (or, after Jackson, of black *mater*) as "gathering space" here, I do not mean space as delimited container. Rather, I mean it in a Longian or elliptical way. Which is to say, with this language I gesture toward an alternate cosmology, a cosmology of a black world or of blackness as ever-expanding, always emergent worlds. These are worlds ever and always beginning, existing in and as becoming and, in this way, as vitalistic be-*ing*. As the italics suggest, I want to place philosophical stress not on *to be* as a static state. This is not a project aimed at continuing modernity's project of ontology, which is a project of ontotheology and a project of onto–political theology. Rather, the stress here is on the gerund be-*ing* as the eventfulness of existence as such, the vitalism of matter as such. So eventful is the vitality of *mater*ial existence that mat(t)er spawns worlds that constantly begin (again), constantly expand, which is to say, that constantly enfleshes itself as entangled, unpredictable multiplicities. What I am trying to begin to formulate and think through here is what might be called a vitalist and therefore anticolonial imagination of matter.[71] *Cosmos*, then, means not so much a singular world but possibilities of pre- or ante-worlds in constant beginning(s). Such pre- or ante-worlds as possibilities or, again, as *mater* are marked by what feminist theologian Catherine Keller has called "tehomic depth." This comes through in Keller's arresting reading of the Bible's Genesis 1:2 across her book *The Face of the Deep: A Theology of Becoming*. Here's Genesis 1:2: "And the earth was without form, and void [*tohu vavohu*]; and darkness was upon the face of the deep [*tehom*]. And the Spirit of God moved upon the face of the waters" (King James Version with transliterated Hebrew interspersed).

In *The Face of the Deep*, Keller attends to the myth character of this passage so as to expose the normative theological tradition's repression of its own myth character. That repression has occurred through a certain way of understanding "God," first in bordered difference from creation, and then by feat of logos declaring the supremacy or, to use the theological language, the sovereignty of the former as superordinate Creator to the latter as created or subordinate creature. In this way, Creator is the name of that which upholds the single origin or *archē* of *the* world *as such*. This ontotheological maneuver is what is designed to repress the whiff of myth. It is what is designed to repress or otherwise cover over the anoriginal entanglement of Creator and creation in an ongoing unfolding wherein the entanglement of the surface of things and the depth of things are disavowed. The name of that repression is the Word or logos of God in disavowal of the tehomic depth or texture of the words and things. Indeed, in repressing its own myth character in the interest of the idea of the stable Word, the normative Christian theological tradition, as a tradition of doctrine or, again, as a tradition of stability or stable words (*logoi*) out of which to build a stable world (*the* world *as such*, in Zakiyyah Jackson's formulation), has worked to establish the terms of the political as ontotheological terms of order, property and (dis)possession, and lordship or sovereignty.[72] And yet, notwithstanding all that with Keller I've here said, what remains the case is that the Word or logos is itself a mode of myth. We might call it an imperial mode of myth. In claiming logos or the *archē* of reason and rationality as its ground, this is myth that disavows itself precisely as myth, as a type of fiction, as something made up (*poiēsis*). Logos is myth in the mode of violent disavowal of its own myth or made-up character so as to further disavow and plunder the tehomic depth of things, the very texture or thingliness of things, though at the level of thingliness or of the *mater* of *mater*iality and of matter itself, *tehom* or depth constantly in-surrects in things and against plunder. As has been said, "Objects can and do resist," but this is because Silence, indeed the "sovereignty of quiet," "an insistent previousness evading each and every natal occasion," imbues things. That quiet previousness opens onto other worlds. Nowhere.[73]

Against the backdrop of Genesis 1:2 understood in such a mythic way and thus as hosting an alternate imagination of matter, ellipsis as a figure of black *mater* is akin to *tehom*. Black *mater* is tehomic *mater*, queerly entangled mat(t)ering. Via Genesis 1:2 as a discourse of mythic mat(t)ering, *mater*iality manifests as a bottomlessness covered by the surface-level skirt of the ocean, beneath which are currents or rhythms (*ythms*, poet Nathaniel Mackey would say, anagrammatizing the word *myth* and clipping or cutting the word *rhythm*; we're coming to him in just a moment) vibrating with animating, in-carnating spirit or depth. As oceanic depth, all things entangle as flesh. One might resort to the language of incarnation to speak of the kind of mattering being spoken of here in terms of depth and surface or the depth of surface, but again theologian Catherine Keller ups the ante on this very language by her poetic extension of the language of incarnation to "intercarnations." Her effort at radicalizing relationality so as to clarify with the language of intercarnation the meanings or depths of matter-ing is quite consonant with Medine's elaborations of Longian ellipsis. Indeed, Keller is worth quoting in her own right, for intercarnation as she means it "witnesses to the multiplication and entanglement of any and all becoming flesh. Affirmations of the corporeal, the carnal, the mattering of matter, of all its materializations are, in the meantime, proliferating promiscuously in theory."[74] With this language she herself is pointing to the spiritual vocation that is internal to matter as such and that after Jackson I've been talking about in terms of black *mater* and after Long in terms of ellipsis and anarchy (as *anarchē*). With the notion of a spiritual vocation or of enfleshment as a vocation of pan-spirituality, of pan-breathing, in mind, I further highlight what Keller says about the matter of flesh:

> Intercarnation highlights the intermittencies, the intervals and inter-dependencies, of *world* relations. Does it describe a panentheism of all flesh in God and therefore God enfleshed in all? Perhaps not quite so neatly. For only in the twists and tangles of creaturely becoming, which is always a becoming bodily, does the subject matter of theology matter now. Or, then, ever. The carnal manifold of the world may indeed compose a living all, *pan*, not as the unity of all bodies but as the innumerable entity of "the flesh of the world." But the turbulent diversity of all that vulnerable flesh, the entanglement of all creatures in their neighbors and in their strangers, mostly involuntary, demands now relentless attention. In the perspective of all of that intercarnational activity, the ancient incarnation does not matter less. On the contrary, it may matter all the more when we emulate its own shift of attention from itself.[75]

With what Keller says here in mind, we can return to the Longian notion of ellipsis (and Medine's analysis, which more than any analysis of Long on ellipsis has been most helpful in helping me think) as signaling what I would call the depth and texture of matter, the depth of black *mater*iality as matter(-ing) otherwise. Charged with depth, with a depth charge, black *mater* is of such an imagination or rather is imaginal or mythic. As Zakiyyah Jackson has said, "When the black female (maternal) figure appears, if she appears, she appears as the work and revelation of myth."[76]

All of this, I propose, Long's language of ellipsis as a language of anarchy, or as a discourse on an-original, *mater*ial gathering space, suggests, provided one understands what I'm calling here "an-original gathering space," after Catherine Keller but with reverberations of Sarah Jane Cervenak on "black gathering" and Alexis Pauline Gumbs on the paraontological as a pan-ontological scale of breathing. As a language of anarchy, ellipsis voices a mythopoetics of be*ing* or existence.[77] In signaling more than the blackness that whiteness created, blackness in its irreducibility to racial category points to just such a mythopoetics. Indeed, so understood, blackness—which we might further annotate perhaps as blackness' (blackness-prime) or as ~~blackness,~~ or with Long as "opacity," or with Jackson as "black *mater*," or with Ferreira da Silva as "virtuality" and as "infinite canvas"—is generative, nonimperial myth.[78] That is to say, blackness is differentially elliptical, differing within itself in differing from itself. Precisely as alternate-mythifying or as suggesting a mythography of entangled difference is how I understand Long's language of ellipsis, and it is certainly what, thinking with and extending Long, I mean by *anarchy* (*an-archē*). Ellipsis is anarchy, is cosmology, is stylistics, a form of be*ing* and thinking, of be*ing* and un/knowing.

But if ellipsis is this, if it is in this way tehomic or bespeaks a spirit-infused and nonrepresentational mythopoetic cosmology of the deep, and that invites a thinking-in-différance or a thinking through extension and "repetition . . . that does not consist in . . . duplication" or reiterations of sameness, then we can understand the force of what I take to be Medine's most crucial point about Longian ellipsis.[79] As a figure of blackness and black thought, or as another way of talking about what R. A. Judy as recently called "*poiēsis* in black," ellipsis connotes spiritual as *mater*ial praxis.[80] It is a figure, alas, of religion, albeit off-kilter or disordered.

More precisely, ellipsis is a figure of *black religion*. It is a figure of the anarchy of black religion, a figure of black (religious) anarchy. By this I mean that ellipsis is a figure of an alternate mode of sacrality, an alternate imagination or poetics of "the sacred," one that is internal to blackness. What is meant by "the sacred" here ought not be heard as still within logics of soteriology (a traditional theological discourse of salvation) that require sacrifice. James Cone has helped us understand that such sacrifice lynches or is connected to the lynching tree.[81] A destabilization of the very category of religion as central to the *archē* of modernity and a hiatus that breaches the order of the human and that operates as a loophole of retreat, the seriality of black religion announces some other orientation. Like ellipsis, it is a figure not of purity but of entangled contact, in light of which alternate ways of being (again, as be*ing*) can be experimented with or mythopoeticized. In this respect, black religion is religion's apophatic unsaying, a movement of thought and practice around mystery. Purloining from poet John Keats but with a longer view in view, by which I mean with what Charles Long opens up in view, we might think of black religion as a mode of aesthetics, that is, as practices animated by "negative capability." Keats thought of the artist as having "access to truth without the pressure and framework of logic or science. Contemplating his own craft and the art of others . . . Keats supposed that a great thinker is 'capable of being in uncertainties, Mysteries, doubts, without any irritable reaching after fact and reason.'"[82] Such is how I hear Medine's elaboration of Long's notion of ellipsis as "origin thinking 'anew'" or in the "hiatus" as a "pause" and thus from the liminal, vestibular threshold of anarchic im/possibilities, the abyss, "between the act of liberation and the actualization of freedom."[83]

The Poetry of Black Religion

In the next and final chapter of this book, I want to consider poet Nathaniel Mackey's practice of the poem, meditating on it as an instance of Long's notion of ellipsis and thus as a way of delving further into what I am trying to get at with the notion of anarchy and specifically the anarchy of black religion, where *black religion* refers at best only secondarily to any formal religious institutions or even to atheistic rejections of religion as tied to institutions and functions more as the name of an orientation in matter and of material existence. For Long, black religion is an elliptical orientation in matter, an occupation in and preoccupation with the hiatus. We might even call this elliptical orientation a dis/orientation in whose praxis there is a disidentification with the category of religion, though that disidentification takes place from within that very category. As I've thought with Long over the years, I've increasingly felt that it is in the practice of poetry or experimental writing that we glimpse the force of his thinking about religion, of his consideration of black religion and indeed of blackness as dis/orientation of beginnings, foundations, or *archē* into ongoingness, without origin. Indeed, one of the writers who has particularly seized me in this regard is poet, novelist, essayist, and sometimes lunch or dinner conversationalist Nathaniel Mackey. The next chapter is really the unfolding of a question: What happens when we consider Mackey's practice of the poem, his practice of artistic, experimental writing, as instancing black religious anarchy, as instancing ellipsis? What becomes available to black (religious) studies and to an understanding of the spiritual vocation of black radicalism if Mackey's practice is approached in this way? Indeed, if we dare imagine poetry in this way? What becomes available should black aesthetics and black religion be thought in the blur of blackness?

Let's see . . .

Chapter Five

Anarchy Is a Poem, Is a Song . . .

For Nate, in gratitude

[The poem is] addressed to the spirit; it's a spiritual. It's speaking to the spiritual vocation of music, the spiritual vocation of art, the spiritual vocation of poetry.—NATHANIEL MACKEY, *Paracritical Hinge* (2005)

Poem

As already noted, this chapter and the previous one are a speculative unit. Together they are an attempt at thinking black (religious) anarchy or the anarchy of black religion. In the previous chapter, I read Charles Long's notion of ellipsis, a key term for his account of black religion, as providing a way into his late notion of anarchy. That is, via the geometry of the ellipse, I tarried with ellipsis mathopoetically. In this chapter I turn to Nathaniel Mackey's poem practice, generally, and to one of the poems in *Eroding Witness* (1985), "Song of the Andoumboulou: 6," specifically, to further my consideration of black (religious) anarchy. Through a slow reading of the poem, what I propose is that Mackey's poetics is a praxis of mystery. Indeed, it is a praxis of that elliptical anarchy that marks black religion understood as an angle or vector through which to understand blackness. Here black religion, like blackness, is a poem of life, just as anarchy, too, understood with Mackey in mind, is a poem. Black (religious) anarchy is a song, a poem-song. Mackey's practice of the poem invites us to think in this direction. Ultimately, by way of this consideration of Mackey's poetics, I want to amp up or bring into further aesthetic relief the anarchy of black religion as a cross-cultural poetics in fugitive refusal of the logics of the state and the reigning logics of the hu/Man, all of this in the constructive interest of imagining alternative ways of life together, with each other, with the earth, an alternate we-ness in diffused or dispersed, differential unity (not uniformity).

In the prior chapter, I offered a preliminary introduction to Mackey's two long poems—*Song of the Andoumboulou* and *Mu*. While the two poems are independent of each other, they have grown over the years such that, as Mackey puts it, "the two [are to be] understood as two and the same, each the other's understudy. Each is the other, each is both, announcedly so in this book [*Splay Anthem* (2006)] by way of number, in earlier books not so announcedly so. . . . [Each] is the other's twin or contagion, each entwines the other's crabbed advance."[1] I now want to add a few more opening remarks about the poems as we make our way into the specific concerns of this chapter. Particularly, it is worth noting that Mackey's "two and the same" poems each take inspiration from a piece of music that is bound up with myth. As such, they are understudies of each other in being (under)studies in myth; they are mythic re-soundings. Experimentalizing language itself, dwelling with and in the "creaking of the word" where language is a scene of jouissance, where pleasure and passion, desire and suffering, converge in an ecstatics of escape, Mackey's two long poems are instances of black mystagogy, a mythography of blackness manifest in cross-cultural movement. Hence, the constant movement across the poems in which at the drop of a hat or, as is more likely in the poems, at the sound of a new song on the ubiquitous jukebox, the wayfarers move from one place to another, from one locale to another. The movement is of an "imagined we be- / yond all calculation."[2] Sometimes called a "wandering we," sometimes with Rastafarian inflection an "I-" and "We-Insofar," sometimes a quantum we, sometimes a "philosophic posse," the poems' incalculable we beyond measure is "a lost tribe of sorts, a band of nervous travelers" that "echo . . . flight and fugitivity."[3] One minute they're in Los Angeles, the next in Bogotá, the next in New Orleans, the next still in Jaipur or some Bedouin commune, and before that in the hold of a slave ship, and so on and so forth. In other words, this is an ecstatic we, the we of an alternate mythic imagination that in its ongoingness, in ellipsis, in incompletion, or in the unbinding that binds it as unbound, this otherwise we defies constitution into a homogeneous society of the same, a society of the One (and the Many as a species of the One), into a nation, a state, a "We the People." What is called *politics* is here decidedly of some other sort. As it's put in one of the *Song of the Andoumboulou* poems, "Space was our claim to kinship."[4]

Mackey's poems incessantly circle in and through and around such matters, the potentials of other worlds, other imaginations of the social at the scene of loss, apocalyptically unveiled on catastrophe's occasion. Under conditions of wounding, there is always more, always more going on. I'm thinking about the relationship between the wound and the blessing, severance and severalness, or communion in/as broken yet entangled multiplicity. Mackey's poetics traffics in this, and it is just this that makes his practice of the poem of particular interest for the black study of religion as practices of fugitive un/binding. For in Mackey's practice, the poem offers itself as a site of ellipsis, as discussed earlier in considering Long; of ongoingness; of release from the sentence, from being sentenced or under sentencing. Here the poem is a site of black religion, expansively, aesthetically, parareligiously understood, as I have been considering it here under the rubric of anarchy (*an-archē*). Mackey brings ellipsis and anarchy into view as *mythopoēisis* at the scene of the sentence, of loss. I want to think about this with particular attention to *Song of the Andoumboulou* generally and then with respect to one of the poems in the *Song* series, namely, "Song of the Andoumboulou: 6," which can be found in Mackey's first book-length collection of poems, *Eroding Witness* (1985). This collection offers the notion of "erosion" itself as a figure of ellipsis and thus of black religion. I'm interested in what "Song: 6" offers to the black study of religion, how Mackey's *Song* enacts a spiritual vocation, an anarcho-poetics, by virtue of advancing a different orientation to matter and mattering, by virtue of its practice of rapture, which is a falling into matter's depths, into the depths of language itself at the scene of loss and catastrophe. There's an unveiling, an apocalypse (in that sense already spoken of with theologian Catherine Keller in mind), that's at stake in Mackey's poetics, though what's unveiled is not to be had or owned in the sense of being possessed like property. There is no telos (of property) here. Here we have to do with the materiality of spirit possession, something beyond propertied self-possession, beyond the logic of the individual, self-owned "I," beyond the condition of ownership or extractive grasping after things. Mackey's poetics is apocalyptic. His practice of the poem discloses this. Through the obliquity or the angularity of the language making up his poem-songs, their "jagged clippings of speech," as one critic has put it, Mackey as poet and experimental writer makes available to readers an alternate sense of things.[5] The poet follows the poem, existing in its poetry. An eroding witness to the poetry of things, the poem creates, builds out, or paramythographizes an interiority that's unbeholden to capture, unbeholden to any and all givens. Releasing readers who undergo its contagion from the surface of things, the poem is a trace of the imaginal or the virtual, "beyond this narrow Now," as W. E. B. Du Bois once put it, to dream earth dreams.[6]

Practice

To appreciate this, let us consider Mackey's long poem-song, his *Song of the Andoumboulou*, more generally. What lies behind the title of this poem? What is at stake in the ongoingness of the poem, its quality of incompletion or unfinishedness? I argue here that at stake is nothing less than the spiritual intensity, the fundamental virtuality, of matter itself—lost matter's, lost maternity's ani*mate*riality.[7] That intensity has everything to do with the black study of religion in its study or contemplation of black (religious) anarchy.

Song of the Andoumboulou finds its point of inspiration in Mackey's hearing in the early 1970s of the album *Les Dogon*, François Di Dio's 1956 recording of Dogon music. On the recording is a track titled "Song of the Andoumboulou," from which Mackey's still-being-written long poem takes its title. The music is funerary, part of the burial rituals of the Dogon people of West African Sudan. Informing those rites is a cosmology that resounds in and through the music. The music, Mackey tells us, "begins with sticks marking time on a drum's head, joined in short order by a lone, laconic voice—gravelly, raspy, reluctant—recounting the creation of the world and the advent of human life. Other voices, likewise reticent, dry, join in, eventually building into song, a scratchy low-key chorus."[8] In due course, however, the singing gives way to "another lone voice," emerging this time not to recount creation but now to eulogize the life of the deceased. The voice "[recites] his genealogy, [bestows] praise, [and] lists all the places where he set foot while alive," taking listeners on what amounts to a journey through the local countryside that can be heard as matching on a smaller local or societal level the earlier cosmic recounting of the creation of the world.[9] Once the story of the departed has finished, an antelope horn blasts, evoking, Mackey says, referring to Di Dio's liner notes, "the wail of a new-born child, born into a terrifying world."[10] The wail of the horns as the sounds of a newborn marks a moment of transit, transition, or movement, that is to say, "the entry of the deceased into the other life."[11] This is the birth of the dead, of what's born in death.

And so here we have a funerary articulation of the beginning of creation (cosmic birth), a storying of the deceased life (the storying of a life at the site of death), and, finally, a recursive turn back to life but now changed, altered in death and by death. The music of the Dogon is a music of movement as the deceased enter the other life (birth again), all of this wrapped in or articulated through voice and song. But there's one more crucial layer to Mackey's cross-cultural paramythographic exchange with Dogon myth, as his reception of the myth becomes interspersed with his interest in the myths, stories, legends, significant stories, and the like of many other cultures, all of this providing a kind of imaginal backdrop for his own long poem, his paramythic, and, as I also like to think about it, his mystic song. That layer concerns the very figure of the "Andoumboulou." Who are the Andoumboulou of the "Song of the Andoumboulou" track on the album *Les Dogon*? Why are they compelling for Mackey?

Though Mackey's encounter with Dogon cosmology and mythology goes back to the early 1970s and even the late 1960s, it wasn't until the late 1980s, after reading French anthropologists Marcel Griaule and Germaine Dieterlen's *The Pale Fox*, that Mackey learned specifically about the Andoumboulou and their place in Dogon cosmology. At the heart of the matter regarding the identity of the Andoumboulou is the question of the human. This comes through in an interview conversation between Mackey and fellow poet and scholar of religion Peter O'Leary in which Mackey explains his take on the Andoumboulou. I ask in advance the reader's patience (and forgiveness) in quoting both so much and at such length in what follows, but it is hard to beat Mackey's own words regarding the Andoumboulou and the grip they came to have on his imagination and his work as an artist. To O'Leary he says:

> The Andoumboulou are, in Dogon mythology and cosmology, an earlier form of human beings who are flawed and failed to sustain themselves or failed to be the thing that human beings would eventually be. So they're a version, an earlier attempt, an earlier draft of human being that didn't work out. But they are invoked at the time of Dogon funeral ceremonies; the "Song of the Andoumboulou" is a Dogon funeral song. It is as if they are harking back to the failure of the Andoumboulou as a pre-figuration of mortality in the more fully realized form of human being that the Dogon are, that we are. I haven't read anything that has explained that, so I've had to guess. Why do they sing the "Song of the Andoumboulou" at funeral time? Why do they hark back to these failed earlier human beings? My understanding of it is that the Andoumboulou become relevant in a ritual that is marking death and mortality, the failure of human life to sustain itself indefinitely, because they are figures of frailty and failure. Mortality is a reminder of frailty and failure. But the song is also a song of the spirit of the person who has died and is moving on to another realm. It's a song of lament and rebirth.[12]

From here Mackey elaborates on the impression the music itself made on him, the ineradicable effect it had on his thinking. The raspy tonality in the voice of the singer, the trumpet-like instrument that blows to announce the movement of the deceased into another realm—of all of this, he says, "I was struck by it, by the music of it, the sound of it."[13]

This point about "the music of it" and "the sound of it" brings us to the threshold of why Mackey is so taken with the "Song of the Andoumboulou" to the point that he names his poem after it. In the same interview with O'Leary, Mackey suggests that what seized his attention is not so much what the "Song of the Andoumboulou" *is* as what it is *doing*, what it addresses and, by extension, I take it, what his own long poem in its recursive ongoingness, as a poetics of ellipsis, is doing, is addressing: "It's addressed to the spirit; it's a spiritual. It's speaking to the spiritual vocation of music, the spiritual vocation of art, the spiritual vocation of poetry. In that way it's related to what the figure of the phantom limb and the other things you've alluded to are getting at. And it's related in my mind to *duende* and to flamenco by that raspy tonality that is resorted to in the voice of the singer of the 'Song of the Andoumboulou.'"[14] And so, as the *Song* is a spiritual, so too, in its crosshatching with the *Song*, is Mackey's poem a kind of spiritual. It is a musical, as in being the poet's, and a poetic, articulation of the vocation of the spirit. Or as Mackey says in another interview given not long after the publication of the collection *Nod House* (2011), the poem-song is a venture in soul-making, soul-building, soul-questing as in the questing for (a) soul, the questing for an otherwise to what is or to what passes itself off as all there is or could ever be. That is, the poem-song as a spiritual is a hymn of questing for a more-than beyond current quagmires and catastrophes, even as that questing occurs under conditions in which, as one of the lines from one of the poems in *Nod House* puts it, "No one wanted to / know / what soul was."[15] This inattention to soul as more-than and less-than ontology, as more-than and less-than what is, this inattention to alternatives, bespeaks not just shortsightedness. It goes to something Mackey hears in the very notion of the Andoumboulou beyond just the Dogon. In the Andoumboulou he hears something of our own "andoumboulouousness" (a Mackey neologism).

The move here, in which taking up the Andoumboulou of Dogon mythology slides into an occasion for addressing and redressing present-day "andoumboulouousness," by way of a practice of the poem or the spiritual vocation of experimental writing, is something Mackey attends to in another interview. Speaking to the various resonances between the sound that comes through in the Dogon's "Song of the Andoumboulou," particularly the stridency and raspiness of voice that moved him so upon hearing the music, and also, for instance, the sound of flamenco, also known as *cante jondo* or the dark, "deep song" of the Spanish musical tradition, or also the raspiness and stridency found in African American blues music—about this strident raspiness of voice and sound across a number of traditions, Mackey in an interview says:

So I'm bringing the Andoumboulou and the Song of the Andoumboulou into harmonic interplay with a number of other references and traditions. . . . [At issue here,] for me, is the range of things that this figure can apply to. I haven't found out a great deal about the Andoumboulou as the Dogon conceive them. In the three or four books on Dogon cosmology that I've read, there isn't a whole lot on the Andoumboulou, so it's not finding out [about them] in that sense [of becoming informed about them]. It's partly finding out and it's partly making. It's not a passive active finding out; it's also constructing, creating what "andoumboulououousness," which is a neologism that comes up in [the poetry collection] *Whatsaid Serif,* means. It's really extending the implications and resonances that reside in the figure as it presides over certain areas of my life and work. It becomes more inclusive and more elastic and, again, vibrates with other traditions and with my own experience. I've taken to joking lately that the Andoumboulou are a form of failed, flawed human being and that that's something I can identify with.[16]

What Mackey here jokingly puts forth in this 1998 interview becomes more serious by the time of his meditations in *Splay Anthem*'s preface. Here he says, "From Griaule and Dieterlen I learned that the Andoumboulou are a failed, earlier form of human being in Dogon cosmology, one of the results of the pale fox of Ogo's cosmic revolt and incestuous penetration of the earth in pursuit of his lost female twin. The Andoumboulou along with the Yeban who were born of that union and in turn gave birth to them, live underground, inhabiting holes in the earth."[17]

The Andoumboulou of Dogon cosmology allow Mackey a way to consider the human not as something ontologically given, and thus as static and final, but as drafts or genres or versions, some of which might need to be scrapped, others experimented with, or even virtual ones in play perhaps in a hidden or unseen way at the same time as other, more dominant versions are operative and wreaking havoc. On this latter point, we get a sense of this when Mackey speaks of the Andoumboulou and the Yeban "living underground, inhabiting holes in the earth," inhabiting the holes of history.[18] "Song of the Andoumboulou" is a ritual music to what has been lost or buried. But it also sonically conjures what has been buried but in some sense is yet alive within the earth, subterranean or surreal to the current arrangement of things. To tap into this underness, to that within, to that lost within, is to be involved in organizing. It is to press toward some other organization of things precisely in their baseness or fundamental thingliness, that is, as *mater*, as matter. Such striving or aspiring or reaching Mackey at one point calls a "religioerotics," this itself being bound up with his respect for "mystical traditions" and for "the intuitive, the uncanny, the oneiric, the sympathetic, the coincidental, the ecstatic, the intangible, the paradoxical, the oceanic, the quirky, the psychosomatic, the quixotic . . . and so on."[19] The religioerotic reaching, this reaching that occurs at the level of the ecstatic and the uncanny, reflects an aspiration for a buried, which is to say, a nonmonumentalized, nonrepresentational but yet available alternative mode of existence. This way of being—and here I hark back to the meditation on be-*ing* that I introduced in the previous chapter in talking about Long and ellipsis, with assistance from Carolyn Jones Medine and Catherine Keller—signals a disposition not predicated on logics of property as logics of possessing, owning, grasping. The elliptical ongoingness that is central to Mackey's practice of the poem aims to be of this nongrasping disposition in which the aspired-for alternative turns out to be something "you have but don't have."

> You have it in the form of a disposition but that disposition is not the same as the possession of it. So you have it as a reaching toward something. In many ways, you have it as a reaching through things, so that there's a way in which that reaching is not satisfied even when it does seize upon something. It goes on reaching. The phantom limb bespeaks that reach, which continues beyond the grasping of something. It speaks of loss, it speaks of lack, but it also speaks of an insufficiency that's indigenous to the very act of reaching. Reaching wants to go on in some sense that's troubling to the things it does settle upon and take hold of. It's not that it empties those things. It simply finds that those things are in place in a certain way that the reaching wants to continue to be free of.[20]

It's this "quality of discontent," as he calls it, this quality of elliptical ongoingness, we might say in a fusion of Longian and Mackeyan terms, that manifests in Mackey's poem and poetics as a practice of refusal. Such refusal is the refusal of the standpoint of a coherent or sovereign "I," the capital *I* that grasps or attains a self or itself as the condition of grasping or taking hold of things. This refusal of standpoint is the refusal of achievement, this itself being a refusal of the desire for standing.

All of this comes through in the final poem of Mackey's first collection of poems, titled *Eroding Witness*. That final poem in *Eroding Witness* is itself titled "Dogon Eclipse." The poem both culminates the book (thus leaving the book under the sign of eclipse as itself a type of solar or lunar erosion of sorts as sun or moon becomes visibly unseeable through the interposition of some other unseeable entity) and culminates the final section of the poetry collection, which bears the apocalyptic name, after French composer, pianist, experimentalist, and Holocaust survivor Olivier Messiaen, "Septet for the End of Time." Not, as one might expect, the seventh poem of the "Septet," but as the last poem "Dogon Eclipse" is actually the eighth poem, that which falls out of the sequence of seven. It's worth noting that Mackey has a certain fascination with the number eight, the number that falls outside of the series of seven, taken within a certain Christian imaginative appropriation of the book of Genesis and the Hebrew Bible to be the number of perfection or completion. Eight is of the Outside. As regards ordinal arrangements of completion, the number eight ordinates Silence as the fulsomeness of incompleteness. Put differently, with mathematician Kurt Gödel's Theorems of Incompleteness coupled with Long's mathopoetics in mind, we might say that the incomplete number eight is of the ongoingness of ellipsis.[21] In this respect, Mackey's *Eroding Witness* is an incomplete book, an elliptical book of the number eight. I'm about to quote from Mackey's eighth and final poem of *Eroding Witness*, the poem that culminates or "completes" his poetically, elliptically incomplete collection that inaugurates both his *Song of the Andoumboulou* and *Mu* serial poems as well as his serial, epistolary novel (presently in five volumes), *From a Broken Bottle Traces of Perfume Still Emanate*. As I do, I invite you, dear reader, to consider the way the first-person pronoun *I* shows up in the poem, how it eclipses and ellipses, how it erodes:

> I wake up waved at, said goodbye
> to, wondering what now,
> what "I" keeps me up.
> I
> wake up eyeless, blinded, eyed,
> watched by armies,   cautious,
> caught.
> Waved at by lines of disappearing
> kin . . .
> Withered lid of an eroded "I,"
> Ogotemmêli overlooks the lit city
> outside . . . [22]

If there's an "I" somehow operative in this poem, it's the I of some altered or surreal, dreamlike, semiasleep, semiawake condition. That is, the I, or, rather, the I's (multiple), move curiously through this poem. The I, for instance, of the first line of the poem is an active I. It is the I who wakes up. However, by the poem's third line, the I is split, diffused, diffracted, scattered, apocalyptically revealed as, in fact, multiple. What I mean is that by the time the reader gets to the third line of the poem, what is disclosed, or perhaps dis-en-closed, is that the I of the first line of the poem is revealed to have been in a kind of vertigo state. At the edge of reason, the I is trying to reckon with its condition, with the state of things, or maybe not even with its condition or state but with its being without state, its statelessness, its wandering. The I, the poem says, is wondering what to make of its ecstatic condition. More specifically, the I wonders what "I" is keeping the I of the first line awake. Interestingly, the second I is put in scare quotes as "I," differentiating it from the first I. This "I" both is and ain't the first I. Could this "I and I"-ness, this doubling without duplication, this doubled consciousness perhaps, be a figure of what the Rastas spoke of as "I 'n I"?

Then, in line 4, which opens a new unit or section of the poem, the I of the first line of the poem, having encountered the "I" of the third line, reappears, waking up (again). This time, however, in the face of the nonidentical doubling of the "I" that appeared in line 3 of the poem, the I appears in what is line 4 of the poem stranded at the end of the line. The I is on a precipice, as it were, teetering on the brink of the line. The I is on edge, at the edge of the line, near the end of the (poetic) line. Perhaps in this eighth poem, the I is an "Octet at the End of Time," which is to say, at the end of the line. That I is, we are told, eyeless, without sight, under surveillance, caught, even as lines of kin wave the I goodbye. As we scoot down the line, further into the poem, we get to a line in which we are told that we are dealing with an I that is under erosion, an "I" whose relationship to normative, self-owned subjecthood or to the normative self-composed and supposedly coherent I is . . . well . . . eroded. Finally, we are told that the "eroded 'I'" is Ogotemmêli, the Sudanese elder who in a series of recordings in the 1950s conveyed to the French anthropologist Marcel Griaule a sense of the philosophy and myths of the Sudanese Dogon people. This is something that I've already mentioned in this chapter. My additional point now is simply that what we've become poetically privy to is the apocalypse as an eclipse, an apoc-eclipse, of the I (and the I's). The I, which is to say, the I's of the poem, is multiple. Nonidentical in their serial repetition, they are like the dots that congregate or gather as an ellipsis. Which is to say, the poem's I is not the self-possessed, stable I. Indeed, the I of the poem is reckoning with an apocalypse, a revelation, of its own indeterminacy and multiplicity. What comes finally through in the poem is that Mackey's poetic I operates under the sign of fracture, fragmentation, and finally erosion. More still, this poetically eroding "I"-in-multiplicity has a certain paramythic-parareligiosity about it. It does so under the "primitive" sign of West African Dogon mythology. This sign or symbol, this eroding I/eye (witness), registers an alternate semiosis that noisily, silently, murmuringly creaks (within) the mythic order of Western modernity. That murmuring "I"-in-multiplicity witnesses to the presence of a surreal aliveness that insurgently persists from within the constraints of racial capitalist modernity. The one who stands in for this destabilizing presence that both is in and exceeds the terms of the modern is, as I've already noted, Ogotemmêli, who is postured toward, so we learn in the poem, "the lit city outside."

It is fitting that, situated as it is between the themes of erosion and the outside, Mackey's eighth poem should bear the name "Dogon Eclipse," a title that has echoing within it because of the word *eclipse* the additional word *ellipsis* and further still the word *apocalypse* as presented under the figure of "primitive" religiosity or Dogon "bad religion," where such bad religion marks the practices of an other semiosis of ex-istence. These are practices of a certain Outside-ness (more on this shortly) that entails dwelling at that limit where the "real" and "imaginary" increasingly lack distinction. Here we move from a determinate mythology that in the name of Reason, with a capital *R*, denies itself as myth (I mean here "the political" and "the human" as themselves terms within modernity itself as a myth of origins, as a number of thinkers from Theodor Adorno and Max Horkheimer to Hans Blumenberg have made clear) to a mythography of what escapes origin myth.[23] Here is where I locate "poëisis in black" as para-mythography of the surreal that obliquely cuts across what counts as real.[24] It is to be involved, in Mackey's case, in an ecstatics of experimental writing. About this oblique cutting, which in his serial novel *From a Broken Bottle Traces of Perfume Still Emanate* is referred to at one point as the "sexual cut," Mackey says, "There's something very spiritual."[25] Or, as I'd put it, there's some other practice of the sacred as matter in play here, one that is driven by "discontent" and that for this reason lends itself to spiritual striving, which again I offer here as a figure of ellipsis. Propelling the striving here is a "ghostliness" or "absence and incompletion" that themselves "suggest a spiritual supplement to the world that both invests it with a certain urgency and divests it of any ultimacy."[26] *Song of the Andoumboulou* sings the spiritual supplement, the obliquity of the surreal.

It is worth tarrying just a bit more on the elliptical as a spiritual supplement that drives Mackey's long poem-song, giving to his poetry the character of a constant reaching beyond, the character of extension. This reaching beyond or extending is itself already part of a dynamic of being moved by or under the sway of an alternative that already unsettles the reigning terms of order. This unsettling manifests as a praxis of ecstasy or what Mackey calls, after the Spanish poet Federico García Lorca, "duende," which is a kind of spirit possession (more on this in a moment), and what he thinks of in conversation with poet Jack Spicer as a "practice of Outside," of being in conversation with the dead.[27] In this respect, what is called *the self* is always in some sense besides itself, more than a singular self, an elliptical "constant less than one," Charles Long might say mathopoetically with the ellipse in mind, as explored in chapter 4. Indeed, as Mackey says in an interview with Paul Naylor, "A lot of theory and criticism that has been coming from Europe is simply trying to catch up with the unspectacular practice of outside and to keep in mind the different levels on which a practice of outside is understandable."[28] Between *duende* and "practice of Outside," Mackey advances what I would call a poetics of spirit possession behind which stands what I would also characterize as the spiritual intensity of the imagination or the imaginal. That intensity comes, for Mackey, in the form of creative practices—let's call these the black arts—animated by conversations with the dead in their ongoing aliveness, their ongoing presence. The absent presence of the alternative, of other possibilities, is another way of thinking of the force of *duende* on the imagination. Communion with an absent presence, with an unidentifiable and even unrepresentable "(re)Source," an unrepresentable Outside or more-than, is a way of speaking of the interplay between loss and gain in Mackey's creative work as driven by the spiritual intensity or the depths of matter as such, its capacity to generate forms.

Literary scholar Nadia Ellis has helped me think about this dynamic of spiritual intensity at the scene of language itself in Mackey's poetics and how this may be understood as Mackey's own version of what Zakiyyah Iman Jackson called "troping the trope of African religion."[29] For Mackey, that troping of the trope of religion or his anagrammatic or ythmic troping of myth operates by unhinging language from the prerogatives of the liberal humanist subject, which is to say, from the project and certitudes of the Human. Ellis speaks of language operating in Mackey's work as a "possessive force" wherein aesthetics occasions "metaphorized spiritual manifestations" under conditions of the kind of loss indicative of Middle Passage, the loss indicative of transatlantic scattering.[30] That scattering created an insistent perception of lost connection and kinship, the loss registering affectively or sensorily the way a phantom limb registers presence at the location of a lost limb and thus at the locus of absence. Through such practices as the limbo dance (where internal to the word *limbo* is *limb*), loss, felt as phantom presence or as a phantom limb, is negotiated with a view not to recovering the lost limb but to entering into a liminal state (a state of statelessness, a state of being spirit possessed, as it were), a state of invention or countercreation. Limboed black performance and the practices of Vodun with which the limbo dance is connected are "variables of an underworld imagination."[31] Importantly for my purposes, Yoruba-based Vodun as a dimension of what is called New World African or black spirituality and the black Atlantic World more generally must be understood as part of this underworld imagination of compensatory invention, invention in compensation of loss. Mackey himself

has found a particular inspiration for his poetics from one of the orishas or dei-
ties of the Yoruba pantheon, namely, Legba (or Eshu-Elegba, from which Legba
derives). What is crucial here is that Legba is the orisha deity or "God of the
Crossroads," an "intercessor" that in Haitian Vodun is "imagined . . . as an old
man with a limp," a limp that Mackey thinks of as stemming from a lost limb
in consequence of crossing from the Old to the New World.[32] Thus, as Ellis explains, "in Mackey's narrative, Legba is the most portable [of the gods]," this god
being an incapacitated, nonableist, or limping deity.[33] The name now clipped as
a result of coming through Middle Passage, from Eshu-Elegba to now just Legba,
this deity's limboed or limping name, Ellis says in her beautiful rendering of
Mackey's outlook here, is "like a wishbone that can be cleanly split, easily cast in
one direction or another. His philosophical embodiment as juncture means he
can signify the side of both loss and potential connection."[34] For this reason, as
Robert Farris Thompson notes, Legba is "the ultimate master of potentiality."[35]
Mackey's poetics—both the creative or experimental writing of his poetry, novels, and criticism and the theoretical outlook driving his practice—tropes the
Legba-inspired, parareligious potentiality I am here describing. As with Legba,
god with a lost limb, his poetics conjoins surplus and lack to fuel spiritual intensity. Mackey sees this troping of religion in the troping of Legba as a crucial dimension of diaspora aesthetics more generally, diaspora itself being a condition
of liminality or limbo. Not just loss but compensatory ongoingness, improvisatory extension. As Mackey (quoted by Ellis) says:

> The master of polyrhythmicity and heterogeneity, [Legba] suffers not
> from deformity but multiformity, a "defective" capacity in a homogeneous
> order given over to uniform rule. Legba's limp is an emblem of heterog-
> enous wholeness, the image and outcome of a peculiar remediation. *Lame*
> or *limping*, that is, like *phantom*, cuts with a relativizing edge to unveil im-
> pairment's power, as though the syncopated accent were an unsuspecting
> blessing offering anomalous, unpredictable support. Impairment taken to
> higher ground, remediated, translates damage in disarray into a dance.
> Legba's limp, compensating the difference in leg lengths, functions like a
> phantom limb. [His] deficit leg [transforms] into invisible supplement.[36]

This notion of a supplement via a limp, via creative fabrication, via critical
fabulation to rework loss, directly connects for Mackey to notions of possession or being possessed. Indeed, speaking to Mackey's indebtedness to Lorca's
notion of *duende* ("for Mackey, the duende represents the mysterious presence
of a spirit but inspires the flamingo singer"), Ellis calls attention to the relationship for Mackey between, on the one hand, limbo as dance in liminal passage

as the enslaved engaged in this dance on the decks of slave ships but also as they were cramped or squashed together below deck in holds and, on the other, the spiritual troubling that propels black music, giving it a sense of "forking of the voice, so that we hear the intersection of two lines of articulation—doubling the voice, splitting the voice, breaking the voice, tearing it."[37] That doubling, splitting, breaking, and tearing marks an ellipsis of the voice, we might say, a "surplus articulation [that] is also a disturbance of language such that the conventional understanding mutates into something else, the articulation itself [poetry, experimental fiction in Mackey's case] takes on the non-representational quality of music."[38] Black music, in other words, becomes the scene or practice of alternate myth, as swing, as rhythm—as (rh)ythm, where *ythm*, Mackey tells us, is both anagrammatic *myth* and clipped rhythm.[39] Under the spiritual inspiration of *duende*, the voice reveals an "eloquence of another order, a broken, problematic, self-problematizing eloquence."[40] More specifically, "spiritual inspiration occurs when seemingly absent, not strictly identifiable, though probably ancestral, forces bend expression so that it is both less than communicative language (no one can say what this duende is) and, of course, more than communicative language (for no one can say whence this surplus)."[41] This is "a poetics of unconventional comprehensibility—like music, symbolic and lacking an easy transfer between sign and meaning."[42] That disjunction between sign and meaning where words are wrung out of joint, made to limp, as it were, dancing in limbo, is the site of a spirituality of the "crossroads," of the unrepresentable nowhere that we might call *utopia*, albeit of some other strange or queer sort.[43] This "other utopianism" is marked by "distinct onto-epistemological affects" and has "historical roots in slaves running away, marronage, piracy, heresy, witchcraft, vagrancy, vagabondage, rebellion, soldier desertion, and other often illegible, illegitimate, or trivialized forms of escape, resistance, opposition, and alternative ways of life" and practices of assembly or congregationality.[44] This alternative "collectivity" enacts a "politics" of escape, a politics that escapes institution, most especially the state, and manifests a sacrality stripped of command, stripped of stately sovereignty.[45]

Such is the spiritual vocation of ellipsis and of anarchy that marks Mackey's practice of the poem in its recursive questing for an alternative sociality beyond "*the* world *as such*," to use Jackson's formulation, beyond the world taken as given.[46] Such is the vocation of a poetry that refuses what Homi Bhabha once called the "continuous progressivist myth of Man."[47] So elevated has this "true story" become that it claims the hegemony of common sense. In other words, through the hegemony of the empirical and of empiricism, myth in its imperial mode aims to halt potentials by imposing "*the* world *as such*" on top of the earth and on top of the imagination, in this way sedimenting in place a propertied or propertizing relationship to the earth.

But also, so elevated has been this story, the imperial myth of the One (world) that's seemingly populated in Newtonian fashion by individual, self-possessed, able-bodied Subjects, that it has claimed the domains of reason and representation, the domain of the empirical, for itself as if that domain is all there is. In claiming the empirical for itself and as all there is and can be, mythic Reason as a story and practice of the blackening of matter, its transubstantiation into property, denies itself as just that, a problematic mode of myth. In other words, the notion of representation and the confidence in the empirical, the "belief" that there's nothing beyond the empirical nor beyond how our senses have been trained or disciplined to the empirical (let's call this *empiricism*, and let's also call it, after W. E. B. Du Bois, the "religion of whiteness," which he linked to empire, property, and extractive capitalism), are themselves the effect of the imperial myth of the human.[48] The denial, and even repression, of myth in the name of "modernity," and on the part of those deemed properly human and thus given to enlightenment rationality, operates ideologically, which is to say, racially. It is part of the architectonics of the "global idea of race."[49] Which is further to say, the denial of myth, a running from it as a feature of being caught within it, operates as part of the *archē* that grounds what is deemed properly political (including what is properly legal or of "law and order") and what is properly scientific.

The black study of religion—and within the framework of such study, what has been called black religion and maybe even what has been called black theology—returns us to and reengages the domain of myth. This is what Mackey's practice of the poem (as well as Charles Long's notion of ellipsis and anarchy, and Zakiyyah Jackson's notion of "troping the trope of African religion") gifts to us. The black study of religion contends that myth cannot be bypassed. Rather, myth must be reworked, apophatically unsaid. In its spiritual vocation and operating out of the sphere of the symbolic or the imaginal, the region of limitless nonrepresentation or the imagination, black radical aesthetics implicitly understands that this is where the struggle is. Myth is where our fundamental struggle is. It's to that domain that the black study of religion returns us under the acknowledgment that black radicalism is an ongoing, serial practice of upheaval, of re-turning to the imagination or, following M. NourbeSe Philip's Rastafarian inflecting of this word, to the "i-magination." Through i-maging and i-magining— that is, through magic-like, conjure-like practices from a consciousness of the I-n-I or the I-in-eroding-multiplicity—black radicalism brings some other collective consciousness comes into view.[50] This involves a ritual, ceremonial reworking of *loss* that itself is extraceremonial—after Sylvia Wynter, Alexis Pauline Gumbs speaks of this under the rubric of "finding ceremony"—to the ceremonial *archē* of modernity and its ceremony of religion and the human. That re-working of loss is an anguished re-turning to the wound of severance. And so, in black radical re-turning, there is a re-working, a torquing, a limboed twisting, a re-troping at the site of the wound. In that re-turning, which is a turning over and over again, in that overturning, something is generated, something found, something glimpsed, improvisationally invented in the space of cramped confinement.[51]

Song

Of course, much of what I'm saying here turns on a certain understanding of what *loss* means. This is a term that I mean in the direction Mackey's poetically summoned, mythically conjured character "N.," who in due course we discover to be a poet and musician, takes it in the poem "Song of the Andoumboulou: 6." N. may be a faint namesake of Mackey's, though "Nathaniel" has been whittled down, eroded down to an alphabetic letter and a punctuation mark, a period. This whittling down or erosion of the name, in fact, takes us to the significance of the title of the poetry collection in which we find "Song: 6," namely, *Eroding Witness* (1985). *Eroding Witness* is composed of several sets of poems. It might be thought of as a book of books, a set of sets (like a jazz set), a book of sets. One of its sets is the first seven poems, which launch the long poem that is *Song of the Andoumboulou*. (The first *Mu* poems make their appearance here as well.) Among the first seven *Song of the Andoumboulou* poems, "Song: 6" is peculiar in that in contrast to the first five poems before it, this sixth poem breaks form. That is, if the first five poems have the look and feel of a poem (limited four- and five-word phrasings on lines, sometimes just one word or none at all on a line, lines indented off the left side of the page in nonuniform ways to create interesting visual looks down the page, and so on), the sixth poem breaks from the form of the poem to become an epistle or a letter written to an outside party unknown to the reader of the poem-letter. N., who figures as the poet or the writer of the poems, addresses his letter ("Song: 6") to an "Angel of Dust." "Dear Angel of Dust" is how the letter-poem opens. Bringing together the angel and dust, the name fuses together an angelic spirituality and materiality, albeit at the level of dust as particulate and thus at the level of the microscopic, perhaps even the quantum level. The name suggests a spirituality, where things operate at a material but unseen level, the level of dust, and where language, too, operates, at the level of the syllables within words, and of the sounds (gutturals, labials, and the like) for which letters and syllables stand in as signs. If "Dear Angel of Dust" is how the letter-poem opens, "Yours, N." is how it closes. The poem further concludes by noting three cc's, or carbon copies. One cc is to US poet Jack Spicer, known for the notion of "Outside." Another is to Spanish poet Federico García Lorca, known for the notion of *duende*. And, finally, a last copy of the letter is cc'd to poet Charles Olson by directing it not directly to Olson but to an idea found in an essay of his. The idea to whom N. copies his letter is "H-mu." A reference to wave theory, "H-mu" was Olson's formulation for inquiring into what might be called the physics of communication or into what in language makes communication possible.[52] In cc'ing Olson's "H-mu" idea, "Song: 6" as I read it is speaking to the quantum of language, to its interiority or the inner world(s) or, better, to the *mater* as the matter of language as such. The nature of that interiority and the alternate, nonrepresentable "solidarities" it affords, particularly when we understand language as bound up with loss, with lost ground, with erosions of various sorts—of place, kinship and connection, and the like—is what the letter, among many other things, invites us to consider, what it speaks to.

Precisely on this issue of the form and content of "Song of the Andoumbou-lou: 6," it is also worth noting why N. writes this poem as a letter. We learn in reading the poem-letter that N. has sent one of the earlier poems (the third of the *Song of the Andoumboulou* poems, "Song: 3," as it were) to a friend, Angel of Dust, who in turn responded with a series of questions about that poem. What is now the sixth poem in the *Song of the Andoumboulou* sequence is N.'s letter-as-poem response to a query about loss that Angel discerns as animating "Song: 3," if not all of the poems in the sequence on some fundamental level. It is also worth noting that N.'s letter-poem is responding to a letter from Angel of Dust that we as readers do not ourselves have access to, though it remains a surreal or eroded presence via the letter-poem that is "Song: 6." All of this is to say that generative erosion underwrites Mackey's practice of the poem. A material angel-ology of erosive, elliptical loss, where loss so understood becomes "re: Source," propels his practice and becomes a formal object of concern in "Song: 6." In addressing the theme of loss, erosion, or underness, the sixth letter is the effect of the very erosion or loss that it addresses. The letter-poem is an "eroding witness" to the very loss or erosion that's being addressed such that in Mackey's practice of the poem, form itself erodes or transubstantiates into new form. Dying or erosion generates (more) form. What I'm trying to get at here is how the experimentalism at work in this practice of the poem apocalyptically discloses (where apocalypse speaks to an unveiling or revelation in catastrophe) a distinct poetics of being-with as becoming, as an alternate sociality or, to use the poem's own language, "solidness" or "solidarity." In other words, the practice of the poem here is a practice of ellipsis in which form itself becomes or differentially (re)generates form in and as difference. That becoming is the questing after alternate communions or solidarities. These are elliptical solidarities, unsimple in their "solidity," in their diffused, dispersed, differential unity.

How does this play out within the poem-letter itself? I have already noted that "Song: 6" is N.'s response to questions Angel of Dust raises about loss as a signal element in "Song: 3." Here's how N. poses the issue in the opening of "Song: 6":

> Dear Angel of Dust,
> In one of your earlier letters, the one you wrote in response to *Song of the Andoumboulou: 3*, you spoke of sorting out "what speaks of speaking of something, and what (more valuably) speaks *from* something, i.e., where the source is available, becomes a resource rather than something evasive, elusive, sought after."[53]

Here N. quotes Angel's letter, which again we as readers are not privy to, back to Angel. Compelled by "Song: 3," Angel of Dust had asked N. how loss was working in the poetry. "More valuably" still, Angel of Dust wants to know what his poetry "resources," what it draws from, in the face of loss, in the face of "the theft of assembly," in the face of that "breach in human solidarity," that violation of kinship, community, connection that we now labor under.[54] There is an answer to this—if *answer* is even the right word for it—that comes through in N.'s letter-poem in "Song: 6." But before getting to the poem's "answer" about that resource that is to be drawn on in addressing loss, I want to set up the rest of the reading of "Song: 6" I am working out here by going through one of Mackey's most cited and theoretically sophisticated essays of criticism, his "Sound and Sentiment, Sound and Symbol." At stake in large part in both this essay and "Song: 6" is the question of origin or *archē*.

In "Sound and Sentiment, Sound and Symbol," Mackey advances the claim that there is a music that arises both within and as a response to the condition of being orphaned, "where in back of 'orphan' one hears echoes of 'orphic,' a music that turns on abandonment, absence, loss."[55] This music offers song that is "semi-wept, semi-sung."[56] In this later essay, Mackey turns, once again, to myth, this time that of the Kaluli of Papua New Guinea, for whom myth is a site of music often sung at funerals, "semi-wept, semi-sung," and of poetic language, to elaborate what he means. What Kaluli myth (and this can be said of Mackey's reception of Dogon myth and music as well, as we saw earlier) offers, Mackey says, quoting musicologist Victor Zuckerkandl, is "a musical concept of the external world" internal to which is "a critique of our concept of reality from the point of view of music."[57] That critique points to the orphic dimensions of reality, to the fact that, as Mackey puts it in his own words but in light of Zuckerkandl, "music bears witness to what is left out of [our] concept of reality, or, if not exactly what, to the fact that something *is* left out."[58] That "left-out-ness" is the condition that Long early on calls silence and then, later, ellipsis. It is what the music makes audible precisely in its left-out-ness. It is what ellipsis, what left-out-ness, what, to invoke another Mackey formulation, "destination out," sounds like.[59] We might even say, it is what silence sounds like, how silence thinks. It thinks as a gathering of inflections or tones or dynamic symbols that constantly point-beyond-themselves as part of a nonrepresentational sphere of meaning, saying, and signification. Kaluli myth, cross-culturally connected with other forms of myth—for example with Dogon mythology as Mackey engages with it through his poetry—invites us to think about music itself as a modality or vehicle of myth. It invites us to think about the symbolicity or the musicality of the world. Like tone as a dynamic symbol in music that points beyond itself, so too the world is better understood as poetry wherein words operate nonrepresentationally, even elliptically. That is, what the more-than and the left-out or the ellipsis of music (and poetry) teach is that "the tangible and visible cannot be the whole of the given world. The intangible and invisible is itself a part of this world, something we encounter, something to which we respond."[60] More specifically, "music encourages us to see that the symbolic is the orphic, that the symbolic realm is the realm of the orphan. Music is prod and precedent for a recognition that the linguistic realm is also the realm of the orphan, as in Octavio Paz's characterization of language as an orphan severed from the presence to which it refers and which presumably gave it birth."[61] This helps make sense of why one definition of poetry has been that it is "an order of words that as movement and tone (rhythm and pitch) approaches in varying degrees the wordless art of music as a kind of mathematic limit"—like an ellipse, which "contains two foci that define the locus of a point that moves so that the ratio of the distance from a fixed point is always a constant less than one."[62]

This approach to loss and orphanage through a musical, paramythic yearning in broken assembly for a new kind of solidarity that is somehow exemplified in poetry as work of "myriad words," if not wayward wording, is foreshadowed in the letter-poem that is "Song: 6." The letter opens with N. quickly going to the topic of "resource" (and, relatedly, source and origin). His aim is to clarify his meaning about the topic, given comments made by Angel of Dust in a letter to N. (we are not privy to the letter) about the poem "Song of the Andoumboulou: 3," which Angel, it seems, has read. I submit that the letter-poem that is "Song: 6" may be understood as speaking toward or in light of an understanding of poetic language as mytho-musical language—as is the case in both Kaluli myth and Dogon myth, and, I'd add, as is the case with ellipsis and anarchy as paramythic figures of black religion or, more precisely, of the blackness of black religion. That at stake for N. is a critique of the concept of reality from the vantage point of the symbolic as orphic and orphaned realm, the realm of ellipsis as the unrepresentable, the realm of what's left out, comes through in the statement N. offers immediately following his citing of Angel of Dust's request that N. clarify for Angel of Dust how loss and resource (loss as resource) work together. Responding to this request, N. says, "We not only can but should speak of 'loss' or, to avoid, quotation marks notwithstanding, any such inkling of self-pity, speak of *absence* as unavoidably an inheritance in the texture of things."[63] N. goes on to elaborate for the rest of the letter—I mean, the poem—that his concern is precisely with this absence, this depth, that materially animates things, giving them a kind of tone or "texture." Indeed, N. says that he's consumed with this absence, this depth, as an inheritance. It is a "preoccupation" of his, he says. But the preoccupation here, the concern, is not about "[believing] in [or holding] out for some first or final gist underlying it all" and toward which all things are tending.[64] This, in other words, is not about teleology—which means that if myth is what, in fact, is at issue (and across this book, I have been making a case that at issue both in our current cultural and political woes and in racial capitalism, more generally, is myth), N.'s concern is with a mode of myth that exceeds myth as we know it. His interest is in myth, albeit of a different sort. It is in myth unhinged from myth's typical gesture of securing how a people, how a tribe, storifies, imagines, or, as it were, mythifies through stories about origins and endings, and how it thereby establishes, often through deathly sacrifice, a sacred-political center or orientation for itself so as to ground peoplehood and endow the idea of "the people" with would-be coherence. In his own way, then, N. is addressing myth's political force. N.'s critique of myth, which also entails a fundamental revising of its terms, is the basis of what amounts to his chiding of his angelic friend for seemingly holding on to a problematic approach to myth. By contrast, N. says that his concern or preoccupation with "origins and ends," which is to say, with myth, "is exactly that: a pre- (equally post-, I suppose) occupation."[65] In other words, N. announces an interest in a mode of myth that is anterior to myth as typically understood. It is a pre-occupation with myth that unsays myth, as it were, from within. Hence, rather than performing the typical mythic gesture of seizing or laying claim to origins, to an *archē*, so as to settle a land or found a nation or ground peoplehood and the like, N. poeticizes from an imaginary of what's been left out, an imaginary that is both anterior to (or pre-) and posterior to (or post-) a logic of occupation, that is both pre- and post- a logic in which property is always already theft. At work here is an "apophatic logic," an apophasis of myth, wherein the pre- in N.'s pre-occupation with myth and the post- in his post-occupation with the same do not operate according to the terms of a linear temporality and its logic of an *archē* that founds or grounds the terms of order.[66] Rather, N.'s concern is with what I have termed across this book with Charles Long in mind *the anarchic* or *anarchy*, where the anarchic is that which inheres in the texture, in the *mater*, of things. At stake is how to think of matter not as origin but as open field, how to think it as *mater*, how to think it at the level of the texture of things, at the level of feel(ing) and touch(ing) insofar as texture invokes feel and touch. This is what N. is getting at when he further says in elaborating on that anarchic, that elliptical absence that is to be felt and touched, that feels and touches, that pre- (and post-) occupies him, and, finally, that (the) black study (of religion) is given to study: "I [that is, N., speaking to Angel of Dust] see the things of your world as *solid* in a way the world my 'myriad words' uncoil can't even hope to be. *Not* 'ethereal,' mind you. Not insubstantial, unreal or whatever else. Only an other (possibly Other) sort of solidarity, as if its very underseams—or to be more exact, those of its advent—sprouted hoofs. . . . What was wanted least but now comes to be missed *is* that very absence, an unlikely Other whose inconceivable occupancy glimpses of ocean beg access to."[67]

N. is playing with the solid in *solid*arity. Not all solidness is the same. Hence, N. here speaks of a feeling and touching of things that contrasts with Angel of Dust's approach to (the) matter. N. articulates a coming into contact with or being in touch with things, their *mater*iality or solidness, that is different. More still, the different imagination of solidness or imagination of matter that N. says his myriad words aim to uncoil or otherwise give voice to supposes a different kind of solidarity, a sociality otherwise. In other words, Mackey's N.'s myriad words work in relationship to the open quiddity or the inherent nature or what-it-is-ness of a thing, as the medieval scholastics might say, the wild quantum (rh)ythms that constitute matter's "solidity," N. might say beyond the scholastics.[68] This (rh)ythmic solidity as the quiddity or the thingliness of things is bound up with the *mater* of speech. Alternate materiality and alternate sociality move together not just in solidarity but more radically in solidity. Indeed, the move from Angel of Dust's conception of "the things of your world as *solid*" (in the sense of remaining only at the level of a realism or empiricism) to an understanding of matter, of things, as imbued with an absent presence, that is, with potentials and virtualities that suggest "an other (possibly Other) sort of solidarity"—this is what N. insists on. More still, it is by way of the poet's "myriad words" that uncoil worlds that the presence of an elliptically absent more-than comes through in its irreducibility to the reigning order of signification. In this, what N. is working to bring into some sort of view is the addressing of loss by means of a mythopoetic inauguration of an-other ceremony. "The ceremony must be found," it has been said.[69] That other ceremony through the poet's "myriad words" happens in catastrophe, though that other ceremony is not reducible to the catastrophe that occasioned it.

Loss here, then, is a curious, a peculiar *resource*. So curious is it that N. poeticizes this word, opening *resource*, thought of as origin or as *archē*, to an "outside," in order to approach what is at stake. We see this in N.'s closing of the letter-poem. I want to conclude with a few final remarks on N.'s terse, one-sentence paragraph that concludes his letter to Angel of Dust: "Not 're-source' so much for me as re: Source."[70]

Here we see Mackey's N. break open *resource* between the prefix (*re*) and the main word (*source*), which appears first as "re-source" and then as "re: Source." How we interpret "re-source" (is the hyphenated *re-* a doubling of *source*?) in its distinction from "re: Source" (is *re:* a shortening of the notion of "with reference to" or "regarding"?) is, for me, secondary to a first observation that I'd like to make. What has my attention as a first point is the very fact that the seemingly solid word *resource* has within it, shall we say, other musical tones, other (rh)ythms. Is it "resource" or "re-source" or "re: Source" that we're dealing with or that is dealing with us? The point I am making here is that Mackey is drawing attention to the fact that this word, *resource*, and indeed words as such, has a creaking within it. They are not as solid as they would seem. The seemingly solid, seemingly one-dimensional word gives way or opens up to some other interior, which is also an exterior. Some other "lit city outside," to bring back that phrase from "Dogon Eclipse," the eighth poem of the Septet sequence, presents itself as the burning, fiery halo, as in an eclipse, surrounding the word *resource*. In this, Mackey invites a vertiginous, an elliptical thinking that is in keeping with what I have been aiming to articulate as a key feature of black (religious) anarchy and the black study of religion. As black religion is the troping (and not merely the duplication in blackface but the troping of what has been called *religion*), so too does Mackey's N. here trope the idea of a resource and its root word, *source*. In N.'s troping the trope of resource, which tropes the notion of a *source* or origin or *archē*, we are, in fact, poetically released from the notion of source as singular or solid origin. We are released into the texture of things. That release takes place as a kind of ecstasy. Indeed, N. suggests that there is an ecstasy advanced through the transmutative event of writing, where writing takes place as a circling around or as an elliptical passage through loss. Circling and ellipsis here connote a poetics through catastrophe that registers a matrixial Outside, a "re: Source." N.'s "myriad words" are, in this regard, parareligiously, parametrically, parasemiotically vertiginous. They signal a cross-cultural solidarity that is not the effect merely of *re*-sourcing or of laying claim to a lost or more pure and proper origin. Rather, in the movement from "re-source" to "re: Source" (and now I am highlighting what I perceive as a distinction N. seems to want to make between "re-source" and "re: Source"), I read a poetics operative through the poet's "myriad words," one that is suggestive of myriad worlds, one that hosts the countersolidness or alter-solidity of other materialities, other solidarities or socialities, some nonexclusionary "we" in transit. "Re: Source" does not bespeak a pure *archē*. Rather, what is meant by "re: Source" here concerns, N. says, "an unlikely Other" occupying poetic language, giving it an orientation of the oceanic. In this way, the poet's "myriad words" are under the sway of some other cosmology. This I read in conjunction with the myth-reading in the previous chapter of Genesis 1:2 and the discussion of "tehomic depth," tehomic *mater*, the oceanic, and "darkness upon the face of the deep." The poem re-turns or moves around this depth-cosmology, which is a cosmology in which the horizon is ever receding, ever expanding, ever descending and in this way ascending, ever deepening. The poem is elliptical, by which I mean it enacts ellipsis. What I am suggesting is that via Mackey (with Jackson, Long, Robinson, et al.) the anarchy of black religion or the black study of religion comes into view as a para-mythifying "practice of Outside." This is not an "Outside" that has an "inside" as its dialectical counterpoint, its binary opposite. Rather, this is an Outside that is out from that, an Outside that undoes an outside-inside, transcendence-immanence dialectic. The undoing happens from within that dialectic or binary that works to constitute what we take as reality, as a solid-ness that is reduced to a certain empiricism of "*the* world *as such*" and that operates to ground the idea(l) of the human. That other "Outside" that is not of the transcendence-immanence dialectic is *mater*ially tehomic. As such, it is a sociopoetically disruptive and divining force, "that within" that is the *mater* to which blackness points.

To try to clarify a bit more, by a sociopoetically disruptive because dynamic or driving force, I also mean what has sometimes been called (often negatively so due to certain normative theological prejudices) "daemonic." I mean *daemonic* in the sense that Sylvia Wynter, on Nijah Cunningham's reading of Wynter's "Black Metamorphosis," invokes in reference to Walter Benjamin's understanding of the hidden force at work in the work of art. In Cunningham's provocative take on Benjamin's essay "Goethe's Elective Affinities," "the daemonic corresponds to the forceful interruption of something unexpected that bears a semblance or glimmer of the secret dwelling in the artwork."[71] Insofar as the daemonic as an aesthetic-religious category points to the secret within the artwork, the daemonic is apocalyptic. It signals revelation. Cunningham mobilizes this understanding of the daemonic to think with Wynter about the sociopoetic force that blackness hosts. That force "both destabilizes the racial logics that undergird the modern idea of the human and also defies" or exceeds the practices of critique that we've inherited insofar as "critique cannot explain and has little interest in addressing the practices, sensibilities, affects, attachments, capacities, aspirations, and general rhythms of social life that unfold in, alongside, and as the effect of the racialized processes of subjugation that throw into question black life's status as human. The daemonic, in turn, enables a specific attunement to the potentialities that gather inside the cultural void and nothingness that the philosophical category of the human engenders."[72] What Cunningham here observes regarding the Wynterian daemonic, or what I'd adumbrate as the socio-poetic, Sycoraxian force of a blackness that is related to but that exceeds racial category, I read as kindred to the Mackeyan notions of "re: Source" and Outside, of that beyond within matter, of the *mater* of writing and speech that I have been elaborating. Indeed, where Cunningham, explicating Wynter by way of Benjamin, speaks of the daemonic, Mackey with Federico García Lorca in mind speaks of *duende*, where *duende* indicates a surge, an urge, and an in-surgency, indeed, something emerging within and perhaps even an emergency in speech and writing. Mackey goes on to speak of *duende* as a kind of "gremlin" in the voice, and I'd say, by extension, in his practice of the poem, thus making the voice (and the artwork that is the poem) spirit possessed. In this way, Mackey's poetics gets at something similar to Wynter's in that both *duende* and the Wynterian "demonic ground" speak to that *mater*ially sociopoetic force that dwells in the artwork and that blackness signals.[73] The daemonic as a gremlin-like sociopoetic force, which is to say, as a kind of divine force that blackness heretically signals in pointing to some other mode of sacrality, deterritorializes so as to unground or unsettle what is called "reality," to unground or unsettle an empirical (as imperial) absolute, thereby releasing the alternative as given elliptically in the very texture, in the ani*mater*iality, of things.

In conclusion, in what I've just said, I tried to think Mackey's poetic idea of "re: Source" beyond an ontotheological approach to matter and origin. I've thus attempted further to display what I see as a convergence between his practice of the poem and Long's poetics of ellipsis as a figure of the blackness—by which I mean the anarchy—of black religion. Via a Nijah Cunningham–inflected reading of Sylvia Wynter and Walter Benjamin on the daemonic, I mobilized the language of the divine and the daemonic, and by implication the shadow languages of the sacred and the profane, the holy and the unholy, as terms within a religious studies discourse about what has been called *mysterium tremendum et fascinosum*, the mystery that strikes both fear and fascination, to talk about "re: Source" or the *mater* of matter or, in Mackey's case, the *mater* of language, speech, and writing.[74] But my recourse to the notions of the divine and the daemonic to talk about

Mackey's idea of "re: Source" in loss or in "phantom pain," as Harryette Mullen has put it, and as a way to talk about black (religious) anarchy, blurs any hard lines between these terms.[75] In the logics of normative theology as well as in the philosophical tradition of ontotheological metaphysics, there often is a dividing line between the divine and the daemonic, the distinction itself often working to ground a certain hierarchically rooted hegemony—political and otherwise. In this respect, the hard line that has tended to divide the divine and the daemonic or the monstrous operates jurisprudentially as a certain structure of law. With respect to blackness, however, the divine and the daemonic, the divine and the monstrous, the divinely demonic and the monstrously divine, point to a mode of matter-ing in which form in-finitely proliferates more form, form entangles with and generates more form. This is an in-finitude as the in-finity that harkens to a dynamism of form. It is the in-finity of matter, of matter's tehomic depth precisely as mat(t)er. This dynamism of the in-finite has the qualities of what in onto–political theology gets segregated out so as to ground a transcendental hierarchy. By contrast, what I'm trying to describe here in meditating on the philosophical force of Mackey's poetics and Long's notion of ellipsis, pointing as they do toward the spiritual vocation of the black radical tradition, moves otherwise.

Faith

To take one final stab at trying more rigorously to clarify this Otherwise, this anarchic alternative, I want to conclude this meditation by taking leave of the languages of the divine and the daemonic, notwithstanding my unsettling of them by blurring them in order to speak of matter as a network of entanglement and to think of *mater* as that matrixial, originative, or exposing touch of alterity that summons things into ex-istence, ceaselessly proliferating ways or forms of ex-istence. If this has been the concern of this book all along (and in so many ways it has been), then what I have really been pushing toward is an account of blackness, black *mater*, and black religion as anarchic mysticism, a *mate*rial mysticism.[76] Now, let me quickly say that anarchic mysticism is not just a species of transcendental mysticism. It is not transcendental but rather is de-cendental, ante-cendental, even cosmo-cendental and quantum-cendental.[77] This is a mysticism of matter that has affinities with what Fred Moten has called "mysticism in the flesh."[78] As flesh mysticism, anarchy is radical. Which is to say, in its alter-everydayness it operates at the base or root of things. It is a root work(ing) that is fundamental rather than transcendental. It works with what's deemed excremental. Anarchy returns us to the fundament of things. In anarchy, we devote ourselves to, attend to, and give attention to things, to the earth, to earthy and earthly things in their base-ness, in their tehomic depth. Blackness points to matter's mystic, un-sovereign depth, its "mystical foundation."[79] It hosts a cosmology of depth. I read Mackey as writing out of or as experimentalizing or mythographizing or ythmizing (from) that cosmic depth, that "re: Source." His practice of the poem, as I read it, is an instance of "base faith," where I am increasingly given to glossing faith as *creative endurance under and through conditions of duress.*[80] This creative endurance marks faith, beyond ecclesiastical or church dogmatic containment, as a mode of poetics, as a feature of the (black) arts. In short, what I am describing is a mysticism of the mat(t)er of blackness, of the parareligiosity as the ir- (as in *irregular*) religiosity, the poetics, of black religion.

anarchy   is   a poem   . . .

            is   a song   . . .

   . . .

An Anarchic Coda
(A Mystic Song)

"Anarchism" is an open and incomplete word, and in this resides its potential.
—SAIDIYA HARTMAN, FOREWORD TO WILLIAM C. ANDERSON, *The Nation on No Map* (2021)

The poetic is the invention of space in a prison. It animates, it moves a closed, decadent order from within. It is therefore mystic in that it creates movements in the secrecy of a blocked situation, like a burst of saying at the heart of a closed language. . . . [It] opens the depths of a walled-in world, making it all the more explosive. The intensity of the poetic fervor comes from this extreme tension.—MICHEL DE CERTEAU, *Mystic Fable* (2015)

To give a sense of the arresting power of the poetry, prose, mysticism, and poetics of the sixteenth-century Spanish writer St. John of the Cross, Michel de Certeau offered the above words. They are meant to be something of an adumbration of the Carmelite's writings, as their nucleus took shape when he was put in solitary confinement for almost two years in the dungeon of the convent of Toledo for the daringness of his intellectual and spiritual outlook. In its own way, that outlook called out, moved against the grain of, and refused the decadence of the age. That decadence was surely related to the "dark night" of the Age of Discovery and Conquest, which was going into high gear as St. John was writing of the "dark night of the soul."[1] For his daring vision, St. John was imprisoned. But as it turns out, as Certeau movingly explains, St. John's imprisonment was also an occasion for attempting to reconceive religion, to release it from itself, to sing it otherwise. St. John went about this by dwelling in the tension between, on the one hand, the glorious flesh of the mystic craft (where the mystic craft is the writerly craft, the artistic compositional craft, the craft of the poem) and, on the other, the painful, suffering flesh of the prisoner. Here the abundant song of the alternative poetically, explosively, sings itself in and through and as flesh that both hurts and is given to joy. "The music is a riotous solemnity, a terrible beauty. It hurts so much that we have to celebrate. That we have to celebrate is what hurts so much. Exhaustive celebration of and in and through our suffering, which is neither distant nor sutured, is black study. That continually rewound and remade claim upon our monstrosity—our miracle, our showing, which is neither near nor far, as [Hortense] Spillers shows—is black feminism, the animaterial ecology of black and thoughtful stolen life as it steals away."[2] There is some sort of resonance between the song of black study and what St. John, on Certeau's telling, is getting at. St. John produces his prison *canciones* (or poems), his "Spiritual Canticle" (or song), precisely in the sixteenth-century moment when through transatlantic commerce and exchange religion was undergoing antiblack invention.[3] Could there be an elliptically black study of religion, a mysticism of blackness, going on with St. John the Carmelite?

It would perhaps be saying both too much and not enough to say that this book follows the itinerary of St. John's canticles. Its itinerary is related to St. John's, but as an exercise in the black study of religion, or more simply as an experiment in the poetics of study, it has its own inflection of darkness; of blackness; of generative material void or fold; of ecstasy; of rupture; of rapture. (At one point, this book was going to be called *Black Rapture: A Poetics of the Sacred*.) It has a poetic, elliptical "re: Source" it draws from. I have sought in these pages to understand what is called black religion in light of that *poiēsis*, in light of that "re: Source." It is from this vantage that it's been written. I've tried here to tell the story of the blackness of black religion in such a way as to "[create movement] in the secrecy of a blocked situation, like a burst of saying at the heart of a closed language," that language being the language of religion itself.

Hence the book's itinerary. I opened this book, somewhat in lamentation, registering the loss so many have felt, so many have experienced, across the past few years, and that so many yet feel. They have been years not of a single virus but of convergent viruses. This includes the COVID-19 virus, the virus of antiblack police violence, the virus of ecological devastation in pillaging and plundering the earth, and the virus within the body politic, that is, the virus of a fascism that, as the prison intellectual George Jackson some fifty years ago told us, is at the foundation of the United States as a settler colonial nation, that is reaching its most developed phase, and that is at the foundation of Western modernity.[4] The approach I've taken in this book to understand the nature of these viruses, these violences, is to surface the deeper philosophical, theological, and religious history that is not past but lives within and animates the present. My goal has been to take us to the foundations, the *archē*, of (Western) modernity as a racially gendered arrangement of religion and the secular, of religion and culture. It has been to demonstrate how a problematic imagination of matter as bound up with a certain imagination of religion is what besets us, what incarcerates us, what politically and in many respects quite literally is sickening us, what has many on ventilators, trying, struggling, to breathe, others with necks kneed into the pavement, also trying to breathe.

However, my task has not only been to diagnose this situation as bound up with the modern (re)invention of religion. It has not only been to take us to the foundations of our current woes, our lamentation. Across these pages I've made a case for a different approach to religion, one that operates under the sign of what has been called *black religion* as hosting an alternative imagination of matter, an alternative imagination of the sacred, and an alternative imagination of the social, an other atmosphere. As socio-aesthetic practices premised on refusing this (racial capitalist) world, built as it is from extraction, indeed, as an alternate imagination of matter, the blackness of black religion advances sharing as our condition of beings (not of being). Black religion constitutes practices that renew our assembly, that renew existence. If the argument of this book turns on understanding the specific blackness of black religion as having taken leave of the Western project of ontology, indeed of ontotheology, and thus as premised on an ante-ontological and therefore nonontologized imagination of matter in light of which life is lived poetically, then the question I've been trying to raise given this is: How do we study this alternative as part of renewing practices of shared existence, as part of the practice of an otherwise, nonexclusionary we-ness that is ever and always on the move, ever and always more and less than itself, more and less than a coherent self? How might we study this other we-ness, the we-ness given in and as entanglement? This is an urgent question insofar as it has been precisely this other we-ness, this other relationality of entanglement in which life is nothing less than diffused, dispersed, and yet gathered generosity. Gentleness. Tenderness. It is precisely this gentle, tender generosity of existence-in-multiplicity, this generosity of matter understood not just as things but as what composes things, what makes things a constantly incomplete composition, a woven or braided fabric that in its ongoing flow re-weaves, re-waves, re-sonates, re-composes, ongoingly re-braids and com-plicates itself—it is precisely this generosity, the tenderness of matter as such, that has been under individuating, racial capitalist assault through logics of property and statecraft that ontologizes matter, subjecting it to regimes of extraction. This approach to matter has been called a "religion of whiteness," a historically specific mode of empire that has been defined as a belief in "the ownership of the earth forever and ever, Amen!"[5]

Dwelling with experimental writing as an aesthetic practice, black feminist theory, and theories of religion and science (particularly, quantum mechanics read with the poetics of matter found in the writings of ancient Roman philosopher Lucretius, who was rediscovered in the late Middle Ages just as the Atlantic trade in slaves from Africa was commencing), I've written this book as the gateway text into a multivolume endeavor that unfolds a new method in the study of religion and that at the same time elaborates what in these pages I've called the spiritual vocation of the black radical tradition.[6] This tradition offers something vital in the face of the political, existential, and spiritual demands of the moment. It offers an alternate imagination of matter(ing) as the basis of a different vision and praxis of sociality. In this book I have explored this imagination of matter through a poetics of fugitivity—or, perhaps better, *refugitivity*, after Gayl Jones's fusion of *refusal* and *fugitivity*—with respect to the modern invention of religion. Housed within refugitivity understood as at once practices of refusal and of fugitivity is a new alternate approach to the study of religion. That approach I have called *the black study of religion*, which is also the general title of this multivolume endeavor that begins with this book.[7] The black study of religion conceives of black religion as instancing a material mysticism that manifests as a distinct *poiēsis* or artistic way of living that as such is anarchic. Such a mysticism in being material and in being of wounded flesh is poetic, which is again to say, it is artistic: an open set of aesthetic practices of the everyday. But not just the everyday but the alternate or the "alter-everyday," as Nathaniel Mackey has put it, where the social undergoes constant renewal, where some other, some alternate human history, some other andoumboulous draft of history, premised on some other mattering, feels its way through, makes a way through, makes contact, makes touch in touching us, and thus through any and every gap, in ellipsis (as a practice of the gap, of and in the break), makes itself . . .   felt.[8]

This practice of artistic living or living in the artistic open given in a preferential option for the alter-everyday is anarchic in precisely that sense that Saidiya Hartman talks about when she says that "'anarchism' is an open and incomplete word, and in this resides its potential"; that anarchism "gathers and names the practices of mutual aid and the programs for survival that have sustained us in the face of unimaginable violence. It unfolds with and as Black feminism and Indigenous struggle"; and, finally, that anarchism "is the history that arrives with us—as those who exist outside the nation, as the stateless, as the dead, as property, as object and tools, as sentient flesh. . . . We are Black in anarchy because of how we have lived and how we have died."[9]

Existing in this way, as "Black in anarchy," to live in material mysticism, where here the mystery in mysticism suggests an aliveness at the convergence of the wound and the blessing, and where the blessing here bespeaks an aliveness, a duended sentience at the rim of the wound and thus in the wake of violence or within the ongoing scene of catastrophic subjection, to live artistically, fugitively, in this way, to *make a way* here, in the wound, with the materials or the matter of *no way*, to conjure apocalyptically through the shards and shrapnel of catastrophe such that while catastrophe wounds, while it hurts, catastrophe is nevertheless also disclosed as neither the first nor the last word—this is what I've been trying to think about, what I've been trying to study in this book. I can't help but be a bit autobiographical, a bit autotheoretical here: it's the stories of my mothers, my mother and grandmother, both gone too late and way too soon. Their lives were stories of surviving and thriving, stories of "surthriving" down in West Philly's "Bottom" and up on that bustling intersection of black love and life, Germantown's Stenton and Washington Lane. Touched by and being of their stories, in the wake of their wakes, I've begun feebly attempting to unfold across these pages an art that I know somehow I picked up from them, that they are somehow channeling through me, that in some measure they handed to me precisely in the craft of study with friends and, yes, with you, too, dear reader. It's the arts of black faith, the arts of things hoped for, as I like to say. This is the black arts of a black faith that imagines alternate ecologies, whose imaginings are premised on an alternate imagination of matter. Here one finds nonindividuated relationalities between each other and with the earth, socioecologies that operate anterior to racially gendered and normatively sexuating logics of property and extraction. Black religion, with a focus on its blackness, its nontransparency or opacity, what in the introduction to this book, after poet Nathaniel Mackey, I called the *it of it*, in its irreducibility to racial category, is the particular instance through which I've tried to think the artistry of this anarchy, the artistry of the alter-everyday to reframe religion altogether.

In other words, I'm pushing toward a poetics of religion as such, a poetics given with and in black religion and the blackness thereof, given with and in black religion's poetics of flesh, with and in the *mater*, the matter, the *mater*ial signs or the semiotics of dispersed life. In beginning to reconceive religion along the lines of the specific materiality of black religion and thus as part of the dark arts of *necromancy* (if I might retrieve another medieval term, the other being the revised *mysticism* that has had my attention in these pages), I've begun to chart a pathway for engaging with the spirit of blackness both in its relationship with racialized blackness and in its constant flying away from or taking leave of the same. Which is to say, in looking away from the racial capitalist ontologization of matter, and thus away from the problem of ontology as a particular way of being, knowing, and conceiving "the World as such," I've begun to engage the material spirituality, the alternate imagination of matter, hosted within black sociality, within black radical practice.

In refusal of a conclusion, in underscoring (its) incompletion, this anarchic coda looks ahead to the more that must be said, to the ongoing song, which is a mystic song.

Notes

AN ANARCHIC INTRODUCTION

1   Daniel Hodges, testimony, July 27, 2021, in a US congressional hearing into the January 6, 2020, insurrection, quoted in Gonzalez, "D.C. Officer."

2   For more on the "religion of whiteness," see Carter, *Religion of Whiteness*. This is the book that I interrupted in a writing frenzy whose result is the book you are now reading.

3   Du Bois, "Souls of White Folk," 56. This statement is part of Du Bois's account of "this new religion of whiteness" that is "dashing . . . on the shores of our time." In developing his argument, he performs the rhetorical cadence of the King James Bible, writing, "I do not laugh. I am quite straight-faced as I ask soberly: 'But what on earth is whiteness that one should so desire it?'" Answering, he responds to his own question, "Then always, somehow, some way, silently but clearly, I am given to understand that whiteness is the ownership of the earth forever and ever, Amen!" (56).

4   On the distinctive American Protestantism of the locking up of religion into the frameworks of church or even cultic histories and the insufficiency—indeed, the failures—of such approaches, see Sidney Mead, *Lively Experiment*. What Mead reveals, in crucial respects beyond the avowed intentions of his book, is that church historical and doctrinal frameworks derived from Old World Europe are insufficient to understanding the phenomenon of American religion because the effort to do so masks deeper settler colonial rationalities. Differently put, they mask settler statecraft as itself a practice of political theology. Whatever the other limitations of Mead's book might be, this insight alone put his 1963 book at the vanguard of the new direction regarding the study of religion as bound up with settlerism. In many respects, this direction in scholarship is only now beginning to come into its own.

5   A. Butler, *White Evangelical Racism*.

6   On the "afterlife of slavery," see Hartman, *Scenes of Subjection*. Thinking with Hartman, Matthew Elia develops the notion of the "afterlife of the master" in his article "Ethics in the Afterlife of Slavery." He more fully develops it in *The Problem of the Christian Master*.

7   This phrase is the subtitle of Hendricks's *Christians against Christianity*.

8   Wimbush, *White Men's Magic*.

9   In speaking of "love improper," I am reading Eddie Glaude's and R. A. Judy's accounts of James Baldwin with and against the grain of each other. Judy's account of Baldwin can be

found in the last chapter of his erudite and pathbreaking book, *Sentient Flesh*. Of course, what sets Glaude's and Judy's Baldwins apart is that the latter's Baldwin is located much more within the context of third worldism and thus within a radical ante- (and not just anti-) Americanism. Which is to say, Judy's Baldwin is quite unstately. He is an avatar of what might be called *unstately black religion*—indeed, of the anarchy of black religion.

The example to which Judy turns to exemplify what he means is the mutual engagement, while Baldwin was in Paris, between Baldwin and the Algerian-born French novelist Nabile Farès. Judy tracks the interlocutions between the two writers, with his attention riveted to Farès's on the significance of Baldwin's writings, why he's moved by them. Specifically, Farès is taken with what he discerns as Baldwin's "rejection of integration qua assimilation as a prerequisite for social justice and freedom" (432). The rejection that Farès picks up on in Baldwin's writings, Farès interprets as the "OUTLANDISH hope" of "a life ARTISTICALLY LIVED" (430). Only such an outlandishly artistic life "can yield any meaning, or give evidence of meaning other than that of political slavishness," which is to say, other than being enthralled by or held captive "to the reigning political line" or reasons of state (430). But this is possible only because at the heart of such poetic or artistic living is a specific mode of being, to wit, "black being," where "black being is a being-on-the-line" (433). Such being is being in exposure or "in ruination without [recourse to] any mitigating redemptive metaphysics or theology" (433). This includes the redemptive metaphysics that comes with and through Christianization as stately Americanization or as assimilation into the body politic as a citizen. Which is to say, the Christianization as the Americanization of the black, the imposition of a burdened individuality of freedom upon the Negro to remake the Negro into the would-be African American, is nothing less than a soteriological operation. It is a feat of political theology by any measure, be it Schmittian or otherwise. Instead, in Baldwin's wake and in the wake of a certain reading of the term *Middle Passage*, Judy proposes an understanding of black being as otherwise to political theology and its redeeming of sacrifice, its logics of redemptive sacrifice for the eschatological salvation of the settler nation-state. As being-on-the-line, black being

> is emergent with the separation of space and time from the everyday practice of living and from each other that occurred in the Guineaman's hold—the architecture of which purposefully aimed at smeltering the preexistent formations of the enslaved's socialities, in order to extract from them dynamic human energy, which, liquefied, is poured into the capitalist mold of the Negro as exchangeable labor-property, where it resolidifies as such. Black being is being in ruination because the smeltering is imperfect. There are elements from before in the fluidity, cannot be expelled, or melted away, which have enough residual cohesion to be manifest in the solidified form. That cohesion in liquefaction is black being; which, neither reducible to the Negro or any longer circumscribed by the preexistent formations, is being on the line of animality and humanity, and so, perpetually exhibiting the material processes of harmonization, without requiring the veneer or conceit of civilization as the legitimation of violent carnage. (433–34)

Much of what Judy says here under the inspiration of Baldwin's and Farès's engagements with each other I explore across chapters 1 to 3 of this book as I think with and between black feminist theory via Kara Keeling's and Zakiyyah Iman Jackson's work and via

Charles H. Long's work on alchemy, the fetish, and the problem of religion. We'll get to that. For now, what has my attention is Judy's Baldwin-inflected, radicalized thinking about the politicality, if we can even call it that, of black being on the line and in ruination. I say "if we can even call it that" because what Judy's Baldwin proposes is not so much a theological or eschatological redeeming of the political and thus a redeeming of America via the sacrifice of black people, nor is it a bringing-together of the cross and the lynching tree. Rather, he offers something much more akin to a revolutionary ante-politicality that emerges artistically, poetically, and cosmologically on the farside of settler politicality and thus on the farside of the political as we know it, on the farside, rhythmically and stylistically, of political theology.

It is this beyond, this farside, that Farès heard in Baldwin-as-artist. He heard in Baldwin's bluesy artistry black being-on-the-line, which entails being-in-common. Such being-in-common has no truck with the logics of individuation or the bordered separability that drives modern statecraft and that's internal to the figure of the citizen as political avatar of the properly human. Here, the state and the citizen, as figures of bordering, are premised on property logics, which have legitimated the theft of land and life and attendant practices and discourses of (settler) sovereignty. Baldwin's name for the artistic alternatives of poetic living as being-in-common is *nonexclusionary love* or what Judy calls "love improper." Love is what is revolutionarily anterior to, what is anarchically on the farside of, political theology's stately machinations. Such love is political to the extent that it revolutionarily undoes rather than reforms the political. It is such practices of love in refusal of and, at some base level, fugitive from theological capture that marks black being as a mystic song.

10   Long, "Understanding Religion and Its Study." Because of its centrality both for Long and for my own engagement with it, I leave *archē* italicized throughout this book.

11   I borrow this formulation from scholar Zakiyyah Iman Jackson. I think extensively with Jackson (and Kara Keeling) in chapter 1 of this book. For now and in the interest of elaborating on this phrase, "the world as such," and how I do not take "the world" as given, I here further reference Jackson. With this phrase her focus is on

> the particular problem of the definite article "the," as a qualifier of "world." In light of the work of Quentin Meillasoux and other realist approaches to "world" and anti-correlationalist stances (i.e., some new materialist approaches), I have argued for a disenchantment of the idea(l) of "the world" as a knowable concept, while holding on to the notion of incalculable and untotalizable worldings. "The world," and especially "the world as such," I argue, fails as a concept (at knowability) but succeeds as an idea(l) of imperialist myth predicated on the absent presence of what I call the black *mater*(nal). This critique is not limited to any particular representation of "the world" but is a rejection of the concept of "the world." (Z. Jackson, *Becoming Human*, 230n11)

On the world as conceptual idea(l), see also Gabriel, *Why the World Does Not Exist*. I am quite in agreement with Jackson's take on the problem of "the world" as rooted in imperialist myth or, as I argue here, as lodged in the problem of modernity's (re)invention of religion and extractive (anti)blackening of the earth. It is this imperialist idea(l) of "the world" and a concomitant understanding of the political that has been imposed on top of the earth. I should also note, Jackson's argument about "the world as such" as "an idea(l) of imperialist myth" resonates with the work of Denise Ferreira da Silva, whose presence courses through the pages of this book.

12   Wynter, "Unsettling the Coloniality of Being."

13   Hartman, *Scenes of Subjection*; and Ferreira da Silva, *Toward a Global Idea of Race*.

14   The notion of refusal beyond resistance runs through my attempt to understand black religion as practices of endurance in opacity. I've found quite helpful cultural anthropologist Carole McGranahan's take on refusal, its relatedness to resistance, and its being about more than just resisting or saying no to domination. See McGranahan, "Theorizing Refusal." She observes that "to refuse is to say no. But, no, it is not just that. To refuse can be generative and strategic, a deliberate move toward one thing, belief, practice, or community and away from another. Refusals illuminate limits and possibilities, especially but not only of the state and other institutions. And yet, refusal cannot be cast merely as a response to authority, or an updated version of resistance, or a concept to subsume under already existing scholarly categories" (319). If refusal is not merely negative or oppositional, if it is not just to say no, then how to think about it? Refusal activates and summons or generates alternate socialities and possibilities. Referencing specifically Audra Simpson's work in indigenous and settler colonial studies and more specifically Simpson's analysis of Kahnawà:ke Mohawk refusals, McGranahan clarifies "that available concepts of resistance or recognition remain insufficient *in that they often overestimate the place of the state*" (322, emphasis added). In its unstateliness, "refusal . . . rejects external state and institutional structures. For the Kahnawà:ke Mohawk [as Simpson shows] this can be to call forward 'the prior,' that is, all that preceded, and desires now to succeed, settler colonialism. This stance challenges the presumption and enactment of inequity in, for example, state-society relations. If resistance involves consciously defying or opposing superiors 'in a context of differential power relationships' . . . , then refusal rejects this hierarchical relationship, repositing the relationship as one configured altogether differently" (322–23). I'm interested in "the prior" to "hierarchy" of which McGranahan, following Simpson, speaks. That is, I'm interested in that anterior to the *archē* in hierarchy, which links to the *an-* of anarchy. I want to think black religion in the mode of refusal. What if, strangely, black religion is the refusal of (the hier-*archē* of) religion (and the secular) that grounds the terms of order? (More on the significance of *archē* in short order.)

       I must also say before concluding this endnote that McGranahan's account of refusal, which builds on Simpson's work, resonates with attention to refusal in black studies, which also informs my thinking on the topic. For example, Tina Campt posits refusal as "a rejection of the status quo as livable and the creation of possibility in the face of negation, i.e., a refusal to recognize a system that renders you fundamentally illegible and unintelligible; the decision to reject the terms of diminished subjecthood with which one is presented" is in McGranahan's language not just to say no. Rather, the negation activates; it, Campt says, is "a generative and creative source of disorderly power to embrace the possibility of living otherwise." See Campt, "Black Visuality and the Practice of Refusal," 83. See as well the fantastic conversation on refusal between Hartman and Fred Moten, "To Refuse That Which Has Been Refused to You." Finally, I must mention the immensely illuminating and first-rate work of Lindsey Stewart on refusal as a practice of joy. See Stewart, *Politics of Black Joy*.

15 Freud, *Uncanny*.

16 See Long, "Freedom, Otherness, and Religion"; and Long, "Understanding Religion and Its Study."

17 On the reconfiguration of empire, see E. Edwards, *Other Side of Terror*.

18 This is a topic insightfully taken up in Rooks, *White Money/Black Power*; Ferguson, *Reorder of Things*; and Mitchell, "Diversity." Attention has yet to be given to the vital question of the emergence of the critical study of religion in the modern university (and thus outside of the often-confessional context of theological seminaries) through the emergence of "secular" religious studies departments in the 1960s and 1970s, at the same time that the birth of African American studies, ethnic studies, women's studies, and the like was also taking place in the modern university. There is something to be thought together about these two phenomena for how questions of religion function within the intramural and epistemological dynamics of these fields. In its own way, this was a topic that Long started to touch on as part of his work in the critical study of religion generally and in the study of black religion and black social life more specifically. See "The Chicago School: An Academic Mode of Being" and "The University, the Liberal Arts, and the Teaching and Study of Religion," both in Long, *Ellipsis*. . . .

19 Long works this out in several places across his expansive oeuvre, but consider particularly the section titled "The Black Reality: Toward a Theology of Freedom" in Long, "Interpretations of Black Religion in America." Consider also Long, "Oppressive Elements in Religion and the Religions of the Oppressed."

20 As a methodological point, I confess to taking liberties with Long precisely as part of my effort not so much to reproduce his thought as to think with him, while also doing my best to remain close to his approach. This, actually, is a point that holds for virtually all with whom I think, where thought itself is a space of commun(-ion)-ism, a vector of sociality. This practice has been called *study*, that "speculative social intellectual practice undertaken in the undercommons of, in defiance of, the university," as Erica Edwards (*Other Side of Terror*, 323n4) puts it, so nicely summarizing Stefano Harney and Fred Moten (*Undercommons*). In undercommoning with Long, which is to say, in being involved with him in the commun(-ion)-ism of black (religious) study and the black study of religion, my aim ultimately is not to secure his "meanings," if by that one means locking down his use of such concepts as *archē* and his late use of the notion *anarchy*. Rather, my approach to these two Longian notions—the former well developed; the latter emergent closer to the end of his life—is akin to Denise Ferreira da Silva's approach to and engagement with Hortense Spillers's notion of "the captive body," "skin color," and "flesh." See Ferreira da Silva, *Unpayable Debt*, and Spillers, "Mama's Baby, Papa's Maybe." About these, Ferreira da Silva says, "I am not taking [Spillers's] terms as concepts, which would presume both that they do comprehend (whatever they are applied to describe) and that their usage assures comprehensibility" (27n7). Similarly, my taking up after Long of *archē* and *anarchy* for an engagement with (the blackness of) black religion and for a more general engagement with the empire of religion and the secular is irreducible to conceptual lockdown. Instead, as Saidiya Hartman suggests in a statement that I've made the epigraph to this book, "'anarchism' [and by extension *anarchy*] is an open and incomplete word, and in this resides its potential." Hartman, "Foreword," xv–xvi. Its potential for what, one asks? Coming back to Ferreira da Silva, I respond, its potential for "[dissembling and disorganizing]

accounts of both racial and cisheteropatriarchal subjugation" precisely at the symbolic site of skin-colored race-gender within "the post-Enlightenment political architecture" (*Unpayable Debt*, 28) or the *archē* of the present, as I call it after Long. This then, in short, is an investigation of the racial-religious *archē* of modernity brought into view against the backdrop of the ana-conceptuality of anarchy (or *an-archē*). Put differently, my interest is in a parareligious poetics of anarchy. It is in anarchy as an open assemblage that constantly disassembles the *archē*-ological terms of order, the religio-secular "arrangement of the Colonial, the Racial, the Juridical (the State and Cisheteropatriarchy), and Capital at work in the global present" (28).

21 Long, "Indigenous People, Materialities, and Religion," 167–68. See also Long, "Primitive/ Civilized."

22 For an engagement with the full range of this term in Greek philosophy, see Gourgouris, "Archē." Besides Stathis Gourgouris's fuller arguments about *archē* in *The Perils of the One*, there are important considerations of *archē* to be found in Martin Heidegger, Jacques Derrida, and Reiner Schürmann. See Derrida, *Of Grammatology*; and Schürmann, *Heidegger on Being and Acting*. Finally, with the phrase *terms of order*, I do indeed mean to connect Long's considerations of *archē* and religion to Cedric Robinson, a key thinker within black studies and black radicalism who was also concerned with order. The suggestion here is that at the heart of black radicalism as a form of speculative study generally and of Robinson's oeuvre particularly is an investigation of the terms of religion, if not the term *religion*. See Robinson, *Terms of Order*.

23 Wynter and McKittrick, "Unparalleled Catastrophe for Our Species?"

24 Wynter, "Unsettling the Coloniality of Being." On Wynter's taking of Blumenberg's notion of "reoccupation" to understand raciality or the emergence of a global idea of race as a reoccupation of certain scholastic or medieval theological protocols, see Garba and Sorentino, "Blackness before Race and Race as Reoccupation."

25 On the problem of extraction as it relates to issues of energy sources and the making of present petroleum culture, see Ghosh, *Nutmeg's Curse*; Lord, *Art and Energy*; Rowe, *Of Modern Extraction*. Notwithstanding Ghosh's work, more work needs to be done that explores the connections between the rise of our current petroculture and practices of petrocapitalism, on the one hand, and racial capitalism, on the other. Fortunately, Macarena Gómez-Barris has jump-started this work. See Gómez-Barris, *Extractive Zone*.

26 Ferreira da Silva, *Unpayable Debt*, 13–14, and more generally chapter 1 of that book.

27 Ferreira da Silva, *Unpayable Debt*, 15, 16.

28 On "collective preservation," see E. Edwards, *Other Side of Terror*, 20. On the maternal ecology, see Williamson, *Scandalize My Name*.

29 Ferreira da Silva, *Unpayable Debt*, 78.

30 Ferreira da Silva, *Unpayable Debt*, 273. See Long, "Silence and Signification," 66.

31 Ferreira da Silva, *Unpayable Debt*, 273.

32 This is a good place to offer a statement about how I will render the word *blackness* (and *black*) throughout this book. Given how as a term *blackness* can have multiple senses—it can be a term of racial categorical denigration, a term that exceeds the racial and colonial freight loaded into it, or both of these all at once—there is a case to be made for capitalizing

Blackness or rendering it in lowercase as *blackness*. There is also a case to be made for going between uppercase and lowercase, depending on the sense of the term one wants to invoke in a particular instance. For the sake of making as smooth a reading experience as possible, I have decided to render *blackness* (and *black*) in lowercase throughout this book and will trust the reader to discern my sense of the term in the context of the specific argument or claim being made.

33 Despentes, "Preface," 17.

34 Preciado, *Apartment on Uranus*, 29.

35 Du Bois, *Souls of Black Folk*; Du Bois, *Problem of the Color Line*; Lowe, *Intimacies of Four Continents*; Ferreira da Silva, *Toward a Global Idea of Race*; and Ferreira da Silva, *Unpayable Debt*.

36 In addition to *Unpayable Debt* and its reflections on matter, see Ferreira da Silva, "1 (Life) / 0 (Blackness)."

37 Wynter, "Unsettling the Coloniality of Being"; Ferreira da Silva, "Before Man"; Ferreira da Silva, "Hacking the Subject"; and Z. Jackson, *Becoming Human*.

38 This account of the medieval as a temporal signifier but also an unrepresentable threshold that I'm aligning with mysticism and with blackness is indebted to a thinking with Aimé Césaire and literary scholar David Lloyd. See Césaire, *Discourse on Colonialism*; Césaire, *Journal of a Homecoming*; and Lloyd, *Irish Times*.

39 See Federici, *Caliban and the Witch*.

40 West, *Race Matters*.

41 Z. Jackson, *Becoming Human*.

42 On "Man 1" and "Man 2" and the Christian theological architecture of his production, see Wynter, "Unsettling the Coloniality of Being." See also McKittrick, *Demonic Grounds*.

43 See both Echeverría, *Modernity and "Whiteness"*; and Carter, *Religion of Whiteness*.

44 Ferreira da Silva, *Toward a Global Idea of Race*; and Ferreira da Silva, "Hacking the Subject."

45 Ferreira da Silva, "On Difference without Separability."

46 See Barad, *Meeting the Universe Halfway*; Salamon, *Assuming the Body*; Snorton, *Black on Both Sides*; Preciado, *Apartment on Uranus*; and Preciado, *Can the Monster Speak?*

47 My investment in metaphysics as poetics should be evident. But also, this book may be understood as informed by a turn to Lucretius in certain quarters of philosophy and classics. In other words, Lucretian naturalism and a certain black religious naturalism or a physics of blackness is also something that is emergent in this book. See Holmes, "Deleuze, Lucretius, and the Simulacrum of Naturalism"; Nail, *Lucretius I*; Nail, *Lucretius II*; Nail, *Lucretius III*; Nail, *Theory of the Earth*; and M. Wright, *Physics of Blackness*.

48 The literature on this is vast and growing, but particularly helpful are Bennett, *Being Property Once Myself*; Bhandar, *Colonial Lives of Property*; Cervenak, *Black Gathering*; and Nichols, *Theft Is Property!*

49 See particularly Locke, *Second Treatise on Government*.

50 The literature on the (Christian) religiosity of secularism is growing. On the topic and drawing them into the context of the black study of religion, I am perhaps most in conversation with Gil Anidjar, Talal Asad, and Saba Mahmood. See Anidjar, "Secularism"; Anidjar, *Semites*; Anidjar, *Blood*; Asad, *Formations of the Secular*; Mahmood, *Politics of Piety*; and Mahmood, *Religious Difference in a Secular Age*.

51 Moten and Harris, *I Ran from It*.

52 The phrase *loophole of retreat* is the title of chapter 21 in Harriet Jacobs's 1861 slave narrative, *Incidents in the Life of a Slave Girl*. In this chapter, Jacobs, writing under the name "Linda Brent," tells the story of her occupation for several years, as a runaway or fugitive slave, of an almost coffin-size attic or garret space atop a small shed. From this space she watched over her children until she could secure their freedom along with her own. See Jacobs, *Incidents*, 137–41.

53 From "Brother B's Rumpstruck Recital" in Mackey, *Nerve Church*, 30. Here's the fuller context of the "it of it" formulation in that poem:

> . . . Was it over
>
> now,
> we asked him, could you let go, let it go, be
> done with it, move on. He said he long since
> cut it loose but no way, we knew, could that
>
> be
> so . . . The tumbling out of it the it of it, the it
> of it going on. Was it love or the love song he
> cut loose but couldn't cut loose we wondered,
>
> an-
> other Anuncio in love with the sound or the
> song of it, barred entry but entranced. We wanted
> to know was it a state he would give it up for, some
> just and a joint array of others wanting voice, the
>
> we
> our cresting récit mused and made mention of,
> the we he'd make real we hoped. . . .

54 Z. Jackson, "'Theorizing in a Void.'" I first encountered the term *parareligion* from Justine Bakker in a Zoom conversation and then in an email exchange. To get some leverage on what *the black study of religion* might be about, I've recruited Bakker's term into my efforts, along with such ideas as paratheology and paraliturgy (Carter, "Paratheological Blackness"; Carter, "Excremental Sacred"), paraontology (Chandler, *X*) and its uptakes and extensions (by Moten, "The Subprime and the Beautiful"; and into "ante-ontology" by Ferreira da Silva, *Unpayable Debt*), and parasemiosis (Judy, *Sentient Flesh*). I engage this mix of conceptual poeticisms in chapter 4 of this book.

55 Gumbs, *M Archive*, 100, 112.

56 Robinson, *Terms of Order*, 197.

57 Along with Long's "Bodies in Time and the Healing of Spaces," in thinking about this I have found exceptionally helpful Jaudon, "Obeah's Sensations"; Paton, "Obeah Acts"; and Rusert, "Plantation Ecologies."

58 Robinson, *Black Marxism*, 136, where he draws on Michael Craton's *Sinews of Empire* in advancing his argument.

59 Robinson, *Black Marxism*, 136, where he again references Craton's *Sinews of Empire*.

60 Stewart, *Politics of Black Joy*, 107.

61 See Moten, "Knowledge of Freedom."

62   Long, *Ellipsis . . .* (particularly, the introductory essay); and Brody, *Punctuation*, particularly ch. 2.

63   Fanon, *Black Skin, White Masks*, 206.

64   Judy, *Sentient Flesh*; and Spillers, "Mama's Baby, Papa's Maybe."

65   Bruce, *How to Go Mad*; Crawley, *Blackpentecostal Breath*; and Stewart, *Politics of Black Joy*. See as well what Georges Bataille called his "atheological summa" (that summa is composed of *Inner Experience, Guilty*, and *On Nietzsche*) and his "unfinished system of nonknowledge" (see *Unfinished System of Nonknowledge*), both of which he saw as driven by incompleteness and as reframing what has been called *mysticism*, albeit without any "God" or stabilizing god-terms to otherwise complete it. "The Mystic Song" of this book's subtitle as well as the notion of "prayer" that I've just spoken of with respect to Fanon's *Black Skin, White Masks* and to anticolonialism and decolonialism more generally registers this as well.

66   E. Edwards, *Other Side of Terror*, 31. On life lived artistically or poetically, see Judy, *Sentient Flesh*.

67   Long, *Significations*, 9.

68   Anderson, *Beyond Ontological Blackness*.

69   Anderson, *Beyond Ontological Blackness*, 61.

70   Much of what I'm saying here is indebted to and in unending conversation with Fred Moten. See Moten, *Black and Blur*.

71   Cervenak, *Black Gathering*; L. Harris, *Experiments in Exile*; and Mackey, "Quantum Ghosts."

CHAPTER ONE. BLACK (FEMINIST) ANARCHY

Epigraphs: Keeling, *Queer Times, Black Futures*, 155; Z. Jackson, *Becoming Human*, 211; and Z. Jackson, *Becoming Human*, 90–91.

1   Spillers, "Fabrics of History: Essays on the Black Sermon."

2   Sharpe, "Black Studies."

3   Keeling, *Queer Times, Black Futures*, 32.

4   Keeling, *Queer Times, Black Futures*, 32.

5   Keeling, *Queer Times, Black Futures*, 155.

6   This phrase, *the black study of religion*, is itself a gift of black study. More specifically, it emerged out of a quick flyby telephone conversation I was having with my ongoing intellectual collaborator in black study and sometimes writing partner, Sarah Jane Cervenak, who deployed this term in describing what I do. When she said it, I was like, "Damn, what'd you just say? . . . Thanks for that . . ."

7   Nongbri, *Before Religion*, 15. Within this quote, Nongbri's reference to a notion of religion as "simply there" draws from historian of comparative religion Eric J. Sharpe. However, Nongbri insists that this naturalist understanding of religion is not just a scholarly statement or an assumption among scholars. Rather, it distills a more popular or commonsense assumption about religion as a natural thing or, again, as "simply there." Nongbri interrogates and takes down this assumption, and across the pages of this book, I, too, interrogate and take it down, though giving more texture than Nongbri does to enslaving architectures internal to the production of religion as a colonial technology. That is,

via thinking with Charles Long and black feminist/black critical thought, I explore the racial capitalist making of religion as a natural thing or as "simply there."

8 Nongbri, *Before Religion*, 16 (emphasis mine).

9 Nongbri, *Before Religion*, 154.

10 Here is where such pacts as the Peace of Westphalia (1648) should be understood as a function of what Sylvia Wynter has called *the coloniality of being*. See Wynter, "Unsettling the Coloniality of Being."

11 Ferreira da Silva, *Toward a Global Idea of Race*.

12 Gumbs, *Undrowned*, 9.

13 Freeburg, *Black Aesthetics and the Interior Life*; and Freeburg, *Counterlife*.

14 Freeburg, *Counterlife*, 3–4.

15 Interestingly, my computer autocorrected the final word of this sentence, *anarchē*, to *anarchaic*, which I then read or rather "heard" in my head as *ana-archaic*. By autocorrecting to *archaic*, my technology for writing (my computer) went astray by introducing the idea of the primitive or the original (the *archaic*) into my writing of anarchy. I deal with the notion of the "primitive" in the context of critically reflecting on the notion of the fetish and in the production of the very idea of black religion in chapter 3 of this book. Notwithstanding that, autocorrect, going astray, has introduced it now. But also, in affixing (in my head at least) the prefix *ana-* to *archaic* so as to have *ana-archaic* erupt inside of *anarchē* or inside of the *anarchic*, we get the sense (with the Greek prefix *ana-*) of an outside. More precisely, we get the sense of that which is anterior to or exceeds (these are all possible understandings of the Greek prefix *ana-*) and therefore is in insurgent refusal of the trope of the primitive and, relatedly, of a discourse of origins or genesis. We've now made a Glissantian slide—a slide, that is, to something close to Édouard Glissant's countermythic, paramythic, and paraphilosophical notion of *digenèse* (digenesis), by which he offered a critique that was a refusal of "genesis," beginnings, stable origins, or, alas, *archē*.

   Introduced in *Traité du tout-monde* (*Treatise on the Whole-World*), digenesis, as John Drabinski beautifully summarizes, turns on "the division that *di* enacts upon its conjoined term *genesis*." This is important "precisely because it forces us to think through the problem of beginning as mixed and split and chaotic, rather than pure, conceptual space. The experience of the Middle Passage, then the border crossing in and on the Plantation, requires such a shoreline thinking. The fecund dimension [of the term] lies in how *digenesis* compels a re-thinking of beginning as the persistence of possibility in survival; history's violence is born by an impossible memory, and that memory makes a world. Even the slave ship is a womb. Destruction is never pure or absolute, nor is survival driven by nostalgia and reactivation. Loss arrives at the shore, then, in the Plantation. *Contact is cosmology*—this is everything" (Drabinski, *Glissant and the Middle Passage*, 92–93).

   When one looks to the actual quotation from which Drabinski is drawing to offer his summary of Glissant's critique of origins and beginnings, what becomes clear is that Glissant's notion of *digenesis* is itself paramythographic, a scrambling of modernity's mythic terms of order. Emergent from the oceanic, from the belly of the slave ship, *digenesis* names a mythopoetic orientation that refuses the notion of the singular root or singular origin such as that which animates a normative Western Christian doctrine of

Creation as rooted in a certain reading of the Genesis stories and that with Sylvia Wynter in mind we might say came to be reoccupied and thereby transubstantiated in producing the racial capitalist scene of modernity. (See Wynter, "Unsettling the Coloniality of Being.") This reading posits God as a sovereign, mastering Creator, the "I Am" whose singular Word settles matter's motion-filled, oceanic unruliness. That unruliness is in the priestly Genesis narrative (Genesis 1:1–2:3) called "earth" and is further elaborated as being "formless and empty," a watery "void" and "the face of the deep" (Gen. 1:2). Creation occurs in God's Word establishing order and thus meaning over matter. This is myth, specifically cosmogonic myth: myth in an imperial mode. Here is Glissant's reading of the situation:

> The putting of atavistic cultures into contact in spaces of colonization has given birth, in those places, to composite cultures and societies, which are not generated by Genesis (adopting the Myths of Creation that come from elsewhere), and for that reason their origin does not lose itself in the night, which is obviously of the historical and non-mythic order. The Genesis of creole societies of the Americas melt themselves on another obscurity, that of the belly of the slave ship. This is what I call a digenesis.
>
> In coming to terms with the idea of digenesis, you grow accustomed to its example, you take leave with the impenetrable demand of the excluding unicity. (Glissant's *Traité du tout-monde*, 36, as translated in Drabinski, *Glissant and the Middle Passage*, 93; see also the more recent translation of this passage in Glissant, *Treatise on the Whole-World*, 21.)

This is a long endnote, beginning as it does with a meditation sparked by a wayward autocorrection and taking us to Glissant on the notions of beginnings, digenesis, and myth. My point in taking time with this is to indicate that with the notion of anarchy I am, in fact, pointing to the problem of myth, something I consider more intently in connection with Nathaniel Mackey's poetry and poetics in the last chapter of this book. More still, I am setting out the idea that as a focal point of black religious studies or maybe more precisely of "black (religious) study," what has been called *black religion* concerns itself with black paramythic (Mackey might say, scrambling the word *myth*, ythmic) possibility. When I say anarchy (*anarchē*) I am gesturing in this sociopoetic direction. Also, Glissant's notion of *digenesis*, where *di* cuts or divides *genesis*, is doing similar work of taking flight from modernity's cosmogonic origins and thus from genesis as it tends to be thought about in terms of a singular root or stable beginnings and pure origin.

16 Keeling, *Queer Times, Black Futures*, 155.

17 Spillers, "Mama's Baby, Papa's Maybe," 67.

18 Sharpe, *Monstrous Intimacies*.

19 Via Long, I am here thinking between Willie James Jennings's rigorous examination of what he calls "the Christian imagination" as it congealed in a new way via transatlantic commerce and exchange and Gil Anidjar's exhaustive and illuminating account of the logics of blood set loose in this period as well and how blood informs a Western biopolitical and/as aesthetic-religious imagination. See Jennings, *Christian Imagination*; and Anidjar, *Blood*.

20 See Rodríguez, *White Reconstruction*.

21 *Melancholy* surely invokes the Sigmund Freud of "Mourning and Melancholy" here, though it is Anne Anlin Cheng's reading of Freud on melancholy through and with race that I'm most inflecting here. See Cheng, *Melancholy of Race*, particularly her engagement with Freud in the introduction and chapter 1.

22 See McKittrick, "Mathematics Black Life."

23 Again, by way of the black study of religion, I am extending research that has emerged in the critical study of religion that puts pressure on the very concept of religion through interrogating its invention. On this score, there is Nongbri's *Before Religion*, which I briefly engaged in opening this chapter. But there are also, to mention a few works that I have found most helpful in thinking through religion's discursive production, Masuzawa, *Invention of World Religions*; Barton and Boyarin, *Imagine No Religion*; Josephson, *Invention of Religion in Japan*; Chidester, *Savage Systems*; and Chidester, *Empire of Religion*.

   Much of this research has been greatly aided by taking on board postcolonial criticism and, more hesitantly, settler colonial analysis. However, at best, the best of this work comes to the threshold of race analysis and halts. Here I am crossing that threshold by thinking the race-religion nexus as an invented and singular, discursive regime—an "imagination of matter," to use Charles Long's potent formulation—that worlds Man in an extractive or propertizing relationship to the earth. That worlding is predicated on a transubstantiating of matter, including transubstantiating of persons, some into the commodity form or property, meant to generate value for other persons who have also been transubstantiated, these into commodity or property owners. This structure or imagination is "whiteness." In short, this analysis of religion (the black study of religion) thinks the invention of religion as bound up with, indeed as one with, racial capitalism. So understood, racial capitalism is a religious formation, a formation of religion. Understanding religion as a global regime of raciality (as I set forth beginning in this chapter and continuing in the next two) helps the deeper stakes of this project come into view. I pose it as a question: Given the invention of religion, which I show to be built on the antiblackening, by which I also mean a certain racial-engendering, of matter and on logics of separability for producing exchange value, how ought one understand what has been called *black religion*? My answer is that black religion is a practice of anarchy with respect to the very category of religion that it both is embedded within and exceeds. This is what I aim to unfold with the notion of the anarchy of black religion (chapters 4 and 5).

24 Z. Jackson, *Becoming Human*, 4.

25 Hartman, *Scenes of Subjection*.

26 Z. Jackson, *Becoming Human*, 4.

27 Z. Jackson, *Becoming Human*, 4.

28 Z. Jackson, *Becoming Human*, 4.

29 Z. Jackson, *Becoming Human*, 4. On "White Being," see Rodríguez, *White Reconstruction*.

30 Z. Jackson, *Becoming Human*, 10–11.

31 Z. Jackson, *Becoming Human*, 47–48.

32 See Kant, *Pure Reason*.

33 Z. Jackson, *Becoming Human*, 39.

34 Z. Jackson, *Becoming Human*, 70.

35 Z. Jackson, *Becoming Human*, 75.

36 Z. Jackson, *Becoming Human*, 61.

37 Z. Jackson, *Becoming Human*, 61; and Morrison, *Beloved*, 13, quoted in Z. Jackson, *Becoming Human*, 61.

38 See chapter 10 of Douglass, "Narrative (1845)."

39 See Curry, *Man-Not*.

40 Z. Jackson, *Becoming Human*, 62, quoting Morrison, *Beloved*, 11.

41 Z. Jackson, *Becoming Human*, 63.

42 Z. Jackson, *Becoming Human*, 64.

43 Z. Jackson, *Becoming Human*, 62–63, quoting Morrison, *Beloved*, 260.

44 Z. Jackson, *Becoming Human*, 64.

45 Z. Jackson, *Becoming Human*, 66.

46 Z. Jackson, *Becoming Human*, 66 (emphasis mine).

47 Jackson, in fact, offers a devastating critique of Heidegger's project in chapter 2 of *Becoming Human*. More still, the critique she offers is part of a deeper critique of how Heidegger in the end simply extends Georg Wilhelm Friedrich Hegel's philosophical project, which is predicated on the antiblackening of the world. It is here that I situate the critique Jackson advances in continuity with Ferreira da Silva's equally crisp critique of Hegel (and by a certain extension of Heidegger too) in *Toward a Global Idea of Race*. Last, I mention here the dissertation of a student I was privileged to work with, Desmond Coleman. Coleman has developed a vital reading of Hegel's philosophical project as predicated on processes of ancient alchemy and notions therein of "blackening" or *melanosis*. See Coleman, "Alchemy and Blackness." When thought with Jackson and Ferreira da Silva, Coleman provides further bolstering of Jackson's argument about the operations of blackening in Heidegger's thought by way of the figure of the animal therein and by way of Heidegger's philosophy of worlding.

48 This paragraph draws on the account of Porete in Sells, *Mystical Languages of Unsaying*. Also see Porete, *Mirror of Simple Souls*. Finally, see my engaging with Porete's mysticism in Carter, "Black Malpractice."

49 While the phrase *black mysticism* is gaining increasing circulation in certain quarters of black studies, I'm specifically thinking here of Jayna Brown's recent development of a mystic spirituality that she ties to the black radical tradition via the likes of Sojourner Truth and Rebecca Cox Jackson, musicians like Alice Coltrane and Sun Ra, and speculative fiction writers like Samuel Delany and Octavia Butler. See Brown, *Black Utopias*.

50 Muñoz, *Disidentifications*.

51 Spillers, "Mama's Baby, Papa's Maybe," 80.

52 Z. Jackson, *Becoming Human*, 69, quoting Morrison, *Beloved*, 86 (emphasis is Jackson's).

53 Z. Jackson, *Becoming Human*, 69, quoting Morrison, *Beloved*, 85.

54 Z. Jackson, *Becoming Human*, 69.

55 Z. Jackson, *Becoming Human*, 71.

56 Z. Jackson, *Becoming Human*, 71.

57 Z. Jackson, *Becoming Human*, 81.

58 Z. Jackson, *Becoming Human*, 66.

59 Z. Jackson, *Becoming Human*, 66, quoting Moten, *In the Break*, 46, 63.

60 Hartman, *Wayward Lives, Beautiful Experiments*, 228; and Brown, *Black Utopias*.

61 Z. Jackson, *Becoming Human*, 111. The fetish is a theme I take up further in chapter 3.

62 Z. Jackson, *Becoming Human*, 113.

63 See Ferreira da Silva, *Toward a Global Idea of Race*; and Judy, *Sentient Flesh*.

64 In his *Lectures on Logic* (as edited by Gottlob Benjamin Jäsche in 1800), Kant bottom lines his entire philosophy down to the question of the human. He says,

> Philosophy . . . is in fact the science of the relation of all cognition and of all use of reason to the ultimate end of human reason, to which, as the highest, all other ends are subordinated, and in which they must all unite to for a unity.
>
> The field of philosophy in the cosmopolitan sense can be brought down to the following questions:
>
> *What can I know?*
> *What ought I do?*
> *What may I hope?*
> *What is man?*
>
> *Metaphysics* answers the first question, *morals* the second, *religion* the third, and *anthropology* the fourth. Fundamentally, however, we could reckon all of this as anthropology, because the first three questions relate to the last one. (Kant, *Lectures on Logic*, 538)

For more Kant on race, religion, and the human, see Carter, *Race*.

65 Kant, "Religion within the Boundaries of Mere Reason," 23.

66 Brown, *Black Utopias*; and Moten, *In the Break*.

67 With the phrase "thinking in disorder," I have in mind Judy, *Sentient Flesh*. While this is not the place to make the case, I contend that there is a serious interlocution to be had between Judy's work and Long's, just as I'm more widely arguing in this book via Long read through black feminist theory for how black studies has been an ongoing improvisation through the question of religion. That improvisation is the practice of a troping of the trope of religion so as to enact what Spillers might call the countermythic alternative and what Nathaniel Mackey might call the seriality of the alternative (as the poet says, in "Song of the Andoumboulou: 64," "In the alternate world another alternate world") and what Long himself might call the stylistics or the rhythmics of the alternative given in the figure of the ellipsis. See Mackey, *Nod House*, 21; Long, *Significations*, 9, along with Long, *Ellipsis* . . . To trope the trope of religion is to be spirit possessed by and thus practice the parareligious, the antereligious and antesecular "consent not to be a single being." It's to be involved in the practices of parasemiosis. See Alexander, *Pedagogies of Crossing*; Hurston, "Hoodoo in America"; Hurston, "High John de Conquer"; Hurston, "Shouting"; Hurston, "Sanctified Church"; P. Johnson, *Spirited Things*; P. Johnson, "Toward an Atlantic Genealogy of 'Spirit Possession'"; Judy, *Sentient Flesh*; Moten, *Black and Blur*; and Strongman, *Queering Black Atlantic Religions*. The phrase "consent not to be a single being" comes from Fred Moten, who borrows it from Édouard Glissant. It provides the general title for Moten's trilogy of books, *Black and Blur* (2017), *Stolen Life* (2018), and *The Universal Machine* (2018).

Some of the material in this chapter formed part of the William H. Scheide Lecture on Religion and Global Concerns focused on religion and the natural environment I presented at the Center for Theological Inquiry, Princeton, NJ, in March 2022, and a talk on Charles Long's imagination of matter presented to the American Society for the Study of Religion in April 2022.

Epigraphs: Z. Jackson, *Becoming Human*, 47–48; and Eliade, *Forge and the Crucible*, 8.

1   Walker, "'Bringer of Problems.'"
2   Z. Jackson, *Becoming Human*, 91.
3   Long, "Mircea Eliade and the Imagination of Matter," 117.
4   Long, "Mircea Eliade and the Imagination of Matter," 117.
5   Long, "Mircea Eliade and the Imagination of Matter," 117.
6   Long, "Mircea Eliade and the Imagination of Matter," 117.
7   Long, "Mircea Eliade and the Imagination of Matter," 117.
8   Long, "Mircea Eliade and the Imagination of Matter," 117.
9   Long, "Mircea Eliade and the Imagination of Matter," 119.
10 Long, "Mircea Eliade and the Imagination of Matter," 119.
11 Long, "Mircea Eliade and the Imagination of Matter," 120.
12 Long, "Mircea Eliade and the Imagination of Matter," 120.
13 Long, "Mircea Eliade and the Imagination of Matter," 120.
14 Long, "Mircea Eliade and the Imagination of Matter," 121.
15 Long, "Mircea Eliade and the Imagination of Matter," 124.
16 Long, "Mircea Eliade and the Imagination of Matter," 124.
17 Eliade, *Forge and the Crucible*, 8, quoted in Long, "Mircea Eliade and the Imagination of Matter," 125.
18 Eliade, *Forge and the Crucible*, 8–9.
19 Eliade, *Forge and the Crucible*, 42, 41.
20 Eliade, *Forge and the Crucible*, 8.
21 Eliade, *Forge and the Crucible*, 9.
22 Eliade, *Forge and the Crucible*, 8, 52.
23 Long, "Mircea Eliade and the Imagination of Matter," 125.
24 For general orientation to this field, see Davis-Floyd, Sargent, and Rapp, *Childbirth and Authoritative Knowledge*; Davis-Floyd, *Birth as an American Rite of Passage*; and Bordo, *Unbearable Weight*.
25 Sharpe, *In the Wake*.
26 Morgan Barbre, email exchange, July 20, 2021. See also Barbre, "Motherhood Enjambed."
27 This is a point that Adrienne Rich also makes. See Rich, *Of Woman Born*.
28 On logistics, logisticality, and hapticality, see Harney and Moten, "Fantasy in the Hold." My claim here is that as a function of enslavement and extraction, logistics ought to be understood as parts of the operations of transatlantic alchemy or what might also be called transatlantic transubstantiation. As such, modern logistics is part and parcel of religion's modern reinvention. I explore this in more detail in the next chapter.
29 Z. Jackson, *Becoming Human*, 3.

30 Glissant, *Poetics of Relation*, 7.

31 Glissant, *Poetics of Relation*, 6.

32 For their engagement with Glissant's "sexual geography," particularly as developed in *Caribbean Discourse*, and how it relates to a sexual economy in Frantz Fanon's writings, see Tinsley, *Thiefing Sugar*, 177–79.

33 Hartman, "Belly of the World," 166.

34 Morgan, *Laboring Women*, 2, 3; and Nash, *Birthing Black Mothers*, 7.

35 Gumbs, M *Archive*, x.

36 Gumbs, M *Archive*, x.

37 Gumbs, M *Archive*, xi.

38 See Ferreira da Silva, "Toward a Black Feminist Poethics"; and Ferreira da Silva, "Black-light." Both Long and Glissant independently of each other develop notions of opacity or theories of nontransparency. See Glissant, *Poetics of Relation*; and Long, *Significations*. On "life lived artistically," see Judy, *Sentient Flesh*.

39 Gumbs, M *Archive*, xi.

40 For more on this, see Philip, "Notanda," the essay included with the poem *Zong!*

41 I offer fuller engagements with Philip's *Zong!* that make this point. See Carter, "Other Worlds, Nowhere"; and Carter, "Mystic S/*Zong!*"

42 Philip, "Sycorax, Spirit, and '*Zong!*'"

43 In my reading of Jackson's work, I have come across no indication that she is consciously drawing on alchemy in setting forth the notion of black *mater*, though as I gestured toward in my consideration of Jackson's work in chapter 1 and as I show below, Jackson does set forth this notion with the problem of the origin (the *archē*) of religion and the fetish in mind. In this, she converges with Long.

44 Eliade, *Forge and the Crucible*, 47 (emphasis mine).

45 Eliade, *Forge and the Crucible*, 149.

46 Eliade, *Forge and the Crucible*, 149.

47 Eliade, *Forge and the Crucible*, 150, 153–57.

48 Eliade, *Forge and the Crucible*, 157.

49 See Judy, *Sentient Flesh*; and Quashie, *Black Aliveness*.

50 Long, "Mircea Eliade and the Imagination of Matter," 126 (emphasis mine).

51 I have been tremendously aided in my ongoing journey into and study of physics by the work of Carlo Rovelli and physics' mediation into the critical humanities in the work of Karen Barad, Denise Ferreira da Silva, and more recently Thomas Nail. See Barad, *Meeting the Universe Halfway*; Barad, *What Is the Measure of Nothingness?*; Ferreira da Silva, "Toward a Black Feminist Poethics"; Ferreira da Silva, "On Difference without Separability"; Nail, *Lucretius I*; Nail, *Lucretius II*; Nail, *Lucretius III*; Rovelli, *Reality Is Not What It Seems*; and Rovelli, *Helgoland*.

52 Z. Jackson, *Becoming Human*, 39.

CHAPTER THREE. ANARCHY AND THE FETISH

Epigraph: S. Johnson, *African American Religions*, 103.

1 On "the world as such," see Z. Jackson, *Becoming Human*, 230n11. See a fuller elaboration in note 11 to the introduction of this book. As for matter as "underlying substance" and

"as primordial and ultimate undemonstrable principal," these are all formulations that Long linked to the Greek word *archē*. For more on this, see my discussion of this term in the introduction and chapter 1. But also see Long, "Indigenous People, Materialities, and Religion," 167.

2 Moten, *In the Break*, 26.

3 On incompleteness, see Harney and Moten, "Refusing Completion." The black radical tradition, as Harney and Moten and others in thinking with Cedric Robinson talk about it, operates out of a praxis that refuses the metaphysics of "completion," where completion, to put it in the terms I am using throughout this book, is to be understood as racial capitalism's *archē*, the *archē* or principle grounding modernity. Moten conveys what the idea of completion is about in recounting the story of, as he puts it,

> a devil in Costco in a red T-shirt, the shirt decorated with an outline of the United States map, on top of which are the words 'USA: Running the world since 1776.' And he's in fucking Costco with no fucking mask on and this little old lady asks him to put on a mask and he charges her, screaming, accusing *her* of aggression. He is the literal embodiment of The Man whose anger is given in and as the very making, the very expression, and the very protection of himself. This is absolute self-fashioning held in a claim not simply of ownership but, deeper still, of the ownership of the right to own. (12–13)

Here ownership as ownership of the very right to own is radically violent completion. By contrast, incompletion entails "a common social refusal of self-possession. . . . the anger of a common love," which isn't to be confused with some sort of humanist romantic love (13). Incompletion points to a sharing that is the anoriginal and *mater*ial condition. "The flash of sharing, of love, of riot . . . that's where the nonlocal is, that's black quantum life, that's the fugitive wormhole, the whole physical sociality that Denise [Ferreira da Silva] teaches us. That's where the order of one and the other, resistance and regulation, gets disordered, continually, where symmetry slips, and in a flash there's a party going on. We work under the assumption that we are shared even if it only comes to us in the flash of a match, of a smile, or a touch" (8). Described here is the condition of ani*mater*ial *an-archē* that here I associate with the practice of black (religious) study and with the anarchy of black religion.

4 On blackness as a genre of existence beyond the human as a structure of racially and juridically distributed Life and Death, see Ferreira da Silva, *Toward a Global Idea of Race*; and Ferreira da Silva, "NO-BODIES." See also Hong, *Death beyond Disavowal*.

5 Long, "Indigenous People, Materialities, and Religion," 168.

6 Long, "Indigenous People, Materialities, and Religion," 168.

7 Long, "Indigenous People, Materialities, and Religion," 169.

8 Long, "Indigenous People, Materialities, and Religion," 169. There is a connection here between the genealogy Long presents on the idea of *civilization* and that presented recently in Graeber and Wengrow, *Dawn of Everything*.

9 Long, "Indigenous People, Materialities, and Religion," 169.

10 Long, "Indigenous People, Materialities, and Religion," 169.

11 See Ferreira da Silva, "On Difference without Separability."

12 Long, "Indigenous People, Materialities, and Religion," 169.

13 On keeping open "the ontological dimension," see Long, "Silence and Signification," 66. On "the ontological totality," see Robinson, *Black Marxism*, 168.

14 Robinson, *Terms of Order*, 196; and Brown, *Black Utopias*, 20.

15 Eliade, *Forge and the Crucible*, 157.

16 See book 1 of Lucretius, *On the Nature of Things*.

17 Eliade, *Forge and the Crucible*, 162.

18 Long, "Indigenous People, Materialities, and Religion," 169.

19 Du Bois, *Black Reconstruction in America*, 237.

20 On America as an invention, see Long, "Primitive/Civilized." See also Long, "Interpretations of Black Religion in America," 151, where he explains the invention of America in terms of its counterrevolution against its depth *archē*, which here I am interpreting as settler colonial counterrevolution against anarchy (or *an-archē*). The counterrevolution aims to interdict the implicacy between various African persons, Native peoples, and poor and exploited European settlers. As for the phrase the "whiteness of the West," which here I've rendered as "the White West," this emerged in a fruitful email conversation with Denise Ferreira da Silva on October 1, 2020.

21 Keeling, *Queer Times, Black Futures*, 38, quoting Snead, "Repetition as a Figure of Black Culture."

22 On the powerful idea of engulfment, see Ferreira da Silva, *Toward a Global Idea of Race*, 31–33, 71–76.

23 The figures of the Savage and the Slave are explored in Wilderson, *Red, White and Black*.

24 For a recent engagement with these issues, see Orsi, *History and Presence*. I address the issues also in Carter, "Excremental Sacred."

25 The book Long is commenting on is Nelson's *The Idea of Usury*.

26 Long, "Indigenous People, Materialities, and Religion," 171.

27 Long, "Indigenous People, Materialities, and Religion," 171.

28 Long, "Indigenous People, Materialities, and Religion," 171.

29 Long, "Indigenous People, Materialities, and Religion," 171.

30 For more on this, see chapters 4 and 7—respectively, "Animals and Animism" and "Humanity and Divinity"—in Chidester, *Empire of Religion*.

31 Here I am only touching the tip of the iceberg of the problem of the fetish. It has been taken up afresh in J. Lorand Matory's *The Fetish Revisited: Marx, Freud, and the Gods Black People Make*. While this is a very important work on the fetish and its significance for animating critical theory, I do have significant disagreement with a key premise of Matory's argument, namely, that we're all fetishizers, including European theorists from Karl Marx to Sigmund Freud and on down the line. It's just that some acknowledge as much (as is the case with African religionists), while others do not (as is the case with European, critical theory). This maneuver of equalization is profoundly problematic. Matory does not stay with the insight, which was well established by Pietz and amplified by Long and Sylvester Johnson, who both operate out of the field of (black) religious studies, but which Matory, too, advances to an extent, that the fetish is a European creation and imposition. This is evident in a key founding text of fetish discourse, Charles de Brosses's "On the Worship of the Fetish Gods" (2017). That imposition operates in service, as I've been arguing here, of capitalist extraction and for the making of a world structure through separability and sequentiality. The fetish individuates; it is the vehicle of

cultural difference as religio-racialization. There is no recuperating it. Full stop. Curiously, and unless it got by me in teaching Matory's text in a recent seminar, Matory nowhere references Long's engagement with the problem of the fetish and the implications of Long's demonstrating that the fetish funds the racial capitalist world. The fetish is an ur-scene of subjection. For more on de Brosses, see Morris and Leonard, *Returns of Fetishism*.

32 Long, "Passage and Prayer," 282.

33 Long, "Indigenous People, Materialities, and Religion," 174–75.

34 For more details on this, see S. Johnson, *African American Religions*, particularly part 1, which exhaustively and lucidly treats the issues.

35 See Du Bois, *World and Africa*. As David Chidester thoroughly examines and explains, Du Bois critically deconstructs the European notion of the fetish, ultimately rejecting it in *The World and Africa*, understanding it as part of the structure of Western imperial domination. See Chidester, *Empire of Religion*, 210–16.

36 S. Johnson, *African American Religions*, 101. Johnson is quoting from *Purchas His Pilgrimage* (1613), a popular colonial travelogue in which Purchas deploys the notion of "ethnike religion."

37 S. Johnson, *African American Religions*, 101.

38 Long, "Passage and Prayer," 283. "Being for the captor" is a phrase from Spillers, "Mama's Baby, Papa's Maybe," 67.

39 Long, "Passage and Prayer," 283.

40 Long, "Passage and Prayer," 283.

41 Long, "How I Changed My Mind or Not," 422 (emphasis mine).

42 Long, "Gift of Speech and the Travail of Language," 408–9.

43 Gumbs, *M Archive*, 6.

44 "Primitive we," "primitive thingliness," and "flying away" are formulations I borrow from R. A. Judy. There are strong resonances between what he says about the fetish (by way of a critique of Martin Heidegger) and what I am here arguing for (by way of a black feminist tweaking of Long). See Judy, *Sentient Flesh*, 358–61.

CHAPTER FOUR. THE ANARCHY OF BLACK RELIGION

Epigraphs: Long, *Ellipsis . . .* , 8; and Moten, "Blackness," 28.

1 Robinson, *Terms of Order*.

2 See Wynter, "Unsettling the Coloniality of Being"; and Fanon, *Wretched of the Earth*.

3 Ferreira da Silva, *Toward a Global Idea of Race*.

4 In the chapter "The Black Man and Language," Fanon cites this line from the final stanza in Paul Valéry's poem "La Pythie," as found in Valéry's volume of poems *Charmes* (1922):

Honneur des hommes, saint LANGAGE,
Discours prophétique et paré,
Belles chaînes en qui s'engage
Le dieu dans la chair égaré,
Illumination, largesse!
Voici parler une Sagesse
Et sonner cette auguste Voix

Qui se connaît quand elle sonne
N'être plus la voix de personne
Tant que des ondes et des bois!

Honor of men, holy LANGUAGE,
Discourse, both prophetic and ornate,
Beautiful chains that bind
The god gone astray in the flesh,
Illumination, generosity!
Behold a Wisdom speaking,
A Voice, august and resonant,
That when it resounds is
Understood now to be
the voice of no one
Except the waters and forests!

(Valéry, *Idea of Perfection*, 234; translation my own)

As a whole, "La Pythie" is arresting, and the last stanza acutely so. In an email exchange about Fanon's repetition of Valéry's statement about language as "the god gone astray in the flesh" to describe the condition of blackness's relationship to language, poet and cultural theorist David Lloyd noted to me "that it seems as if Valéry is condensing the Greek Delphic oracle or priestess with a woman who is being ridden or possessed. The poem is about the torture and disintegration of the body from which speech issues." I think Lloyd is onto something quite important here, something that, arguably, Fanon was also attuned to when he read Valéry's "La Pythie" and heard in it, as Lloyd suggested to me in our email exchange, a contending with the case of blackness as the condition of modern speech as such. What I propose here (in conversation with Lloyd) begins to come through in an earlier stanza in the poem where the poet writes:

Mon cher corps . . . Forme préférée,
. . . .
Et vos partages indicibles
D'une argile en îles sensibles,
Douce matière de mon sort,
Quelle alliance nous vécûmes,
Avant que le don des écumes
Ait fait de toi ce corps de mort! (224)

My dear body . . . Cherished form,
. . . .
Your inexpressibly soft clay
Divided into sensitive islands,
Sweet substance of my destiny,
We lived united by such bonds
Until the foaming gift of tongues
Transformed you to this husk of death! (225)

In another stanza, the poet writes:

Noirs témoins de tant de lumières
Ne cherchez plus . . . Pleurez, mes yeux! . . .
Ô pleurs dont les sources premières
Sont trop profondes dans les cieux! . . .
Jamais plus amère demande! . . .
Mais la prunelle la plus grande
De ténèbres se doit nourrir! . . .
Tenant notre race atterrée,
La distance désespérée
Nous laisse le temps de mourir! (230, 232)

Black witnesses of so much light,
Search no longer . . . Cry, my eyes . . .
O tears whose deepest sources well
Too deep within the distant heavens! . . .
Never so bitter a request! . . .
A pupil, even opened wide,
Still needs the nourishment of shadows . . .
Keeping us cowed and bound to the earth,
The distance lengthened to despair
Just leave us with the time to die! (231, 233)

If these verses support Lloyd's point, as he put it to me in his email correspondence and as I believe they do, that Valéry's poem condenses the Greek Delphic oracle or priestess with a woman who is being ridden or possessed, that the poem is about the torture and disintegration of the body from which speech issues, that the poem operates as "a coded meditation on the flesh and Blackness," and finally that "Fanon grasped [this] about [the poem]"—if this is all the case, I also propose and extend Lloyd's insight, particularly with the last stanza in mind, that Fanon grasps that the poem is a coded meditation that rewrites the terms of the sacred rendered incarnate in and as the flesh of Jesus of Nazareth, as Christianity would have it. Now we see the sacred gone astray, both wandering and gathering, in the flesh, which is also "the Voice," of black life, where "Voice" here is to be "understood now (as) the voice of no one / except the waters and forests!" There is a socio-ecopoetics, even a hydro-poetics as a recovery of the earth (the woods), at play here in what the poet is suggesting about "the Voice" of blackness. To specify a bit more what I mean, consider the following lines from the poem, which are about the waters that the poet has in mind and that to my ear are suggestive of the waters, perhaps, of the Middle Passage:

Alors, par cette vagabonde
Morte, errante, et lune à jamais,
Soit l'eau des mers surprise, et l'onde
Astreinte à d'éternels sommets!
Que soient les humains faits statues,

Les cœurs figés, les âmes tues. (222)

So may my vagabond and ever
Drifting, and ever moonlit death
Surprise the waters of the sea,
Hold to eternal peaks the waves,
Make men and women stand, sculpted
With frozen hears and silenced souls. (223)

It is here, in these travails, says the poet, that "the honors of the earth" (227) are received ("Rendu des honneurs souterrains," 226). However, not stopping here, the poet reads these travails as part of a set of rituals, an antiblack dramaturgy, at the heart of which is the bruising of blackness within a scene of subjection, a subjecting of black life to sacrifice in the very making of the modern world. The poet gets at this by asking,

Qu'ai-je donc fait qui me condamne
Pure, à ces rites odieux?
Une sombre carcasse d'âne
Eût bien servi de ruche aux dieux! (226, 228)

What did I do to be condemned,
Innocent, to these odious rites?
The blackened carcass of a mule
Would make the gods as good a hive! (227, 229)

It is against this backdrop that the poet, in speaking of language as "the god gone astray in the flesh" (a reference, I take it, to the incarnation of God in the flesh of Jesus Christ, according to Christian theological tradition), glimpses language as having gone even more astray, now dispersed in the flesh of blackness as this is bound up with the flesh of the earthly commons (the waters and the forests). It is this that Fanon has picked up on in Valéry's poem, hearing in it what amounts to a meditation on blackness and language, internal to which is an alternate imagination of the sacred gone astray. Unhinging the sacred from an individuated messiah figure and a sacrificial messianism, the sacred or the holy so revised indexes a semiotic reimagining of the holy in the baseness of the mass(es), which is to say, in the mass, I mean the mess, in the messy mass of blackness, and that in its relatedness to but also nonreduction to the people who have been designated as black(ened) people returns us to the earth that is more and less than and beyond this (racial capitalist) world. In other words, might it be that Fanon has glimpsed Valéry's own contending with black radicalism's mystic song?

I thank David Lloyd for our October 29, 2022, email exchange on Fanon's citing of Valéry's poem "La Pythie" that sent me down this path. The translation of the poem's last stanza, which has the line that Fanon quotes about language as "the god gone astray in the flesh," is mine, though it has been influenced both by the translation Lloyd provided me in our email exchange and the translation found in Valéry, *The Idea of Perfection*. For translations of the other stanzas of Valéry's poem, I have relied (except where indicated) on Nathaniel Rudavsky-Brody's in *The Idea of Perfection*.

5 I've envisioned this in-depth study as a three-volume work with the general title *The Black Study of Religion*. This book is the opening installment.

6 On "aesthetic sociality," see L. Harris, *Experiments in Exile*.

7 E. Edwards, *Other Side of Terror*, 28.

8 Freeburg, *Black Aesthetics and the Interior Life*, 21, quoted in E. Edwards, *Other Side of Terror*, 28.

9 See Ferreira da Silva, "Toward a Black Feminist Poethics," 81; and L. Harris, *Experiments in Exile*.

10 Quashie, *Sovereignty of Quiet*, 104.

11 Quashie, *Sovereignty of Quiet*, 104. Quashie here beautifully draws on poets Aimé Césaire and Carl Philips to make this point. On incompletion as I'm invoking it here, see Harney and Moten, *All Incomplete*.

12 This is quite the point, among many points, that Moten makes both in the essay "Blue Vespers" in *Black and Blur* and the chapter "Chromatic Saturation" in *The Universal Machine*.

13 These formulations are from Moten, *Black and Blur*; and Harney and Moten, *All Incomplete*. With these references I am positioning Harney, Moten, and colleagues within a tradition of prayerful black radicalism and as giving voice to the general material spirituality of the black radical tradition, of black *mater*.

14 Ferreira da Silva, "Hacking the Subject," 27; Ferreira da Silva, "1 (Life) / 0 (Blackness)," 1, 2.

15 Ferreira da Silva, "1 (Life) / 0 (Blackness)," 1.

16 Ferreira da Silva, "1 (Life) / 0 (Blackness)," 1 (emphasis mine).

17 Ferreira da Silva, "Toward a Black Feminist Poethics," 81.

18 Ferreira da Silva, "1 (Life) / 0 (Blackness)," 2.

19 Ferreira da Silva, *Toward a Global Idea of Race*.

20 Robinson, *Terms of Order*.

21 I have here fused the notion of the possible and the impossible to signal the importance of discourses of possibility in black thought, as, for example, in Crawley, *Blackpentecostal Breath*, while also holding onto Sun Ra's statement about impossibility. In an essay on Ra, Brent Hayes Edwards explains, "Sun Ra's use of the word *impossible* is the recognition that the radically different, a radical alterity, is inconceivable, and yet paradoxically exactly that which must be conceived. . . . *The impossible attracts me*, Ra often said, *because everything possible has been done and the world didn't change*." B. Edwards, "Race for Space," 33. Of course, in speaking of the possible that has been done without the world changing, Ra is talking about the possible that the reigning terms of order dictate. Hence, Ra's interest is in that possible that's beyond the measure of this world (order) or that is impossible in terms of this world (order). We aspire toward the beautifully im/possible in the midst of the ending world, that which moves lyrically through apocalypse. For more on this, see B. Edwards, "Race for Space," as well as the chapter on Sun Ra in B. Edwards, *Epistrophies*.

22 See both Keller, *Apocalypse Now and Then*; and Keller, *Facing Apocalypse*.

23 On "moving well together," see the elaboration of a Lucretian ethics of motion in Nail, *Lucretius II*.

24 On black *mater* as matter, see Z. Jackson, *Becoming Human*, whose work I take up in chapter 1 of this book. See also the Hortense Spillers–inflected development of the *mater*nity of Blackness in Moten, *In the Break*, 18. Finally, see Ferreira da Silva, foreword, where she reads Harney and Moten on *jus* generativity in the direction of generosity, where this

indicates an earth ecology of dividuated sharing in refusal of racial capitalist economies of the individual (6–7, 11).

25 Harney and Moten, *All Incomplete*, 19.

26 Harney and Moten, *All Incomplete*, 123.

27 Harney and Moten, *All Incomplete*, 126.

28 Lucretius, *On the Nature of Things*.

29 Fauset, *Black Gods of the Metropolis*; Woodbine, *Black Gods of the Asphalt*.

30 Sells, *Mystical Languages of Unsaying*.

31 Cervenak, *Black Gathering*.

32 In a wonderful email exchange, process feminist theologian Catherine Keller gifted me with the word *blackalypse* in describing back to me what she heard me saying.

33 Cervenak, *Black Gathering*.

34 Brody, *Punctuation*. See, particularly, chapter 2 of Brody's book, which is on the ellipsis as punctuation mark.

35 Richard Wright structures the poem "Between the World and Me" through a series of ellipses, which points in some sense to what I'm trying to describe here about the seriality of the ellipsis as a figure of nonidentical repetition or return. There are four stanzas to the poem, each concluding with an ellipsis. And because this is the case with the final stanza too, the poem itself concludes with an ellipsis, thus making it an unfinished or broken-off poem, a poem without conclusion. But our understanding of the specific work of the ellipsis in "Between the World and Me" can be sharpened, for a careful working through of the poem, which I will resist doing here, reveals that the poem's final ellipsis loops the reader back to the beginning of the poem. The poem becomes a kind of circle, or rather an ellipse, that loops back on itself, back to the beginning. Recursively, it keeps beginning again. But there's an important caveat. Each loop back to the beginning happens in some sort of new critical posture or poetic relationship to the very violence that the poem narrates (the poem narrates a scene of lynching mediated through tropes of religion). That poetic posture hosts potentials to disrupt the violence the poem narrates. There's something that the violence that the poem narrates can't seize. In this sense, the poem not only resists but refuses narrativization even as the violence that the poem would narrate proves to be a scene of exhaustion calling for a capacity for duration, for a kind of endurance in the sun of modern enlightenment. My point is that Wright's poem is predicated on an *unclosed* circularity, on incomplete movement. Yes, the antiblack violence that the poem describes repeats itself. However, I want to read that repetition as always already laced with a certain accumulating criticality that itself reveals that the violence the poem describes operates out of a structure that itself is internally unstable. It's not a closed totality such that the violence is inescapable or otherwise cannot be ended. The instability of which I speak, then, witnesses to fugitive potentials. The questions for me, then, that Wright's poem, finally, begs are: What kind of poem is this? And how might we understand the poetics of ellipsis? How are we to understand the negative, creative capacity that the poem enacts? I conjecture that that negative creative capacity is a capacity to endure and to create in that endurance. Or perhaps better put, the negative capacity that the poem enacts connotes creative endurance and renewal. The poem's nonidentical looping, its elliptical recursivity and

generativity, signals what I would call *black faith*. It is part and parcel of the spiritual vocation of black radicalism.

36 Mackey, *Splay Anthem*, ix.

37 Mackey, *From a Broken Bottle Traces of Perfume Still Emanate*.

38 Mackey, *Eroding Witness*, 35.

39 Mackey, "Sound and Sentiment, Sound and Symbol," 232.

40 P. Nelson, "An Interview with Nathaniel Mackey," 12–13.

41 With the formulation "unendingly 'ungivenness,'" besides Mackey I'm also thinking with Sarah Jane Cervenak on "ungiven life." See Cervenak, *Black Gathering*.

42 On "aesthetic sociality," see L. Harris, *Experiments in Exile*. On the importance of myth and of "troping the trope of religion" in black aesthetics, see Z. Jackson, *Becoming Human*, 91–93, 109.

43 See the riveting essay by Harris, "The Unfinished Genesis of the Imagination."

44 For more on mathopoetics, see the discussion between Zalamea and Moten, "Discussion on Mathopoetics." Also, in the following discussion of mathopoetics and Zalamea's philosophy, I've been aided immensely by Barry Esson and Bryony McIntyre's "Listening to the Voice of Things."

45 Esson and McIntyre, "Listening to the Voice of Things."

46 Zalamea, *Synthetic Philosophy of Contemporary Mathematics*, 87 (emphasis original).

47 Zalamea, *Synthetic Philosophy of Contemporary Mathematics*, 87 (emphasis original).

48 Long, *Significations*, 9.

49 Zalamea, *Synthetic Philosophy of Contemporary Mathematics*, 312.

50 Esson and McIntyre, "Listening to the Voice of Things."

51 Esson and McIntyre, "Listening to the Voice of Things."

52 Long, *Ellipsis . . .* , 8.

53 "ellipse, n." OED *Online*, Oxford University Press. September 2022. https://www-oed-com .proxyiub.uits.iu.edu/view/Entry/60523?redirectedFrom=ellipse (accessed November 06, 2022).

54 Long, *Ellipsis . . .* , 8–9.

55 Zalamea and Moten, "Discussion on Mathopoetics."

56 Helpful in thinking about this issue is Gourgouris, *Perils of the One*. Helpful as well is Mackey's interrogation of the positing of the One (and the Many) in Western philosophy and his poetics of a notion of the "One" that is not simply captured by Western philosophy. See Mackey, "All Accruing to the One." I would also note that Mackey's discomfort with the positing of the One (and the Many) in Western philosophy ought to be thought with Hortense J. Spillers. In "'All the Things You Could Be by Now If Sigmund Freud's Wife Was Your Mother,'" Spillers says,

> What is missing in African American cultural analysis is a concept of the "one." Though there is a hidden allegiance to the idea of "superstar"/"hero"—the emplotments of both the autobiography and the form of the slave narrative are firmly grounded in old-fashioned notions of bourgeois "individualism"—it is widely believed that black people cannot afford to be individualistic. I must admit that most of the black people I know who think this are, by the way, the intellectuals who, in practice, not only insist on their own particularity but in some cases posit

a uniqueness. But if we can, we must maintain a distinction between the "one" and the "individual," even though the positions overlap. The individual of black culture exists strictly by virtue of the "masses," which is the only image of social formation that traditional analysis recognizes. . . . The individual-in-the-mass and the mass-in-the-individual mark an iconic thickness: a concerted function whose abiding centrality is embodied *in the flesh.* (394–95)

57 Long, *Ellipsis . . .* , 9.

58 Long, *Ellipsis . . .* , 9.

59 On "the groundedness of an uncontainable outside," see Moten, *In the Break*, 26.

60 Medine, "Ellipsis," 13.

61 On liminality, see Turner, *Ritual Process*. As for "portal," I am thinking of Deana Lawson's photograph of this title as well as Zadie Smith's essay that comments on it. See Smith, "Through the Portal." Finally, on vestibularity, see Spillers, "Mama's Baby, Papa's Maybe."

62 Moten, *In the Break*.

63 See chapter 2 of Z. Jackson, *Becoming Human*.

64 Silence is a running theme of Philip's poetics. See Philip's *She Tries Her Tongue, Her Silence Softly Breaks*; *Looking for Livingstone: An Odyssey of Silence*; and *Zong!*

65 Open-field poetics is associated with the poets of Black Mountain, North Carolina, generally and with poet Charles Olson particularly. In his seminal essay "Projective Verse," Olson called for a poetry of "open field" composition to replace traditional closed poetic forms with an improvised form in which form itself reflects a poem's content. For more on Olson's poetics as Mackey creatively takes it up, see Mackey, "That Words Can Be on the Page." Also, here I am connecting open field poetics to wildness as a modality of existence, ecology, and womanism or black theological ecofeminism. See Halberstam and Nyong'o, "Theory in the Wild"; Cervenak, *Wandering*; and Williams, *Sisters in the Wilderness*.

66 Medine, "Ellipsis," 14.

67 Medine, "Ellipsis," 14–15. Medine is quoting from Derrida, "Ellipsis," and Nancy, "Elliptical Sense."

68 Keller, *Face of the Deep*; and Pagden, *Lords of All the World*.

69 Again, see Keller, *Face of the Deep*.

70 Ferreira da Silva, "On Difference without Separability."

71 As this sentence states, I'm only at the beginning of formulating this vitalist-as-anticolonial imagination of matter. I've noted that, going forward, working through the vitalism that Lucretius proposes in *De Rerum Natura* (*On the Nature of Things*) will have some sort of place in working this out. However, I want to acknowledge two works that are proving important. The first is Donna V. Jones's *The Racial Discourses of Life Philosophy*. In this work, Jones considers how such *Négritude* thinkers as Aimé Césaire creatively engaged Henri Bergson's thought to advance an anticolonial vitalism. I want to follow some of the trajectories Jones has opened up. The other work I want to think with in filling out an anticolonial imagination of matter or an anticolonial vitalism is the work of Jewish studies theorist Bruce Rosenstock. I am grateful for an extended and vibrant conversation with Rosenstock on the occasion of my visit to the University of Illinois, Urbana-Champaign, on September 28, 2022, to offer the Thulin Lecture. Rosenstock introduced me to his work on Henri Bergson and Oskar Goldberg and to his work more generally

on "the vitalist imagination." Aware of Jones's work, Goldberg made other connections between vitalism, the imagination of matter, and black thought. I am presently working through Rosenstock's *Transfinite Life* and hope to engage his work further as I continue to pursue work toward an anticolonial imagination of matter.

72   Z. Jackson, *Becoming Human*, 39. For more on my reading of Jackson in concert with black religion, see chapter 1 of this book.

73   Reverberating through these sentences is a trio of Moten, *In the Break*; with Quashie, *Sovereignty of Quiet*; and Mackey, *From a Broken Bottle Traces of Perfume Still Emanate*.

74   Keller, *Intercarnations*, 2.

75   Keller, *Intercarnations*, 2–3.

76   Z. Jackson, *Becoming Human*, 109.

77   See Cervenak, *Black Gathering*; and Gumbs, *Undrowned*.

78   Long, *Significations*; Z. Jackson, *Becoming Human*; and Ferreira da Silva, "Toward a Black Feminist Poethics." The marker ~~Blackness~~ (Blackness-strikethrough) I picked up in conversations with both Calvin Warren and my graduate student Desmond Coleman. Coleman interprets ~~Blackness~~ through a remarkable reading of invisibility and exhaustion in the context of research into race and alchemy, the subject of his dissertation. See Warren, *Ontological Terror*; and Coleman, "Alchemy and Blackness."

79   Medine, "Ellipsis," 15 (quoting Jean-Luc Nancy, "Elliptical Sense," 176).

80   Judy, *Sentient Flesh*.

81   Cone, *Cross and the Lynching Tree*.

82   Poetry Foundation, "Glossary of Poetic Terms."

83   Medine, "Ellipsis," 15. The last quote on the abyss is from Long, "New Orleans as an American City," 35.

CHAPTER FIVE. ANARCHY IS A POEM, IS A SONG . . .

Epigraph: Mackey, *Paracritical Hinge*, 294.

1   Mackey, *Splay Anthem*, ix.

2   Mackey, *Nerve Church*, 36.

3   Mackey, *Splay Anthem*, x. I-Insofar (or Insofar-I); We-Insofar (or Insofar-We); He-, She-, and They-Insofar; and even "Insofarians" are formulations that appear in Mackey's poems as various poetic speakers speak of themselves and others individually and collectively. Along with "philosophic posse," these formulations of the Insofar can be found, for example, in several of the poems collected in Mackey, *Blue Fasa*.

4   Mackey, *Nerve Church*, 36.

5   This felicitous phrase, "jagged clippings of speech," Peter O'Leary uses in his interview with Mackey. See Mackey, *Paracritical Hinge*, 295.

6   From "Of the Passing of the First Born," in Du Bois, *Souls of Black Folk*, 510.

7   With this term, "ani*mater*iality," I betray the fact that I'm still in a kind of jam session with Fred Moten. The term itself can be found in Moten, *In the Break*, 18. In thinking with Moten (inside of thinking in this chapter with Mackey), I'm working to fine-tune this question of the task of the black study of religion as the study of an anarchic impulse that in its distinctive *mater*iality takes us out into the thought of black *mater* as matter's entangled depths. To be taken out into this thought is to engage in the ecstasy of thought.

It is to think in ecstasy, in rapture, even as such thinking opens for thought a new vista of the social. In the essay "Blue Vespers," in which he thinks with the visual artwork of painter Chris Ofili, Moten meditates on this animaterial vista as one of chromatic density in which the colors black and blue blur and converge into a sort of indistinction. (See *Black and Blur*, 230–44.) This vista of chromatic density registers a material ecstatics, the rapture of flesh. This is a rapture that does not only rupture the order of things; its in-surgency as an urgency through the order of things reveals precisely at the scene of catastrophe the open secret of alternatives. This is about the revelation of the strange proximity of sorrow and joy, of the wound and the blessing, which is something that my colleague and friend, the poet Ross Gay, has also been helping me think about. (What do I point readers to here? Well, just see anything Ross has written. But short of this, see *Catalog of Unabashed Gratitude* and *Inciting Joy*.) This disclosing, or what I earlier called an anarcho-material impulse, is apocalyptic. Indeed, this anarcho-material impulse moves in relationship to the very production of what is called religion though it parareligiously exceeds religion's invention by virtue of the very blackening that gets religion as a modern invention off the ground in the first place as part of the production of the slave, and alas the Negro, within commodity exchange in the Atlantic World. (For more on this, see chapter 3 of this book.)

If Moten's *In the Break* contributes to the aesthetic genealogy of blackness as a tradition of anarcho-*mater*iality and -animacy, which is to say, after Cedric Robinson, "the black radical tradition" (see Robinson, *Black Marxism*), then the black study of religion, as I'm thinking about it, concerns itself with the spiritual (as a distinct type of material) vocation of that tradition. It studies *mater* as a kind of persistent aliveness, as *mater*ial spirit, we might say, as matter's depths, what Charles Long might call "the stuff" of blackness in its opacity. By "stuff" is meant the *mater* of black *mater*iality. In a wonderful email exchange, Sora Han has helped me further think about this. She's helped me understand that what we are dealing with here, to adapt Jacques Derrida, is what might be called the mystical (precisely as the *mater*ial) foundations of matter. See Derrida, "Force of Law."

I find much of what I am proposing here encased within Moten's notion of ani*mater*iality, which is why I find it generative to think with (even as I find something like what I am proposing here operative in Mackey's practice of the poem, which is the central concern of this chapter). Specifically, Moten in *In the Break* deploys the notion of ani*mater*iality in the context of an analysis of what Karl Marx and Leopoldina Fortunati, a feminist commentator on Marx, miss in their accounts of the slave and the commodity. He observes that "neither Marx nor Fortunati is able fully to think the articulation of slave and commodity," and because of this "they both underestimate the commodity's powers, for instance, the power to speak and to break speech" (17). Moten then elaborates on the commodity's powers by zeroing in on what Fortunati herself faintly picks up on in subjecting Marx's categories to "the corrective of feminist theory." She glimpses that "along with and ahead of Marx, . . . the individual contains value and nonvalue, . . . the commodity is contained within the individual" (17). What Moten draws from this is that "this presence of the commodity within the individual is an effect of reproduction, a trace of maternity. Of equal importance is the containment of a certain personhood within the commodity that can be seen as the commodity's animation by the material trace of the maternal—a palpable hit or touch, a bodily and visible phonographic inscription" (18). Moten's concern is with that materially given maternal trace and its ongoing "transference . . . that takes place on the bridge of lost matter, lost maternity, lost mechanics that joins bondage and freedom, that interinanimates the body and its ephemeral if productive force, that interarticulates the performance and the reproductive reproduction it always already contains and which contains it" (18). This gets to the heart of the story, then, that Moten wants to tell. The story he wants to tell is both "of how apparent nonvalue functions as a creator of value" and "of how value animates what appears as nonvalue. This functioning and this animation are material. This anim*ater*iality—impassioned response to passionate utterance—is painfully and hiddenly disclosed always and everywhere in the tracks of black performance and black discourse on black performance" (18).

8 Mackey, *Splay Anthem*, ix.

9 Mackey, *Splay Anthem*, ix.

10 Mackey, *Splay Anthem*, ix.

11 Mackey, *Splay Anthem*, ix.

12 Mackey, interview by Peter O'Leary, in Mackey, *Paracritical Hinge*, 293.

13 Mackey, interview by O'Leary, in Mackey, *Paracritical Hinge*, 293.

14 Mackey, interview by O'Leary, in Mackey, *Paracritical Hinge*, 294.

15 From the poem "Day after Day of the Dead (mu forty-eighth part)," in Mackey, *Nod House*, 49.

16 Mackey, interview by Brent Cunningham, in Mackey, *Paracritical Hinge*, 317.

17 Mackey, *Splay Anthem*, xi.

18 See Naylor, *Poetic Investigations*, which has a fine chapter on Mackey.

19 Mackey, *Paracritical Hinge*, 327.

20 Mackey, *Paracritical Hinge*, 292–93.

21 See Budiansky, *Journey to the Edge of Reason*. See also my discussions of this in the prior chapter.

22 Mackey, *Eroding Witness*, 104–5.

23 See Horkheimer and Adorno, *Dialectic of Enlightenment*; and Blumenberg, *Work on Myth*.

24 Judy, *Sentient Flesh*.

25 Mackey, *Paracritical Hinge*, 293.

26 Mackey, *Paracritical Hinge*, 293.

27 Mackey, *Paracritical Hinge*, 327.

28 Mackey, *Paracritical Hinge*, 276.

29 Z. Jackson, *Becoming Human*, 91.

30 Ellis, *Territories of the Soul*, 164.

31 Ellis, *Territories of the Soul*, 166. By way of Mackey's essay "Limbo, Dislocation, Phantom Limb" in *Discrepant Engagement* (70), Ellis is citing Wilson Harris's essay "History, Fable, and Myth in the Caribbean and Guianas."

32 Ellis, *Territories of the Soul*, 171–72.

33 Ellis, *Territories of the Soul*, 171.

34 Ellis, *Territories of the Soul*, 171.

35 Ellis here draws on Thompson on Yoruba religion to illuminate Mackey's poetics. Thompson, *Flash of the Spirit*, 19, quoted in Ellis, *Territories of the Soul*, 171.

36 Mackey, "Sound and Sentiment, Sound and Symbol," 244, quoted in Ellis, *Territories of the Soul*, 172.

37   Mackey, "Cante Moro," in *Paracritical Hinge*, 193, quoted in Ellis, *Territories of the Soul*, 166.

38   Ellis, *Territories of the Soul*, 166–67.

39   Mackey, *Splay Anthem*, xiii.

40   Mackey, "Cante Moro," in *Paracritical Hinge*, 182, quoted in Ellis, *Territories of the Soul*, 167.

41   Ellis, *Territories of the Soul*, 167.

42   Ellis, *Territories of the Soul*, 167.

43   In additional to Ellis's work, on this I'm inspired by José Esteban Muñoz and Avery Gordon, both of whom draw on and redirect the utopian thinking of Ernst Bloch. See Muñoz, *Cruising Utopia*; and Gordon, *Hawthorn Archive*.

44   Gordon, *Hawthorn Archive*, viii.

45   Mackey, *Splay Anthem*, xi.

46   Z. Jackson, *Becoming Human*, 233n32.

47   Bhabha, *Location of Culture*, 237.

48   Here I echo Mackey's condensed and beautiful elaboration of a certain attraction on his part to the mystical in its testimony "to other ways of knowing, multiple ways of knowing." Found both within and beyond the West, such traditions acknowledge "the limits of reason." Mackey has in mind, for example, "Henri Corbin's coinage 'cardiognosis' in his book on Islamic mysticism" as well as Harriet Jacobs, who in *Incidents in the Life of a Slave Girl* "[refers] to the heart as a 'mystic clock.'" See Mackey, *Paracritical Hinge*, 327. In subtitling this book "a mystic song," I propose a consideration of (the blackness of) black religion as spirit possessive or hoodoo mysticism, as mystic art or as what I've also called in this book *poiēsis* or poetics. Insurgent with regard to religion as a function of the modernity of racial capitalism, blackness signals not so much religion as a poetics of religion. As for the reference to whiteness as hegemonic, religio-mythic empiricism, see Carter, *Religion of Whiteness*.

49   See Ferreira da Silva, *Toward a Global Idea of Race*.

50   On the "i-mage" in contradistinction from the representational image and the artist as i-mage worker, see M. NourbeSe Philip, "The Absence of Writing or How I Almost Became a Spy," 78–79.

51   See Goldman, *I Want to Be Ready*.

52   I recently asked Mackey about what is behind cc'ing the letter to "H-mu." He referred me to Olson's essay "The Gate and the Center," which is where he came across the notion. The essay can be found in Olson, *Collected Prose*.

53   Mackey, *Eroding Witness*, 52.

54   On "theft of assembly," see Harney and Moten, *All Incomplete*. On a "breach in human solidarity," see Mackey, "Sound and Sentiment, Sound and Symbol," 231.

55   Mackey, "Sound and Sentiment, Sound and Symbol," 232.

56   Mackey, "Sound and Sentiment, Sound and Symbol," 232.

57   Mackey, "Sound and Sentiment, Sound and Symbol," 232 (quoting Zuckerkandl, *Sound and Symbol*, 363, 364).

58   Mackey, "Sound and Sentiment, Sound and Symbol," 232 (emphasis original).

59   "Destination Out" is the title of a barely essay-length piece of writing that Jeanne Heuving identifies as Mackey's manifesto. See Mackey, "Destination Out"; and Heuving, "Introduction."

60 Zuckerkandl, *Sound and Symbol*, 71, as quoted in Mackey, "Sound and Sentiment, Sound and Symbol," 233.

61 Mackey, "Sound and Sentiment, Sound and Symbol," 233.

62 Mackey, "Sound and Sentiment, Sound and Symbol," 233; Long, *Ellipsis . . .* , 8.

63 Mackey, *Eroding Witness*, 52.

64 Mackey, *Eroding Witness*, 52.

65 Mackey, *Eroding Witness*, 52.

66 I am here subjecting both "apophasis" and "apophatic logic" (the latter term I borrow from Islamicist Michael Sells) to black study. See Sells, *Mystical Languages of Unsaying*.

67 Mackey, *Eroding Witness*, 52.

68 Thank you, Catherine Keller, for the gift of "*solidity*."

69 Wynter, "Ceremony Must Be Found." But see also Gumbs, *Dub*, particularly the moving preface.

70 Mackey, *Eroding Witness*, 52.

71 Cunningham, "Resistance of the Lost Body," 114.

72 Cunningham, "Resistance of the Lost Body," 115.

73 On "gremlin" in the voice, see Mackey, "Cante Moro," in *Paracritical Hinge*, 182, 184. Besides Cunningham's adumbration of the Wynterian daemonic, which he unfolds between Wynter's "Black Metamorphosis" and Benjamin's "Goethe's Elective Affinities," throughout this all-too-brief engagement with Wynter in juxtaposition with Mackey, I have had in mind also Wynter's notion of "demonic ground." On this, see Wynter, "Beyond Miranda's Meanings." Katherine McKittrick thoroughly engages Wynter's notion of "demonic ground" as a concept derived from both physics and religious studies discourses and has been most helpful to think with in thinking with Wynter. See McKittrick, *Demonic Grounds*.

74 On *mysterium tremendum et fascinosum*, see Otto, *Idea of the Holy*.

75 Mullen, "Phantom Pain."

76 See Moten, "Blackness and Nothingness."

77 These formulations emerged in conversations with two partners in thought: Jeremy Biles and Sora Han. Specifically, *de-cendental* is one Jeremy Biles rolled out in a recent conversation, while *cosmo-cendental* is the gift of Sora Han.

78 Moten, "Blackness and Nothingness."

79 The echo here is to Derrida, "Force of Law." Again, thanks, Sora, for helping me think about this.

80 Harney and Moten, "Base Faith."

AN ANARCHIC CODA

Epigraphs: Hartman, "Foreword," xv–xvi; and Certeau, *Mystic Fable*, 2:77.

1 See "The Dark Night," in *John of the Cross: Selected Writings*, 155–210.

2 Moten, *Black and Blur*, xiii.

3 See "The Spiritual Canticle," in John of the Cross, *John of the Cross: Selected Writings*, 211–84.

4   G. Jackson, *Blood in My Eye*, 119–20, 129–40. I've found the following reliable guides in thinking with Jackson: Koerner, "Line of Escape"; Reyes, "Can't Go Home Again"; and Rodríguez, *Forced Passages*.

5   Du Bois, "Souls of White Folk," 56.

6   On Lucretius, see Lucretius, *On the Nature of Things*.

7   The idea of refugitivity comes up in G. Jones, *Corregidora*.

8   See the author's note in Mackey, *Tej Bet*, xv.

9   Hartman, "Foreword," xv–xvi, xiii, xvii. For a fuller elaboration of this approach to anarchy, see Hartman, *Wayward Lives, Beautiful Experiments*.

Bibliography

Alexander, M. Jacqui. *Pedagogies of Crossing: Meditations on Feminism, Sexual Politics, Memory, and the Sacred*. Durham, NC: Duke University Press, 2006.

Anderson, Victor. *Beyond Ontological Blackness: An Essay on African American Religious and Cultural Criticism*. New York: Continuum, 1995.

Anidjar, Gil. *Blood: A Critique of Christianity*. New York: Columbia University Press, 2014.

Anidjar, Gil. "Secularism." *Critical Inquiry* 33, no. 1 (Autumn 2006): 52–77.

Anidjar, Gil. *Semites: Race, Religion, Literature*. Cultural Memory in the Present. Stanford, CA: Stanford University Press, 2008.

Asad, Talal. *Formations of the Secular: Christianity, Islam, Modernity*. Cultural Memory in the Present. Stanford, CA: Stanford University Press, 2003.

Bakker, Justine. "'The Vibrations Are Different Here': Parareligious Stories in the African Diaspora." PhD diss., Rice University, 2020.

Bambara, Toni Cade. *The Salt Eaters*. New York: Random House, 1980.

Barad, Karen. *Meeting the Universe Halfway: Quantum Physics and the Entanglement of Matter and Meaning*. Durham, NC: Duke University Press, 2007.

Barad, Karen. *What Is the Measure of Nothingness? Infinity, Virtuality, Justice = Was ist das Mass des Nichts? Unendlichkeit, Virtualität, Gerechtigkeit*. Ostfildern: Hatje Cantz, 2012.

Barbre, Morgan E. "Motherhood Enjambed: Birth Stories, Ritual, and Implicit Religion." *Journal of Beliefs and Values* 43, no. 1 (January 2022): 40–50.

Barton, Carlin A., and Daniel Boyarin. *Imagine No Religion: How Modern Abstractions Hide Ancient Realities*. New York: Fordham University Press, 2016.

Bataille, Georges. *Guilty*. Translated by Stuart Kendall. Albany: State University of New York Press, 2011.

Bataille, Georges. *Inner Experience*. Translated by Stuart Kendall. Albany: State University of New York Press, 2014.

Bataille, Georges. *On Nietzsche*. Translated by Stuart Kendall. Albany: State University of New York Press, 2016.

Bataille, Georges. *Unfinished System of Nonknowledge*. Minneapolis: University of Minnesota Press, 2004.

Benjamin, Walter. "Goethe's Elective Affinities." In *Walter Benjamin: Selected Writings, Volume 1: 1913-1926*, edited by Marcus Bullock and Michael W. Jennings, 297–360. Belknap Press, 2004.

Bennett, Joshua. *Being Property Once Myself: Blackness and the End of Man*. Cambridge, MA: Belknap Press of Harvard University Press, 2020.

Bhabha, Homi K. *The Location of Culture*. New York: Routledge, 1994.

Bhandar, Brenna. *Colonial Lives of Property: Law, Land, and Racial Regimes of Ownership*. Durham, NC: Duke University Press, 2018.

Blumenberg, Hans. *Work on Myth*. Translated by Robert M. Wallace. Cambridge, MA: MIT Press, 1988.

Bordo, Susan. *Unbearable Weight: Feminism, Western Culture, and the Body*. 10th-anniv. ed. Berkeley: University of California Press, 2004.

Brody, Jennifer DeVere. *Punctuation: Art, Politics, and Play*. Durham, NC: Duke University Press, 2008.

Brosses, Charles de. "On the Worship of the Fetish Gods; Or, a Parallel of the Ancient Religion of Egypt with the Present Religion of Nigritia." In *The Returns of Fetishism: Charles de Brosses and the Afterlives of an Idea*, edited by Rosalind C. Morris and Daniel H. Leonard, translated by Daniel H. Leonard, 44–132. Chicago: University of Chicago Press, 2017.

Brown, Jayna. *Black Utopias: Speculative Life and the Music of Other Worlds*. Durham, NC: Duke University Press, 2021.

Bruce, La Marr Jurelle. *How to Go Mad without Losing Your Mind: Madness and Black Radical Creativity*. Durham, NC: Duke University Press, 2021.

Budiansky, Stephen. *Journey to the Edge of Reason: The Life of Kurt Gödel*. New York: W. W. Norton, 2021.

Butler, Anthea. *White Evangelical Racism: The Politics of Morality in America*. Chapel Hill: University of North Carolina Press, 2021.

Butler, Octavia. *Kindred*. 1979. Boston: Beacon Press, 2003.

Campt, Tina Marie. "Black Visuality and the Practice of Refusal." *Women and Performance: A Journal of Feminist Theory* 29, no. 1 (January 2019): 79–87.

Carter, J. Kameron. "Black Malpractice (A Poetics of the Sacred)." *Social Text* 37, no. 2 (June 2019): 67–107.

Carter, J. Kameron. "The Excremental Sacred: A Paraliturgy." In *Beyond Man: Race, Coloniality, and Philosophy of Religion*, edited by Yountae An and Eleanor Craig, 151–203. Durham, NC: Duke University Press, 2021.

Carter, J. Kameron. "Mystic S/Zong!" In *Political Theology on Edge: Ruptures of Justice and Belief in the Anthropocene*, edited by Clayton Crockett and Catherine Keller, 272–312. New York: Fordham University Press, 2022.

Carter, J. Kameron. "Other Worlds, Nowhere (Or, the Sacred Otherwise)." In *Otherwise Worlds: Against Settler Colonialism and Anti-Blackness*, edited by Tiffany Lethabo King, Jenell Navarro, and Andrea Smith, 158–209. Durham, NC: Duke University Press, 2020.

Carter, J. Kameron. "Paratheological Blackness." *South Atlantic Quarterly* 112, no. 4 (Fall 2013): 589–611.

Carter, J. Kameron. *Race: A Theological Account*. New York: Oxford University Press, 2008.

Carter, J. Kameron. *The Religion of Whiteness: An Apocalyptic Lyric*. New Haven, CT: Yale University Press, forthcoming.

Certeau, Michel de. *The Mystic Fable*. Vol. 2, *The Sixteenth and Seventeenth Centuries*. Edited by Luce Giard. Translated by Michael B. Smith. Chicago: University of Chicago Press, 2015.

Cervenak, Sarah Jane. *Black Gathering: Art, Ecology, Ungiven Life*. Durham, NC: Duke University Press, 2021.

Cervenak, Sarah Jane. *Wandering: Philosophical Performances of Racial and Sexual Freedom*. Durham, NC: Duke University Press, 2014.

Césaire, Aimé. *Discourse on Colonialism*. Translated by Joan Pinkham. New York: Monthly Review Press, 2000.

Césaire, Aimé. *Journal of a Homecoming/Cahier d'un Retour au Pays Natal*. Translated by N. Gregson Davis. Durham, NC: Duke University Press, 2017.

Chandler, Nahum Dimitri. *X: The Problem of the Negro as a Problem for Thought*. New York: Fordham University Press, 2013.

Cheng, Anne Anlin. *The Melancholy of Race*. New York: Oxford University Press, 2001.

Chidester, David. *Empire of Religion: Imperialism and Comparative Religion*. Chicago: University of Chicago Press, 2014.

Chidester, David. *Savage Systems: Colonialism and Comparative Religion in Southern Africa*. Charlottesville: University Press of Virginia, 1996.

Coleman, Desmond. "Alchemy and Blackness." PhD diss., Drew University, 2022.

Cone, James H. *The Cross and the Lynching Tree*. Maryknoll, NY: Orbis Books, 2011.

Craton, Michael. *Sinews of Empire: A Short History of British Slavery*. Garden City, NY: Anchor Books, 1974.

Crawley, Ashon T. *Blackpentecostal Breath: The Aesthetics of Possibility*. New York: Fordham University Press, 2016.

Cunningham, Nijah. "The Resistance of the Lost Body." *Small Axe: A Caribbean Journal of Criticism* 20, no. 1 (March 2016): 113–28.

Curry, Tommy J. *The Man-Not: Race, Class, Genre, and the Dilemmas of Black Manhood*. Philadelphia: Temple University Press, 2017.

Davis-Floyd, Robbie E. *Birth as an American Rite of Passage*. Berkeley: University of California Press, 2004.

Davis-Floyd, Robbie E., Carolyn Fishel Sargent, and Rayna Rapp, eds. *Childbirth and Authoritative Knowledge: Cross-Cultural Perspectives*. Berkeley: University of California Press, 1997.

Derrida, Jacques. "Ellipsis." In *Writing and Difference*, translated by Alan Bass, 295–300. Chicago: University of Chicago Press, 1978.

Derrida, Jacques. "Force of Law: The 'Mystical Foundation of Authority.'" In *Acts of Religion*, edited by Gil Anidjar, 228–99. New York: Routledge, 2002.

Derrida, Jacques. *Of Grammatology*. Translated by Gayatri Chakravorty Spivak. Baltimore: Johns Hopkins University Press, 1997.

Despentes, Virginie. "Preface." In *An Apartment on Uranus: Chronicles of the Crossing*, by Paul B. Preciado, 13–19. South Pasadena, CA: Semiotext(e), 2020.

Douglass, Frederick. "Narrative of the Life of Frederick Douglass, an American Slave." In *Autobiographies: Frederick Douglass*, edited by Henry Louis Gates, 1–102. 1845. New York: Library of America, Penguin, 1994.

Drabinski, John E. *Glissant and the Middle Passage: Philosophy, Beginning, Abyss*. Minneapolis: University of Minnesota Press, 2019.

Du Bois, W. E. B. *Black Reconstruction in America, 1860–1880*. Edited by David Levering Lewis. New York: Free Press, 1999.

Du Bois, W. E. B. *The Problem of the Color Line at the Turn of the Twentieth Century: The Essential Early Essays*. Edited by Nahum Dimitri Chandler. New York: Fordham University Press, 2014.

Du Bois, W. E. B. *The Souls of Black Folk*. In *Writings: The Suppression of the African Slave-Trade, The Souls of Black Folk, Dusk of Dawn, Essays and Articles*, edited by Nathan I. Huggins, 357–547. New York: Library of America, 1986.

Du Bois, W. E. B. "The Souls of White Folk." In *Darkwater: Voices from Within the Veil*, 55–74. Amherst, NY: Humanity Books, 2002.

Du Bois, W. E. B. *The World and Africa*. New York: International Publishers, 2003.

Echeverría, Bolívar. *Modernity and "Whiteness."* Translated by Rodrigo Ferreira. New York: Polity, 2019.

Edwards, Brent Hayes. *Epistrophies: Jazz and the Literary Imagination*. Cambridge, MA: Harvard University Press, 2017.

Edwards, Brent Hayes. "The Race for Space: Sun Ra's Poetry." In *Sun Ra: The Immeasurable Equation—The Collected Poetry and Prose*, by Sun Ra, edited by Hartmut Geerken and James L. Wolf, 29–56. Norderstedt: Books on Demand, 2005.

Edwards, Erica. *The Other Side of Terror: Black Women and the Culture of US Empire*. New York: New York University Press, 2021.

Elia, Matthew. "Ethics in the Afterlife of Slavery: Race, Augustine, and the Problem of the Master." *Journal of the Society of Christian Ethics* 38, no. 2 (Fall/Winter 2018): 93–110.

Elia, Matthew. *The Problem of the Christian Master: Augustine in the Afterlife of Slavery*. New Haven, CT: Yale University Press, forthcoming.

Eliade, Mircea. *The Forge and the Crucible: The Origins and Structures of Alchemy*. 1956. Chicago: University of Chicago Press, 1979.

Eliade, Mircea. *Patterns in Comparative Religion*. 1958. Translated by Rosemary Sheed. Lincoln: University of Nebraska Press, 1996.

Ellis, Nadia. *Territories of the Soul: Queered Belonging in the Black Diaspora*. Durham, NC: Duke University Press, 2015.

Esson, Barry, and Bryony McIntyre. "Listening to the Voice of Things." Unpublished paper, Edinburgh, November 2019.

Fanon, Frantz. *Black Skin, White Masks*. New York: Grove, 2008.

Fanon, Frantz. *The Wretched of the Earth*. New York: Grove, 2004.

Fauset, Arthur Huff. *Black Gods of the Metropolis: Negro Religious Cults of the Urban North*. Philadelphia: University of Pennsylvania Press, 1971.

Federici, Silvia. *Caliban and the Witch: Women, the Body and Primitive Accumulation*. New York: Autonomedia, 2004.

Ferguson, Roderick A. *The Reorder of Things: The University and Its Pedagogies of Minority Difference*. Minneapolis: University of Minnesota Press, 2012.

Ferreira da Silva, Denise. "Before Man: Sylvia Wynter's Rewriting of the Modern Episteme." In *Sylvia Wynter: On Being Human as Praxis*, edited by Katherine McKittrick, 90–105. Durham, NC: Duke University Press, 2014.

Ferreira da Silva, Denise. "Blacklight." In *Otobong Nkanga: Luster and Lucre*, edited by Fabian Schöneich, Clare Molloy, and Philippe Pirotte, 244–52. Berlin: Sternberg, 2017.

Ferreira da Silva, Denise. Foreword to *All Incomplete*, by Stefano Harney and Fred Moten, 5–11. New York: Minor Compositions, 2021.

Ferreira da Silva, Denise. "Hacking the Subject: Black Feminism and Refusal beyond the Limits of Critique." *PhiloSOPHIA* 8, no. 1 (Winter 2018): 19–41.

Ferreira da Silva, Denise. "NO-BODIES: Law, Raciality and Violence." *Griffith Law Review* 18, no. 2 (2009): 212–36.

Ferreira da Silva, Denise. "On Difference without Separability." In *Incerteza Viva: 32nd Bienal de São Paulo: 7 Sept–11 Dec 2016*, edited by Jochen Volz, Rjeille Isabella, and Júlia Rebouças, 57–65. São Paulo: Fundação Bienal de São Paulo, 2016.

Ferreira da Silva, Denise. "1 (Life) / 0 (Blackness) = Infinity - Infinity or Infinity / Infinity: On Matter beyond the Equation of Value." *E-Flux* 79 (February 2017). https://www.e-flux.com /journal/79/94686/1-life-o-blackness-or-on-matter-beyond-the-equation-of-value/.

Ferreira da Silva, Denise. "Toward a Black Feminist Poethics: The Quest(ion) of Blackness toward the End of the World." *Black Scholar* 44, no. 2 (Summer 2014): 81–97.

Ferreira da Silva, Denise. *Toward a Global Idea of Race*. Minneapolis: University of Minnesota Press, 2007.

Ferreira da Silva, Denise. *Unpayable Debt*. London: Sternberg, 2022.

Freeburg, Christopher. *Black Aesthetics and the Interior Life*. Charlottesville: University of Virginia Press, 2017.

Freeburg, Christopher. *Counterlife: Slavery after Resistance and Social Death*. Durham, NC: Duke University Press, 2021.

Freud, Sigmund. "Mourning and Melancholy." In *The Freud Reader*, edited by Peter Gay, 584–89. New York: W. W. Norton, 1989.

Freud, Sigmund. *The Uncanny*. Translated by David McLintock. New York: Penguin Classics, 2003.

Gabriel, Markus. *Why the World Does Not Exist*. Translated by Gregory Moss. New York: Polity, 2017.

Garba, Tapji Paul, and Sara-Maria Sorentino. "Blackness before Race and Race as Reoccupation: Reading Sylvia Wynter with Hans Blumenberg." *Political Theology*, published online May 24, 2022. https://doi.org/10.1080/1462317X.2022.2079216.

Gay, Ross. *Catalog of Unabashed Gratitude*. Pittsburgh: University of Pittsburgh Press, 2015.

Gay, Ross. *Inciting Joy: Essays*. Chapel Hill, NC: Algonquin Books, 2022.

Ghosh, Amitav. *The Nutmeg's Curse: Parables for a Planet in Crisis*. Chicago: University of Chicago Press, 2022.

Glaude, Eddie S., Jr. *Begin Again: James Baldwin's America and Its Urgent Lessons for Our Own*. New York: Crown, 2020.

Glissant, Édouard. *Poetics of Relation*. Translated by Betsy Wing. Ann Arbor: University of Michigan Press, 1997.

Glissant, Édouard. *Traité du tout-monde*. Paris: Gallimard, 1997.

Glissant, Édouard. *Treatise on the Whole-World*. Translated by Celia Britton. Liverpool: Liverpool University Press, 2020.

Goldman, Danielle. *I Want to Be Ready: Improvised Dance as a Practice of Freedom*. Ann Arbor: University of Michigan Press, 2010.

Gómez-Barris, Macarena. *The Extractive Zone: Social Ecologies and Decolonial Perspectives*. Durham, NC: Duke University Press, 2017.

Gonzalez, Oriana. "D.C. Officer Testifies: 'It Was Clear the Terrorists Perceived Themselves to Be Christians.'" *Axios*, July 27, 2021. https://www.axios.com/2021/07/27/capitol-riot-terrorists -christians-police-attack.

Gordon, Avery F. *The Hawthorn Archive: Letters from the Utopian Margins*. 1st ed. New York: Fordham University Press, 2018.

Gourgouris, Stathis. "Archē." In *Political Concepts: A Critical Lexicon*, edited by Adi Ophir, Ann Laura Stoler, and J. M. Bernstein, 5–24. New York: Fordham University Press, 2018.

Gourgouris, Stathis. *The Perils of the One*. New York: Columbia University Press, 2019.

Graeber, David, and David Wengrow. *The Dawn of Everything: A New History of Humanity*. New York: Farrar, Straus and Giroux, 2021.

Griaule, Marcel, and Germaine Dieterlen. *The Pale Fox*. 1965. Translated by Stephen C. Infantino. Chino Valley, AZ: Continuum Foundation, 1986.

Gumbs, Alexis Pauline. *Dub: Finding Ceremony*. Durham, NC: Duke University Press, 2020.

Gumbs, Alexis Pauline. *M Archive: After the End of the World*. Durham, NC: Duke University Press, 2018.

Gumbs, Alexis Pauline. *Undrowned: Black Feminist Lessons from Marine Mammals*. Chico, CA: AK Press, 2020.

Halberstam, Jack, and Tavia Nyong'o. "Theory in the Wild." *South Atlantic Quarterly* 117, no. 3 (July 2018): 453–64.

Harney, Stefano, and Fred Moten. *All Incomplete*. New York: Minor Compositions, 2021.

Harney, Stefano, and Fred Moten. "Base Faith." *E-Flux* 86 (November 2017). https://www.e-flux.com/journal/86/162888/base-faith/.

Harney, Stefano, and Fred Moten. "Fantasy in the Hold." In Harney and Moten, *Undercommons*, 84–99.

Harney, Stefano, and Fred Moten. "Refusing Completion: A Conversation." *E-Flux* 116 (March 2021). https://www.e-flux.com/journal/116/379446/refusing-completion-a-conversation/.

Harney, Stefano, and Fred Moten. *The Undercommons: Fugitive Planning and Black Study*. New York: Minor Compositions, 2013.

Harris, Laura. *Experiments in Exile: C. L. R. James, Hélio Oiticica, and the Aesthetic Sociality of Blackness*. New York: Fordham University Press, 2018.

Harris, Wilson E. "History, Fable and Myth in the Caribbean and Guianas." 60th anniv. ed.: Literature and Ideas. *Caribbean Quarterly* 54, nos. 1–2 (March-June 2008): 5–38.

Harris, Wilson. "The Unfinished Genesis of the Imagination." In *Selected Essays of Wilson Harris*, edited by A. J. M. Bundy, 248–60. New York: Routledge, 1999.

Hartman, Saidiya. "The Belly of the World: A Note on Black Women's Labors." *Souls* 18, no. 1 (January–March 2016): 166–73.

Hartman, Saidiya. "Foreword: Black in Anarchy." In William C. Anderson, *The Nation on No Map: Black Anarchism and Abolition*, xiii–xvii. Chico, CA: AK Press, 2021.

Hartman, Saidiya V. *Scenes of Subjection: Terror, Slavery, and Self-Making in Nineteenth-Century America*. New York: Oxford University Press, 1997.

Hartman, Saidiya. *Wayward Lives, Beautiful Experiments: Intimate Histories of Social Upheaval*. 1st ed. New York: W. W. Norton, 2019.

Hartman, Saidiya V., and Fred Moten. "To Refuse That Which Has Been Refused to You." *Chimurenga Chronic*, October 19, 2018. https://chimurengachronic.co.za/to-refuse-that-which-has-been-refused-to-you-2/.

Hendricks, Obery M., Jr. *Christians against Christianity: How Right-Wing Evangelicals Are Destroying Our Nation and Our Faith*. Boston: Beacon, 2021.

Heuving, Jeanne. "Introduction." In *Nathaniel Mackey, Destination Out: Essays on His Work*, edited by Jeanne Heuving, 1–15. Iowa City: University of Iowa Press, 2021.

Holmes, Brooke. "Deleuze, Lucretius, and the Simulacrum of Naturalism." In *Dynamic Reading: Studies in the Reception of Epicureanism*, 316–421. New York: Oxford University Press, 2012.

Hong, Grace Kyungwon. *Death beyond Disavowal: The Impossible Politics of Difference*. Minneapolis: University of Minnesota Press, 2015.

Hopkinson, Nalo. *Brown Girl in the Ring*. New York: Warner Books, 1998.

Horkheimer, Max, and Theodor W. Adorno. *Dialectic of Enlightenment: Philosophical Fragments*. Stanford, CA: Stanford University Press, 2002.

Hurston, Zora Neale. "High John de Conquer." In *Zora Neale Hurston: Folklore, Memoirs, and Other Writings*, edited by Cheryl Wall, 922–31. New York: Library of America, 1995.

Hurston, Zora Neale. "Hoodoo in America." *Journal of American Folklore* 44, no. 174 (October–December 1931): 317–417.

Hurston, Zora Neale. "The Sanctified Church." In *Zora Neale Hurston: Folklore, Memoirs, and Other Writings*, edited by Cheryl Wall, 901–5. New York: Library of America, 1995.

Hurston, Zora Neale. "Shouting." In *Zora Neale Hurston: Folklore, Memoirs, and Other Writings*, edited by Cheryl Wall, 851–53. New York: Library of America, 1995.

Jackson, George. *Blood in My Eye*. Baltimore, MD: Black Classic Press, 1990.

Jackson, Zakiyyah Iman. *Becoming Human: Matter and Meaning in an Antiblack World*. New York: New York University Press, 2020.

Jackson, Zakiyyah Iman. "'Theorizing in a Void': Sublimity, Matter, and Physics in Black Feminist Poetics." *South Atlantic Quarterly* 117, no. 3 (July 2018): 617–48.

Jacobs, Harriet. *Incidents in the Life of a Slave Girl*. New York: Modern Library, 2021.

Jaudon, Toni Wall. "Obeah's Sensations: Rethinking Religion at the Transnational Turn." *American Literature* 84, no. 4 (December 2012): 715–41.

Jennings, Willie James. *The Christian Imagination: Theology and the Origins of Race*. New Haven, CT: Yale University Press, 2010.

John of the Cross. *John of the Cross: Selected Writings*. Edited by Kieran Kavanaugh. New York: Paulist Press, 1987.

Johnson, Paul Christopher, ed. *Spirited Things: The Work of "Possession" in Afro-Atlantic Religions*. Chicago: University of Chicago Press, 2014.

Johnson, Paul Christopher. "Toward an Atlantic Genealogy of 'Spirit Possession.'" In *Spirited Things: The Work of "Possession" in Afro-Atlantic Religions*, edited by Paul Christopher Johnson, 23–46. Chicago: University of Chicago Press, 2014.

Johnson, Sylvester A. *African American Religions, 1500–2000: Colonialism, Democracy, and Freedom*. New York: Cambridge University Press, 2015.

Jones, Donna V. *The Racial Discourses of Life Philosophy: Négritude, Vitalism, and Modernity*. New York: Columbia University Press, 2010.

Jones, Gayl. *Corregidora*. Boston: Beacon, 1987.

Josephson, Jason Ananda. *The Invention of Religion in Japan*. Chicago: University of Chicago Press, 2012.

Judy, R. A. *Sentient Flesh: Thinking in Disorder, Poiesis in Black*. Durham, NC: Duke University Press, 2020.

Kant, Immanuel. *Critique of Pure Reason*. Translated by Werner S. Pluhar. Indianapolis, IN: Hackett, 1996.

Kant, Immanuel. *Lectures on Logic*. Edited and translated by J. Michael Young. Cambridge: Cambridge University Press, 2004.

Kant, Immanuel. "Religion within the Boundaries of Mere Reason." In *Kant: Religion within the Boundaries of Mere Reason: And Other Writings*, translated by Allen Wood and George di Giovanni, 37–230. New York: Cambridge University Press, 2018.

Keeling, Kara. *Queer Times, Black Futures*. New York: New York University Press, 2019.

Keller, Catherine. *Apocalypse Now and Then: A Feminist Guide to the End of the World*. Minneapolis, MN: Fortress, 2004.

Keller, Catherine. *The Face of the Deep: A Theology of Becoming*. New York: Routledge, 2003.

Keller, Catherine. *Facing Apocalypse: Climate, Democracy, and Other Last Chances*. Maryknoll, NY: Orbis Books, 2021.

Keller, Catherine. *Intercarnations: Exercises in Theological Possibility*. New York: Fordham University Press, 2017.

Koerner, Michelle. "Line of Escape: Gilles Deleuze's Encounter with George Jackson." *Genre* 44, no. 2 (June 2011): 157–80.

Lloyd, David. *Irish Times: Temporalities of Modernity*. 1st ed. Dublin: Field Day, 2008.

Locke, John. *Second Treatise on Government*. In *Locke: Two Treatises of Government*, edited by Peter Laslett, 265–428. Cambridge Texts in the History of Political Thought. Cambridge: Cambridge University Press, 1988.

Long, Charles H. "Bodies in Time and the Healing of Spaces: Religion, Temporalities, and Health." In Long, *Ellipsis . . .* , 261–78.

Long, Charles H. "The Chicago School: An Academic Mode of Being." In Long, *Ellipsis . . .* , 89–98.

Long, Charles H. *Ellipsis . . . : The Collected Writings of Charles H. Long*. New York: Bloomsbury Academic, 2018.

Long, Charles H. "Freedom, Otherness, and Religion: Theologies Opaque." In Long, *Significations*, 199–214.

Long, Charles H. "The Gift of Speech and the Travail of Language." In Long, *Ellipsis . . .* , 403–11.

Long, Charles H. "How I Changed My Mind or Not." In Long, *Ellipsis . . .* , 417–24.

Long, Charles H. "Indigenous People, Materialities, and Religion: Outline for a New Orientation to Religious Meaning." In *Religion and Global Culture: New Terrain in the Study of Religion and the Work of Charles H. Long*, edited by Jennifer I. M. Reid, 167–80. Lanham, MD: Lexington Books, 2004.

Long, Charles H. "Interpretations of Black Religion in America." In Long, *Significations*, 139–70.

Long, Charles H. "Introduction." In Long, *Ellipsis . . .* , 1–10.

Long, Charles H. "Mircea Eliade and the Imagination of Matter." In Long, *Ellipsis . . .* , 117–27.

Long, Charles H. "New Orleans as an American City: Origins, Exchanges, Materialities, and Religion." In Long, *Ellipsis . . .* , 25–38.

Long, Charles H. "The Oppressive Elements in Religion and the Religions of the Oppressed." In Long, *Significations*, 145–70.

Long, Charles H. "Passage and Prayer: The Origin of Religion in the Atlantic World." In Long, *Ellipsis . . .* , 279–84.

Long, Charles H. "Primitive/Civilized: Locus of a Problem." In Long, *Significations*, 89–106.

Long, Charles H. *Significations: Signs, Symbols, and Images in the Interpretation of Religion*. 1986. Aurora, CO: Davies Group, 1995.

Long, Charles H. "Silence and Signification." In Long, *Significations*, 61–70.

Long, Charles H. "Understanding Religion and Its Study: An Outline for Continuing Research." In Long, *Ellipsis . . .* , 287–92.

Long, Charles H. "The University, the Liberal Arts, and the Teaching and Study of Religion." In Long, *Ellipsis . . .* , 99–115.

Lord, Barry. *Art and Energy: How Culture Changes*. Washington, DC: American Alliance of Museums, 2014.

Lowe, Lisa. *The Intimacies of Four Continents*. Durham, NC: Duke University Press, 2015.

Lucretius. *On the Nature of Things: De rerum natura*. Translated by Walter Englert. Newburyport, MA: Focus, 2002.

Mackey, Nathaniel. "All Accruing to the One." In Mackey, *Tej Bet*, 215–20.

Mackey, Nathaniel. *Blue Fasa*. 1st ed. New York: New Directions, 2015.

Mackey, Nathaniel. "Destination Out." In *Paracritical Hinge: Essays, Talks, Notes, Interviews*, 239. Madison: University of Wisconsin Press, 2005.

Mackey, Nathaniel. *Eroding Witness*. 1985. Pittsboro, NC: Selva Oscura, 2018.

Mackey, Nathaniel. *From a Broken Bottle Traces of Perfume Still Emanate*. 5 vols. New York: New Directions, 1986.

Mackey, Nathaniel. "Limbo, Dislocation, Phantom Limb: Wilson Harris and the Caribbean Occasion." In *Discrepant Engagement: Dissonance, Cross-Culturality and Experimental Writing*, 162–79. Tuscaloosa: University of Alabama Press, 2000.

Mackey, Nathaniel. *Nerve Church*. Vol. 3 of *Double Trio*. New York: New Directions, 2021.

Mackey, Nathaniel. *Nod House*. New York: New Directions, 2011.

Mackey, Nathaniel. *Paracritical Hinge: Essays, Talks, Notes, Interviews*. Madison: University of Wisconsin Press, 2005.

Mackey, Nathaniel. "Quantum Ghosts: An Interview with Wilson Harris." In *Discrepant Abstraction*, edited by Kobena Mercer, 207–21. London: Institute of International Visual Arts (inIVA) and MIT Press, n.d.

Mackey, Nathaniel. "Sound and Sentiment, Sound and Symbol." In *Discrepant Engagement: Dissonance, Cross-Culturality, and Experimental Writing*, 231–59. Tuscaloosa: University of Alabama Press, 2000.

Mackey, Nathaniel. *Splay Anthem*. New York: New Directions, 2006.

Mackey, Nathaniel. *Tej Bet*. Vol. 1 of *Double Trio*. New York: New Directions, 2021.

Mackey, Nathaniel. "That Words Can Be on the Page: The Graphic Aspect of Charles Olson's Poetics." In *Discrepant Engagement: Dissonance, Cross-Culturality, and Experimental Writing*, 121–38. Tuscaloosa: University of Alabama Press, 2000.

Mahmood, Saba. *Politics of Piety: The Islamic Revival and the Feminist Subject*. Princeton, NJ: Princeton University Press, 2011.

Mahmood, Saba. *Religious Difference in a Secular Age: A Minority Report*. Princeton, NJ: Princeton University Press, 2015.

Masuzawa, Tomoko. *The Invention of World Religions: Or, How European Universalism Was Preserved in the Language of Pluralism*. Chicago: University of Chicago Press, 2005.

Matory, J. Lorand. *The Fetish Revisited: Marx, Freud, and the Gods Black People Make*. Durham, NC: Duke University Press, 2018.

McGranahan, Carole. "Theorizing Refusal: An Introduction." *Cultural Anthropology* 31, no. 3 (2016): 319–25.

McKittrick, Katherine. *Demonic Grounds: Black Women and the Cartographies of Struggle*. Minneapolis: University of Minnesota Press, 2006.

McKittrick, Katherine. "Mathematics Black Life." *Black Scholar* 44, no. 2 (Summer 2014): 16–28.

Mead, Sidney E. *The Lively Experiment: The Shaping of Christianity in America*. New York: Harper and Row, 1963.

Medine, Carolyn M. Jones. "Ellipsis: Deconstructive Practice in the Work of Charles H. Long / Elipsis: La práctica deconstructiva en la obra de Charles H. Long." *American Religion* 2, no. 2 (Spring 2021): 5–24.

Mitchell, Nick. "Diversity." In *Keywords for African American Studies*, edited by Erica R. Edwards, Roderick A. Ferguson, and Jeffrey O. G. Ogbar, 68–74. New York: New York University Press, 2018.

Morgan, Jennifer L. *Laboring Women: Reproduction and Gender in New World Slavery*. Philadelphia: University of Pennsylvania Press, 2004.

Morris, Rosalind C., and Daniel H. Leonard. *The Returns of Fetishism: Charles de Brosses and the Afterlives of an Idea*. Chicago: University of Chicago Press, 2017.

Morrison, Toni. *Beloved*. 1987. New York: Vintage, 2004.

Moten, Fred. *Black and Blur*. Durham, NC: Duke University Press, 2017.

Moten, Fred. "Blackness." In *Keywords for African American Studies*, edited by Erica R. Edwards, Roderick A. Ferguson, and Jeffrey O. G. Ogbar, 27–29. New York: New York University Press, 2018.

Moten, Fred. "Blackness and Nothingness (Mysticism in the Flesh)." *South Atlantic Quarterly* 112, no. 4 (Fall 2013): 737–80.

Moten, Fred. *In the Break: The Aesthetics of the Black Radical Tradition*. Minneapolis: University of Minnesota Press, 2003.

Moten, Fred. "Knowledge of Freedom." *CR: The New Centennial Review* 4, no. 2 (2005): 269–310.

Moten, Fred. "The Subprime and the Beautiful." *African Identities* 11, no. 2 (May 2013): 237–45.

Moten, Fred. *The Universal Machine*. Durham, NC: Duke University Press, 2018.

Moten, Fred, and Theodore A. Harris. *I Ran from It and Was Still in It*. Los Angeles: Cusp Books, 2007.

Mullen, Harryette. "Phantom Pain: Nathaniel Mackey's Bedouin Hornbook." *Talisman* 9 (Fall 1992): 37–41.

Muñoz, José Esteban. *Cruising Utopia: The Then and There of Queer Futurity*. New York: New York University Press, 2009.

Muñoz, José Esteban. *Disidentifications: Queers of Color and the Performance of Politics*. Minneapolis: University of Minnesota Press, 1999.

Naas, Michael. "BLANCHOT. . . . WRITING . . . ELLIPSIS." *Qui Parle* 10, no. 1 (Fall/Winter 1996): 89–112.

Nail, Thomas. *Lucretius I: An Ontology of Motion*. Edinburgh: Edinburgh University Press, 2018.

Nail, Thomas. *Lucretius II: An Ethics of Motion*. Edinburgh: Edinburgh University Press, 2020.

Nail, Thomas. *Lucretius III: A History of Motion*. Edinburgh: Edinburgh University Press, 2022.

Nail, Thomas. *Theory of the Earth*. 1st ed. Stanford, CA: Stanford University Press, 2021.

Nancy, Jean-Luc. "Elliptical Sense." Translated by Peter Connor. *Research in Phenomenology* 18 (1988): 175–90.

Nash, Jennifer C. *Birthing Black Mothers*. Durham, NC: Duke University Press, 2021.

Naylor, Paul. *Poetic Investigations: Singing the Holes in History*. Evanston, IL: Northwestern University Press, 1999.

Nelson, Benjamin. *The Idea of Usury: From Tribal Brotherhood to Universal Otherhood*. Princeton, NJ: Princeton University Press, 1949.

Nelson, Paul E. "An Interview with Nathaniel Mackey." *Amerarcana: A Bird and Beckett Review*, January 2013, 10–24.

Nichols, Robert. *Theft Is Property! Dispossession and Critical Theory*. Durham, NC: Duke University Press, 2019.

Nongbri, Brent. *Before Religion: A History of a Modern Concept*. New Haven, CT: Yale University Press, 2013.

Olson, Charles. *Collected Prose*. Edited by Donald Allen, Benjamin Friedlander, and Robert Creeley. Berkeley: University of California Press, 1997.

Olson, Charles. "Projective Verse." In *Collected Prose*, edited by Donald Allen, Benjamin Friedlander, and Robert Creeley, 239–49. Berkeley: University of California Press, 1997.

Orsi, Robert A. *History and Presence*. Cambridge, MA: Belknap Press of Harvard University Press, 2018.

Otto, Rudolf. *The Idea of the Holy: An Inquiry in the Non-rational Factor in the Idea of the Divine and Its Relation to the Rational*. Translated by John W. Harvey. New York: Oxford University Press, 1958.

Pagden, Anthony. *Lords of All the World: Ideologies of Empire in Spain, Britain and France c. 1500–c. 1850*. New Haven, CT: Yale University Press, 1995.

Paton, Diana. "Obeah Acts: Producing and Policing the Boundaries of Religion in the Caribbean." *Small Axe: A Caribbean Journal of Criticism* 13, no. 1 (March 2009): 1–18.

Philip, M. NourbeSe. "The Absence of Writing or How I Almost Became a Spy." In *She Tries Her Tongue, Her Silence Softly Breaks*, 76–91. 1989. Middletown, CT: Wesleyan University Press, 2015.

Philip, M. NourbeSe. *Looking for Livingstone: An Odyssey of Silence*. Stratford, ON: Mercury, 1991.

Philip, M. NourbeSe. "Notanda." In Philip, *Zong!*, 187–209.

Philip, M. NourbeSe. *She Tries Her Tongue, Her Silence Softly Breaks*. 1989. Middletown, CT: Wesleyan University Press, 2015.

Philip, M. NourbeSe. "Sycorax, Spirit, and 'Zong!': An Interview with M. NourbeSe Philip." By Jordan Scott. *Jacket2*, May 14, 2019. https://jacket2.org/interviews/sycorax-spirit-and-zong.

Philip, M. NourbeSe. *Zong!* As told to the author by Setaey Adamu Boateng. Middletown, CT: Wesleyan University Press, 2011.

Poetry Foundation. "Glossary of Poetic Terms: Negative Capability." May 25, 2021. https://www.poetryfoundation.org/learn/glossary-terms/negative-capability.

Porete, Marguerite. *The Mirror of Simple Souls*. Translated by Ellen Babinsky. Mahwah, NJ: Paulist Press, 1993.

Preciado, Paul B. *An Apartment on Uranus: Chronicles of the Crossing*. South Pasadena, CA: Semiotext(e), 2020.

Preciado, Paul B. *Can the Monster Speak? Report to an Academy of Psychoanalysts*. Translated by Frank Wynne. South Pasadena, CA: Semiotext(e), 2021.

Quashie, Kevin. *Black Aliveness, or A Poetics of Being*. Durham, NC: Duke University Press, 2021.

Quashie, Kevin. *The Sovereignty of Quiet: Beyond Resistance in Black Culture*. New Brunswick, NJ: Rutgers University Press, 2012.

Reyes, Alvaro. "Can't Go Home Again: Sovereign Entanglements and the Black Radical Tradition in the Twentieth Century." PhD diss., Duke University, 2009.

Rich, Adrienne. *Of Woman Born: Motherhood as Experience and Institution*. New York: W. W. Norton, 1995.

Robinson, Cedric J. *Black Marxism: The Making of the Black Radical Tradition*. 1983. Chapel Hill: University of North Carolina Press, 2000.

Robinson, Cedric J. *The Terms of Order: Political Science and the Myth of Leadership*. 1980. Chapel Hill: University of North Carolina Press, 2016.

Rodríguez, Dylan. *Forced Passages: Imprisoned Radical Intellectuals and the U.S. Prison Regime*. Minneapolis: University of Minnesota Press, 2006.

Rodríguez, Dylan. *White Reconstruction: Domestic Warfare and the Logics of Genocide*. New York: Fordham University Press, 2020.

Rooks, Noliwe M. *White Money/Black Power: The Surprising History of African-American Studies and the Crisis of Race in Higher Education*. Boston: Beacon, 2007.

Rosenstock, Bruce. *Transfinite Life: Oskar Goldberg and the Vitalist Imagination*. Bloomington: Indiana University Press, 2017.

Rovelli, Carlo. *Helgoland: Making Sense of the Quantum Revolution*. Translated by Erica Segre and Simon Carnell. New York: Riverhead Books, 2021.

Rovelli, Carlo. *Reality Is Not What It Seems: The Journey to Quantum Gravity*. Translated by Simon Carnell and Erica Segre. New York: Riverhead Books, 2018.

Rowe, Terra Schwerin. *Of Modern Extraction: Experiments in Critical Petro-Theology*. New York: T&T Clark, 2022.

Rusert, Britt. "Plantation Ecologies: The Experimental Plantation in and against James Grainger's *The Sugar-Cane*." *Early American Studies* 13, no. 2 (Spring 2015): 341–73.

Salamon, Gayle. *Assuming the Body: Transgender and Rhetorics of Materiality*. New York: Columbia University Press, 2010.

Schürmann, Reiner. *Heidegger on Being and Acting: From Principles to Anarchy*. Bloomington: Indiana University Press, 1987.

Sells, Michael A. *Mystical Languages of Unsaying*. Chicago: University of Chicago Press, 1994.

Sharpe, Christina. "Black Studies: In the Wake." *Black Scholar* 44, no. 2 (Summer 2014): 59–69.

Sharpe, Christina. *In the Wake: On Blackness and Being*. Durham, NC: Duke University Press, 2016.

Sharpe, Christina. *Monstrous Intimacies: Making Post-slavery Subjects*. Duke University Press, 2010.

Smith, Zadie. "Through the Portal: Locating the Magnificent." In *Deana Lawson: An Aperture Monograph*, 5–9. New York: Aperture, 2018.

Snead, James A. "Repetition as a Figure of Black Culture." In *The Jazz Cadence of American Culture*, edited by Robert G. O'Meally, 62–81. New York: Columbia University Press, 1998.

Snorton, C. Riley. *Black on Both Sides: A Racial History of Trans Identity*. Minneapolis: University of Minnesota Press, 2017.

Spillers, Hortense J. "'All the Things You Could Be by Now If Sigmund Freud's Wife Was Your Mother': Psychoanalysis and Race." In *Black, White, and in Color: Essays on American Literature and Culture*, 376–427. Chicago: University of Chicago Press, 2003.

Spillers, Hortense J. "Fabrics of History: Essays on the Black Sermon." PhD diss., Brandeis University, 1974.

Spillers, Hortense J. "Mama's Baby, Papa's Maybe: An American Grammar Book." *Diacritics* 17, no. 2 (Summer 1987): 65–81.

Stewart, Lindsey. *The Politics of Black Joy: Zora Neale Hurston and Neo-abolitionism*. Evanston, IL: Northwestern University Press, 2021.

Strongman, Roberto. *Queering Black Atlantic Religions: Transcorporeality in Candomblé, Santería, and Vodou*. Durham, NC: Duke University Press, 2019.

Thompson, Robert Farris. *Flash of the Spirit: African and Afro-American Art and Philosophy*. New York: Random House, 1983.

Tinsley, Omise'eke Natasha. *Thiefing Sugar: Eroticism between Women in Caribbean Literature*. Durham, NC: Duke University Press, 2010.

Turner, Victor. *The Ritual Process: Structure and Anti-structure*. New York: Routledge, 1995.

Valéry, Paul. *The Idea of Perfection: The Poetry and Prose of Paul Valéry*. Bilingual ed. Translated by Nathaniel Rudavsky-Brody. New York: Farrar, Straus and Giroux, 2021.

Walker, Corey B. D. "'Bringer of Problems': Charles H. Long and the Basic Question of Humanity." *Black Perspectives* (blog), December 9, 2015. https://www.aaihs.org/bringer-of -problems-charles-h-long-and-the-basic-question-of-humanity/.

Warren, Calvin L. *Ontological Terror: Blackness, Nihilism, and Emancipation*. Durham, NC: Duke University Press, 2018.

West, Cornel. *Race Matters*. New York: Vintage Books, 1993.

Wilderson, Frank, III. *Red, White and Black: Cinema and the Structure of U.S. Antagonisms*. Durham, NC: Duke University Press, 2010.

Williams, Delores S. *Sisters in the Wilderness: The Challenge of Womanist God-Talk*. Maryknoll, NY: Orbis Books, 1993.

Williamson, Terrion L. *Scandalize My Name: Black Feminist Practice and the Making of Black Social Life*. New York: Fordham University Press, 2016.

Wimbush, Vincent L. *White Men's Magic: Scripturalization as Slavery*. New York: Oxford University Press, 2012.

Woodbine, Onaje X. O. *Black Gods of the Asphalt: Religion, Hip-Hop, and Street Basketball*. New York: Columbia University Press, 2016.

Wright, Michelle M. *Physics of Blackness: Beyond the Middle Passage Epistemology*. Minneapolis: University of Minnesota Press, 2015.

Wright, Richard. "Between the World and Me." In *Richard Wright Reader*, edited by Ellen Wright and Michel Fabre, 246–47. New York: Harper and Row, 1978.

Wynter, Sylvia. "Beyond Miranda's Meanings: Un/Silencing the 'Demonic Ground' of Caliban's Women." In *Out of the Kumbla: Caribbean Women and Literature*, 355–72. Trenton, NJ: Africa World Press, 1990.

Wynter, Sylvia. "Black Metamorphosis: New Natives in a New World." Institute of the Black World Records, MG 502, Box 1, Schomburg Center for Research in Black Culture, n.d.

Wynter, Sylvia. "The Ceremony Must Be Found: After Humanism." *Boundary 2* 12, no. 3 and 13, no. 1 (Spring–Autumn 1984): 19–70.

Wynter, Sylvia. "Unsettling the Coloniality of Being/Power/Truth/Freedom: Towards the Human, after Man, Its Overrepresentation—an Argument." *CR: The New Centennial Review* 3, no. 3 (Fall 2003): 257–337.

Wynter, Sylvia, and Katherine McKittrick. "Unparalleled Catastrophe for Our Species? Or, to Give Humanness a Different Future: Conversations." In *Sylvia Wynter: On Being Human as Praxis*, edited by Katherine McKittrick, 9–89. Durham, NC: Duke University Press, 2014.

Zalamea, Fernando. *Synthetic Philosophy of Contemporary Mathematics*. Translated by Zachery Luke Fraser. New York: Urbanomic/Sequence Press, 2012.

Zalamea, Fernando, and Fred Moten. "Discussion on Mathopoetics." Arika, November 23, 2019. https://arika.org.uk/archive/items/episode-10-means-without-end/discussion-mathopoetics.

Zuckerkandl, Victor. *Sound and Symbol: Music and the External World*. Translated by Willard R. Trask. Princeton, NJ: Princeton University Press, 1956.

Index

abjection: anarchic potentials of, 35; and black femininity, 33–39, 42; and plasticization, 37–38

absence, 28, 67–68, 118, 125, 127

aesthetic sociality, 77–78, 86–87, 94

African religion, 33; as bad religion, 44, 70–71, 84, 117; as black(ened), 61; mask as sign of "disordered being," 44; New World African or black spirituality, 118–19; "troping of the trope of," 17, 49, 59, 118, 121, 152n67. *See also* black religion; "fetish"

Afro-surreal, 22, 62

alchemization: counteralchemization, 58–61, 65

alchemy: and (anti)blackening of matter, 48–49, 54, 60–61, 68–69; color phases of, 60, 67; fetus as "super-subject", 54–56; by figures of modernity, 56–57; gynecology and imagination of matter, 53–56; as human intervention in time, 52; as in-gestating/ingestion, 67–68; and the maternal ecology of blackness, 56–62; minerals, as "living" substances, 52–53; racial, 61, 67–68; and transatlantic commerce and exchange, 54, 56–57, 60, 153n28

Alexander, M. Jacqui, 58–59

"alter-everyday," 58, 136–37

an-archē, 148–49n15; of abjection, 35; *ana-archaic*, 148n15; *an-archic*, 8, 19, 65, 73; anarchy as, 24, 32, 34–35, 46, 65, 97, 102, 144n20

an-archic massa confusa, 61

anarchy, 23–24, 75–79; of African coastal enclaves, 73; as alternative, 19, 20, 31, 76; as *an-archē*, 24, 32, 34–35, 46, 65, 97, 102, 144n20; anarcho-material impulse, 165–67n7; "Black in anarchy," 136–37; of black religion, 24–25, 34, 74, 75–76, 86–88, 103–4, 108, 125, 129–30; and counterlife, 30–31; ellipsis as, 20, 103; as "going astray," 35, 148n15; matter as system of, 43–44; of mysticism, 131, 136–37; as para-religious, 24, 31; as poem, 107; resourcing of, 99–100. *See also* refusal

Anderson, Victor, 24

Andoumboulou, figure of, 111–13

Angel of Dust, figure of, 85, 122–24, 126–28

Anidjar, Gil, 149n19

animacy, 7, 97–98, 166n7

animal perspective, 39–43

ani*mater*iality, 46, 110, 130, 134, 155n3, 165–67n7

animism, 70

anthropology, 81, 152n64; of birthing, 54; and Eliade's work, 49; enclosure by, 17; globality as regime of, 12–13, 30; and modern invention of religion, 12–13, 15, 44–45

(anti)blackening of matter, 14–15, 31–34, 48, 64, 87; and alchemy, 48–49, 54, 60–61, 68–69; *archē* of, 23; and black (female)ness, 35–43. *See also* blackening

antiblackness, religion of, 3–6, 9, 23, 44, 75. *See also* modern (re)invention of religion; religion

apocalypse, 59, 81–84, 109, 161n21; apoc-eclipse, 78, 83–84, 116; as disclosure, 81, 83; and dis-en-closure, 81, 115–16; Fanon's words of, 21; and incompleteness, 79–87; as revelation, 78, 81, 83, 103, 116, 123, 129, 165n7

religion, 84–85; unstateliness of, 76. *See also* African religion; "fetish"

Black Skin, White Masks (Fanon), 21–22, 147n64

black study, 22, 75; religious studies subjected to, 49, 59–60; shadow concern with religion in, 28

black study of religion, 11, 23, 25–26, 29, 43–46, 136, 139n4, 143n20, 147n6, 165–67n7; black study of prayer, 22; commun(-ion)-ism of, 143n20; and matter(ing) otherwise, 13–18; problematic orientation toward matter, 64–65; as study of a specific type of anarchy, 75. *See also* critical study of religion

"Black woman," figure of, 27, 29, 32–35, 45

blood, logics of, 149n19

Blumenberg, Hans, 9

Bordo, Susan, 54

breathing, pan-ontological, 102, 103

Brody, Jennifer DeVere, 20, 85

Brown, Jayna, 43, 67, 151n49

Brown Girl in the Ring (Hopkinson), 49

Bruce, La Marr Jurelle, 22

Butler, Anthea, 4–5

Butler, Octavia, 10

Calvin, John, 69–70

Campt, Tina Marie, 142n14

capitalism: as god-term, 14; slavery inseparable from, 32. *See also* racial capitalism

ceremony, 121–22, 127–28

Certeau, Michel de, 133–34

Cervenak, Sarah Jane, 83, 103, 147n6

chaos, 37–38, 60

Christ, and transubstantiation, 60, 69

Christianity, 29, 70, 159n4. *See also* modern (re)invention of religion; religion

circle, figure of, 93, 95–99

civilization, 9, 66–68, 140n9; as god-term, 14, 68; "we-ing" as function of, 16–17; Western notions of, 66, 67

Civil War (US), 4

coherence/incoherence, 16–17, 39–40, 45, 94, 98, 114, 116, 126, 135

Coleman, Desmond, 165n78

collaboration, 53–55

colonial *archē*, 6–7

colonialism. *See* racial capitalism; settler colonialism

"coloniality of being and knowing," 7

commodity, 33, 56, 60–61, 69–71; commodity theo-economics, 69

Cone, James, 103

consciousness, 21, 29, 65; collective, 121; "double," 95, 116; religious, 50–51, 50–52; subjective, 21

coronavirus (COVID-19 pandemic), 1–2, 15

cosmology, 32, 60, 148–49n15; alternate, 8, 11, 18–19, 20, 22, 24, 100; black radical, 77; catastrophic, 9; of depth, 19, 102, 114, 129, 132, 148n15; Dogon, 110–13; ellipsis as, 103; racial capitalist, 6–8, 14–15, 18–19, 23

counteralchemization, 58–61, 65

counterlife, 30–31

countermythic, 28, 152n67

Crawley, Ashon T., 22, 161n21

creativity, 28; of blackness, 22, 58–59, 61–62, 78, 80, 87, 118; of ellipsis, 62, 75, 94; and endurance, 49, 132, 162–63n35; mathematical, 89–90, 94

credit and debt, 17, 79–80, 83; "unpayable debt," 10–11

critical study of religion, 15, 18, 143n18, 149–50n23; history of religions as subfield of, 48, 51–52, 61, 72; as scientific study, 6–8, 16, 44–45, 54, 80, 121; as white science, 4, 44–45, 60. *See also* black study of religion

Critique of Pure Reason (Kant), 37

cross-cultural poetics, 85–86, 108, 126

crossings, 58–59

crossroads, 11, 18, 20, 25, 119–20

Cunningham, Nijah, 129–30, 169n73

daemonic ground, 129–31, 169n73

dead, the: relationship to, 19–20, 59, 86, 110, 117–18, 136

death, 60, 65, 86, 110–11

debt, "unpayable," 10–11

dehumanization, 62; plasticization distinguished from, 36–37

demonic, the, 37–38, 130–31, 169n73

71; a priori and concrete forms of, 50–51; problematic orientation toward in black study of religion, 64–65; re-generative indeterminacy of, 24–25; of religion, 50–53; as scene of extractive subjection, 11–12; spirit as opposed to, 47–48; storage/warehousing of, 33; as system of anarchy, 43–44; thingliness, 7, 17, 73–74, 101, 113, 127, 157n44; trans-substancing of, 9–10; transubstantiated into property, 23, 31, 33, 121, 150n23. *See also* imagination of matter

matter(ing) otherwise, 4, 13, 24, 43, 65, 100, 131

McGranahan, Carole, 142n14

McIntyre, Bryony, 88

McKittrick, Katherine, 9, 169n73

Mead, Sidney, 139n4

medical-scientific authority, 54

medieval, the, 9, 13, 55, 60, 81, 127, 145n38

Medine, Carolyn M. Jones, 88, 97–99, 102, 114

Messiaen, Olivier, 115

metaphysics, 76, 152n64; black feminist, 19, 74; of "completion," 155n3; of matter(ing), 65, 73–74; ~~metaphysics~~, 18, 73–74, 145n47; ontotheological, 131; as poetics, 145n7; redemptive, 140n9; of separability, 66

Middle Passage, 57–58, 148–49n15, 159n4; and loss, 118–20

Milley, Mark A., 2

"Mircea Eliade and the Imagination of Matter" (Long), 49–62, 65, 67

Mirror of Simple Souls (Porete), 40–41

modernity: archaic, primal, or indigenous as necessary to, 65–67; *archē* of, 71, 122, 144n20; denial of myth in name of, 121; Genesis narrative in making of, 148–49n15; gyneco-obstetric affair of, 56–57; plasticization of blackness, 36; as problem of (meta)physics, 69; religion central to formation of, 6–8, 28, 88; religio-secularity as mode of, 11, 87; as scene of subjection, 7, 36; as a terroristic materialism, 12. *See also* transatlantic alchemy

modern (re)invention of religion, 8, 12–15, 75, 79, 134–36, 141n111; alchemy, relationship to, 56–58; and anthropology, 12–13, 15, 30,

44–45; antiblackness, religion of, 3–6, 9, 23, 44, 75; black religion as outside the category of, 45–46, 64–65, 87–90, 94–95; in context of Atlantic commerce and exchange, 13–14; contrasted with "ancient" notion of religion, 29; as ecological crisis, 17; ellipsis, relation to, 99; extractive logic of, 11–12, 15, 23, 48–49, 150n23; and fetish, 69–73; fetish as central to, 71; matter as central to, 9, 13–14, 48; as racial capitalism, 4–6, 77, 80–81; refusal of, 22–23, 30–31. *See also* (anti)blackening of matter; religion

monstrous, the, 7, 33, 131

Morgan, Jennifer L., 58

Morrison, Toni, 38–43

Moten, Fred, 43, 57, 75, 95, 155n3, 161n13, 165–67n7; ani*mater*iality in work of, 165n78; "mysticism in the flesh," 131

movement, 80–82; across poems, 108; of blackness, 78; in Dogon music, 110; and eclipse, 84; and ellipse, 94

Mullen, Harryette, 131

multiplicity, 11, 31, 73, 168n48; of ellipse, 93–94, 96; entangled, 100, 102, 109; existence-in, 135; "I-in-," 115–17, 121; matter as imbued with, 70

Muñoz, José Esteban, 41

music: as concept of reality, 124–25; Dogon, 110–13, 125; flamenco, 112; funerary, 110; and myth, 108, 124–25; orphic, 124–26; rhythms/ythms, 102, 120, 127–28

mystagogy, black, 108

mystery, 70–71, 82, 97–99, 104, 107, 137; *mysterium tremendum et fascinosum*, 70, 130

mysticism, 13, 18–20, 25, 168n48; anarchic, 131, 136–37; black, 41, 151n49; of Porete, 40–41; of sociality, 16

mystic song, concept of, 20, 86, 111, 138, 141n9, 160n4, 168n48

myth: apophasis of, 125–27; denial of Reason as, 117, 121; and digenesis, 148–49n15; imperial, 35, 87, 101, 120–21, 148–49n15; and music, 108, 124–25; of racial capitalism, 19, 121, 126; spiritual vocation of, 121

myth character, 100–101

poem, practice of, 11, 24–25, 112, 114, 120–21, 123–24, 130–32, 166n7; as cross-cultural, 85–86, 108; ellipsis enacted by, 85–87, 104–5, 109, 129; as parareligious, 62; as "re-Source," 87; and spiritual vocation of black radicalism, 79. *See also* Mackey, Nathaniel

poethics, 20, 59, 61. *See also* mathopoetics

poetics, 59, 168n48; atheological, 76; black radical, 84; of black religion, 87; black religion as, 107–8; of black thought, 18; cross-cultural, 85–86, 108, 126; mathopoetics of ellipsis, 24; of performative unsaying, 83; philosophical, 77; of religion, 24, 27, 28, 81, 137; of the social, 16

Poetics of Relation (Glissant), 57

poetry: of black religion, 104–5, 109; letters as, 85–86, 122–23; relationship with blackness and prayer, 78–79; as "re: Source," 87, 123, 128–32, 134; spiritual vocation of, 107, 109, 112. *See also* mathopoetics

poiēsis, 79, 101, 134, 136, 168n48; in black, 87, 103, 117; of mathematics, 89; *mythopoēisis*, 109

police killings, 2

"political, the," 3–4

Porete, Marguerite, 40–41

Portuguese merchants, 70

possibility, conditions of, 61, 79, 89, 99, 142n14, 148–49n15; im/possibility, 81, 161n21

prayer: blackness, relationship to, 21–22, 78–79; of Fanon, 21–22, 76–77, 147n64, 157–60n4; sacrilegious, 22, 25

Preciado, Paul, 11, 16

presence: absent, 28, 67–68, 118, 127; de-stabilizing, 116–17, 123, 125; elliptical, 85; multiple, 70; "real," 68–69

present, the, 6, 10, 13–14, 135, 144n20

primal, the, 65

"primitive, the," 9, 117, 148n15; description of as racializing exercise, 63; "primitive thingliness," 73–74, 157n44

primitive accumulation, 63–64, 68, 90

"prior, the," 20, 142n14

progressivist myth, 12–13, 120

proper reason/improper religion binary, 87

property, 7, 14, 90; blackness as, 36; owner-ship of, 15; settler colonial philosophy of, 17; as theft, 81, 126, 141n9; transubstantia-tion of matter into, 23, 31, 33, 121, 150n23

Protestantism, and beginnings of capitalism, 69–70

Protestant Reformation, 69

Purchas, Samuel, 72

quantum, concept of, 19, 25, 61, 122–23, 131, 155n3

quantum physics, 16, 82, 136

quantum we, 108

Quashie, Kevin, 61, 78, 161n11

Queer Times, Black Futures (Keeling), 32

race-gender, 14–15, 144n20

racial capitalism: *archē* of, 8; cosmology of, 6–8, 14–15, 18–19, 23; and ecological crisis, 12, 35, 48, 134; and individuation, 9, 90; and logics of separability, 13, 15, 19, 58, 73, 150n23, 156–57n31; modern (re)invention of religion as, 77, 80–81; myth of, 19, 121, 126; ontology of, 6, 11, 21, 46; and persistence of crossings, 58–59; and Protestantism, 69–70; as religious formation, 62, 150n23; rise of as alchemical, transubstantiational happening, 62; and sacred-secular divide, 4, 11, 17; scripturalization central to, 5; "unpayable debt" as condition of, 10–11. *See also* settler colonialism

racial dialectic, 7

racial globality: as differential ordering, 12

racialization: blackness as in excess of, 45–46; "Black woman" yokes processes of to political economy, 36; description of "primitive" as exercise in, 63; as religion-ization, 63–64

rapture, 17, 43, 86, 109, 134, 165n7

rationality, 7–8, 13, 17, 76, 102, 121

"raw materials," language of, 10, 67–68

"reality," 62, 78, 94, 124–26, 130

reason, 44–45; as Reason, 33, 117, 121

refugitivity, 136

(socio)poetics, 16, 80, 129–30
solidity, 123–24, 127–29
"*Song of the Andoumboulou*" (*Les Dogon* recording), 110–11
Song of the Andoumboulou (Mackey), 85–86, 107–32
"Song of the Andoumboulou: 6" (Mackey), 86, 107–9, 112–13, 122–29; Angel of Dust, figure of, 85, 122–24, 126–28; "N.," character of, 122–29
soul, the, 86, 112
"Sound and Sentiment, Sound and Symbol" (Mackey), 124–25
sovereignty: animal perspective on, 39–43; *archē* (ἀρχή), 6; and European nationalism, 32; freedom as function of, 7; of "I," 71; prayer without, 22; Westphalian international order, 9
space-time, 10, 12–13, 61, 66–67, 98
Spicer, Jack, 123
Spillers, Hortense, 28, 98, 134, 143n20, 152n67; "female within," 41; on the "one," 163–64n56
spirit, as opposed to matter, 47–48
"Spiritual Canticle" (St. John of the Cross), 133–34
spiritual vocation: of black radicalism, 18–23, 24–26, 46, 65, 77, 121, 129–32, 136, 162–63n35, 166n7; of experimental writing, 112; material, 77, 102, 138; of poetry, 107, 109, 112
state: emergence of, 9; *Homo politicus* as citizen-subject of, 14; reasons of, 63; religiosity of, 3–4, 29–30; "we" of, 15, 108
statelessness, 8, 116, 118, 136
stealing away, 30–31
Stewart, Lindsey, 19–20, 22
St. John of the Cross, 133–34
subject: *archē-form* of, 80; self-determination of, 7, 80
Subject, the: blackening as backdrop for enactment of, 7–8; self-possessed, 7, 13, 81–82; transparent, as white, 14
subjection, 7, 11–12, 36, 137, 156–57n31
Sun Ra, 161n21

surreal, 17, 20, 58, 68, 113, 123; Afro-surreal, 22, 62; at heart of the real, 89; of "I"-in-multiplicity, 115–17
swerving, 22, 76, 78–79, 82
Sycorax, figure of, 40, 59
Synthetic Philosophy of Contemporary Mathematics (Zalamea), 88

Taylor, Breonna, 2
tehomic depth, 100–101, 129, 131–32
"terms of order," 8–9, 41, 101, 144n20, 144n22, 148n15, 161n21; alternatives beyond, 13, 31, 81, 117, 127, 142n14, 144n20; humanist, 38; incompleteness counterposed to, 19; statism as, 76. *See also* order
Terms of Order, The (Robinson), 19
terra mater, 52–53, 55, 60, 65, 67–68
theft, 58, 79, 124; property as, 81, 126, 141n9
theology, black, 46, 121
thingliness, 7, 101, 113, 127; of commodity, 56, 70; of earth, 17, 28; "primitive," 73–74, 157n44; of "world," 36
Tinsley, Omise'eke Natasha, 57
Traite du tout-monde (*Treatise on the Whole-World*) (Glissant), 148–49n15
Transatlantic Alchemy, 57, 60, 153n28
transatlantic commerce and exchange, 3, 9, 12–13, 17, 84, 134, 149n19; and alchemy, 54, 56–57, 60, 153n28; "new" *archē* in emergence of, 6–7, 61–62, 64, 71; rise of as religio-magical event, 53–54. *See also* Atlantic World
Transatlantic Transubstantiation, 60–61, 63, 65–69, 79, 153n28
transparency, opacity as opposed to, 7, 14, 73
transparency and nontransparency, 7, 14, 73, 137, 154n38
transubstantiation: of African into Negro, 64; of black(ened) people, 33, 60; eucharistic language, 67–71; European battles over, 69–70; of matter into property, 23, 31, 33, 121, 150n23; transatlantic, 60–61, 63, 65–69, 79, 153n28; trans-substancing, 9–10
"troping of the trope of" African religion, 17, 49, 59, 118, 121, 152n67

Trump, Donald J., 2–6
Turner, Victor, 98

uncanny (unheimlich), 7–8, 20, 22, 43, 114
undercommons, 143n20
United States, 49; as "America," 68, 156n20;
    fascism, 2, 3, 134; January 6, 2021, assault
    on US Capitol building, 1, 2–3; techno-
    cratic obstetrics in, 55–56
university, 8, 25, 143n18
"unpayable debt," 10–11
un/sayable, apophasis of, 18, 40, 83–85, 121
unstateliness, 8, 22, 65, 76, 120, 140n9
utopianism, "other," 120

Valéry, Paul, 77, 157–60n4
value, 12, 19–20, 150n23, 166n7; "Black
    women" and reproduction as store of, 27,
    31–35, 45, 56–58
Venus (goddess), 67
vibration, 52
violence: of "civilization," 68; domination
    in excess of forced labor, 42–43; against
    ecology, 68; obstetric, 57; of plasticization,
    36, 37
vitalism, 100, 164–65n71
Vodun, 118–19

Walker, Corey B. D., 48
way making, 25, 87, 137
"we," 16–19, 23, 108, 129; alternate/otherwise,
    18–19, 135; anarchic, 22–23; statist, 15, 108
West, Cornel, 13
Western civilization, 9, 16, 56, 68
Westphalian international order, 9, 148n10
whiteness: and binary of Life and Death,
    65; as enactment of cosmology, 14–15; as

ethical-civilizational form, 14; as "owner-
    ship of earth forever," 4, 136, 139n3; as
    settler colonial and capitalist cosmology,
    14; as transparency, 14; white nationalism,
    2–5; white science, 4, 45, 60
"whiteness, religion of," 3, 121, 135–36, 139n3
"White West," 68, 156n20
Wilderson, Frank III., 69
Williamson, Terrion L., 10
Wimbush, Vincent L., 5
witchcraft, 13, 20, 40, 120
women, 36–37, 84, 166n7; "Black woman,"
    figure of, 27, 29, 32–35, 45; witch, figure of,
    13. See also maternal, the
Woodbine, Onaje X., 82–83
Word, as mode of myth, 101
"world, the," 7, 14, 30, 141–42n11; logic of
    religion internal to making of, 23; new ori-
    entation toward, 64; and plasticization, 36
"world as such, the," 7, 64, 79, 138, 141–42n11,
    141n9, 154–55n1; alternative sociality beyond,
    19, 120–21; empiricism of, 129; and myth of
    "God," 101; obstetric invasion of, 62
worlding, 14, 19, 50, 141n11, 150n23, 151n47
wound/wounding, 10, 86, 122, 136–37, 165n7;
    and ellipsis, 99, 109, 134. See also loss
Wright, Richard, 162–63n35
Wynter, Sylvia, 7, 9, 28; daemonic, concept
    of, 129–31, 169n73; Man, account of, 14, 76;
    reoccupation, concept of, 144n24, 148n15

Yoruba pantheon, 118–17

Zalamea, Fernando, 88–89, 94–95
Zong! (Philip), 59
Zong (slave ship), 59
Zuckerkandl, Victor, 124